Praise for *Praying*

"In *Praying for Gil Hodges*, Tom Oliphant has created a small masterpiece: a splendid re-creation of life in the 1950s, a poignant tribute to his parents, and a fabulous story about the central role the Brooklyn Dodgers played in the lives of his and countless other families. Moving effortlessly from an adult's perspective to a child's recollection, shifting seamlessly between the present and the past, he captures the reader's interest at every step along the way. I found myself happily transported back in time, following a warm-hearted young boy as he comes of age in a memorable era."
—Doris Kearns Goodwin, author of the bestselling *Wait Till Next Year*

"A family saga that is universal in appeal, even for readers too young to recall the long-gone world of the 1950s."   —*USA Today Sports Weekly*

"For the way it recaptures a special time and place, *Praying for Gil Hodges* is worthwhile reading for summer's bittersweet last days."
—*The Providence Journal*

"Oliphant has written a significant book that recalls nicely how the Dodgers at last became masters of all they surveyed."
—*The Washington Times*

"The book is a trip to the time of Alan Freed's Rock 'n' Roll Show at the Brooklyn Paramount, Coney Island summers, and, of course, an enchanting team and its bandbox ballpark on Bedford Avenue. Top that for magic, Harry Potter."   —*Newsday* (Long Island, New York)

"Oliphant's timely and stylishly written memoir will warm the hearts and rekindle memories of those who were there. And for those who weren't, it offers a glimpse of America and a team from Brooklyn's history."
—*The Hartford Courant*

"Oliphant has an endearing way of mixing history and biography and, especially for someone who grew up in Brooklyn and spent many Sundays in church hoping to spot number fourteen in a pew, this book is like going home."   —CBSNews.com, Beach Book Bag

In loving memory of Homer and Anna Oliphant,
who knew that my wife, Susan, is the love of my life;
I dream of us all together drinking cream soda
in the bleachers at Ebbets Field.

Contents

Acknowledgments

Almost by definition, *Praying for Gil Hodges* was the kind of project that demanded at least an attempt at mixing apples, oranges, pears, peaches, and strawberries.

For most of my life, I have carried with me vivid memories of the seventh game of the 1955 World Series, but I always sensed that simply reconstructing one of the most exciting baseball games ever played would not do justice to those memories. Fortunately, I had a lot of help as I tried to puzzle through it all.

My wife, Susan Spencer; my best friend and longtime colleague, Curtis Wilkie; and my literary representative, Deborah Grosvenor, would not permit me to take refuge in a one-dimensional reconstruction of a famous baseball game fifty years after it was played. They insisted that I deal with the Brooklyn Dodgers of that long ago October afternoon in context to both explain the power of my own memories and their unusual resonance at the time and ever since in the country.

There was, of course, the game that dramatically ended a literary seesaw World Series. But there was also this unique team that represented part of a city, its wild and usually heartbreaking history, its hold on Americans for whom the underdog is a very easy metaphor, its roots in a special part of New York City that has deep and lasting ties to the rest of the country, its direct relevance to the story of my own family and of my early years, and its special role in helping end the grip racial segregation still had on post–World War II America.

Before I got started I also had the help of two special friends who happen to root for their home team, the Los Angeles Dodgers. Katherine Reback, a deft screenwriter by trade, helped me understand that drama needs pacing and that words can help make narrative almost visual. And Lynne Wasserman, with typical graciousness, helped open some of the first doors that made my research possible and then rewarding.

Because there was so much juggling of topics and narratives, the completion of my first stab at manuscript was just the beginning of my long journey. My editor at Thomas Dunne, Peter Wolverton, was a patient, exacting, and simply marvelous partner in helping shape the draft so that its many digressions had a chance of fitting together. Working at times on a daily basis with his assistant Kathleen Gilligan, was pure joy. I also enjoyed a father's special pleasure—the assistance of one of my favorite writers, my daughter, Wendy, who both pruned much of my verbosity and helped shape the introduction. A final pleasure was the chance to spend a little time learning from two of my writing heroines, the historian Doris Kearns Goodwin and the novelist Marylouise Oates. Doris shared my love for the Dodgers, lived a story not dissimilar from my own, and wrote an inspirational memoir about that special time, *Wait Till Next Year*. Marylouise is both my dear friend and a superb get-to-the-point editor.

As an organization, the Dodgers have always been most careful to preserve and honor their past, including the team's heart-shattering move to the West Coast in 1958. My research spanned the period when their ownership changed from Rupert Murdoch's Fox Entertainment Group to Frank and Jamie McCourt of Boston. Bob Graziano, then the team's president, could not have been kinder in helping me get started. And the McCourts were both gracious and generous. The link for me was a most remarkable person, Mark Langell, who keeps the Dodger flame burning with astonishing dedication and diligence. As the team's historian, he gave generously of his time helping me get in touch with people, recommending books and other research materials, some long out of print, and offering helpful suggestions.

Every writer delving into baseball's past, especially anything associated with the Brooklyn Dodgers, has two special treats in store. The first is the New York Public Library, a huge influence in my childhood and still a unique temple of learning. I spent two unforgettable weeks lost in its newspaper and periodical rooms, a delicious experience tempered only by sorrow that budget problems restrict the great place's hours. The second treat is the research wing of baseball's Hall of Fame in Cooperstown, New York. Baseball lovers who visit are often surprised to discover that anyone can walk into it, ask for some bit of the game's past, and get lost in the joys of history. My days there, helped immeasurably by research associate Gabriel Schecter and his colleagues, were a delight.

It has often been noted that not many of the players who suited up on October 4, 1955, are still living. Just eleven of the Brooklyn Dodgers are still alive, and only a few of them played pivotal roles in the game. Because I was interested in the depth above all, it was vital to talk to the pitchers. The thrill of actually spending a day with the person who dominated Game Seven and gave me the happiest moment of my life up to the age of ten is indescribable. My gratitude to Johnny Podres knows no bounds. But an unexpected delight was another day spent with his opponent that day for the Yankees, Tommy Byrne. Witty and gracious, he was the perfect bookend for Podres.

I am also grateful to players like George "Shotgun" Shuba, who played critical roles in the game's still unbelievable sixth inning, for sharing memories of their brief moments on that stage. It is also sometimes forgotten that some of the Dodgers wrote memoirs that included important facts about Game Seven. Manager Walter Alston wrote two, as did Roy Campanella. Gems are also available from works published by Jackie Robinson, Carl Erskine, and especially the marvelous memoir written by Duke Snider with Bill Gilbert. Above all, in my search for depth and perspective, I am eternally grateful to two icons of Dodger history who made time to help me understand the 1955 triumph in context. Vin Scully shared a morning with me before broadcasting a game from Chicago's Wrigley Field. And E. J. "Buzzie" Bavasi, a truly fascinating man with an institutional memory stretching back to the late 1930s, was kind to spend an afternoon regaling me with stories at his home in La Jolla, California.

To even attempt to understand Brooklyn required, I believe, the assistance of contemporaries who were there—not just that one day, but throughout the Dodgers' tortuous but glorious journey after World War II. Hearing their personal stories as well as their baseball memories transported me back to those days that never really leave me. I cannot come close to adequately expressing my gratitude for the courtesy and generosity showed to me by Florence (Rubenstein) Hart, Jill Schuker, Carey Aminoff, Billy Delury, and Gary Hymel. A pal in politics for many years, I am also grateful beyond words to Hymel for providing what to me is the priceless souvenir of my research—the scorecard he kept from the center-field bleachers in Yankee Stadium that unforgettable afternoon.

Every important American story is punctuated by race. In the case of the Dodgers, the enormous attention that accompanied Jackie Robinson's historic step onto Ebbets Field in 1947 tended to ebb as time passed, in part because the Dodgers were trying to make integration work and not simply to make headlines. In my view, the special impact the Dodgers had on post-war America is incomprehensible without an understanding of this vital element of their inspiring story. To help me put it in context, I was helped by a special person in my life—Vernon Jordan, the civil-rights leader and Washington power broker. Jordan not only added delightful detail to his memories of a Dodger tour through his native Georgia when he was a child (told originally in his widely praised memoir, *Vernon Can Read*), he also helped me understand how huge the Dodgers' frontal challenge to segregation loomed nationally at a time when none of the other race news was good. As if that weren't enough, he also helped hook me up with his own mentor, still in Brooklyn—Reverend Gardner Calvin Taylor.

THOMAS DUNNE BOOKS.
An imprint of St. Martin's Press.

PRAYING FOR GIL HODGES. Copyright © 2005 by Thomas Oliphant. All rights reserved.
Printed in the United States of America. No part of this book may be used or repro-
duced in any manner whatsoever without written permission except in the case of
brief quotations embodied in critical articles or reviews. For information, address St.
Martin's Press, 175 Fifth Avenue, New York, N.Y. 10010.

Book design by Michael Collica

www.stmartins.com

Library of Congress Cataloging-in-Publication Data

Oliphant, Thomas.
    Praying for Gil Hodges : a memoir of the 1955 World Series and one family's love
of the Brooklyn Dodgers / Thomas Oliphant.
        p. cm.
    ISBN-13: 978-0-312-31762-1
    ISBN-10: 0-312-31762-X (pbk)
    1. Brooklyn Dodgers (Baseball team)—History. 2. World Series (Baseball) (1955)
3. Baseball fans—United States. I. Title.

GV875.B7 O55 2005
796.357'64'0974723—dc22

2005040941

First St. Martin's Griffin Edition: July 2006

10 9 8 7 6 5 4 3 2 1

Praying for
Gil Hodges

*A Memoir
of the 1955 World Series
and One Family's Love of
the Brooklyn Dodgers*

Thomas Oliphant

THOMAS DUNNE BOOKS
St. Martin's Griffin ✖ New York

Now in his eighties, Reverend Taylor was kind enough to spend a few hours helping me understand what it was like to be in Brooklyn in the 1940s and '50s. He had not only helped the team take strides forward behind the scenes, he also spoke eloquently and in detail of what it was like to be African-American at that time in that town. He is both a theologian of worldwide repute and a person of deep faith and I am forever grateful for his assistance.

Every writer who has ever tackled a book project with a spouse in the house gets reminded daily why he remains head over heels in love. My Susan was with me long before the takeoff, and through every stage of the research and writing and editing (much of which was based on her famous preference for clarity as one of CBS News' best correspondents). In the face of unconditional love, one does not express gratitude so much as awe. I am also forever indebted to my three children—Tom, Wendy, and Jeremy (along with his wife, Jennifer, who did some of the organizational work that helped me get started)—for their understanding of an often distracted father.

Every writer also begins every project aware of his enormous dependence on others and then grateful in the extreme for the help he has received. In the end, however, I recognize the ultimate truth—that each and every error, whether of conception or execution, is mine alone.

Praying for
Gil Hodges

1

A Bridge in Indiana

I t happened right out of the blue.

I had started early on my way through rural, southern Indiana to spend some time in the university town of Bloomington. After maybe thirty uneventful, placid miles on State Highway 57, I passed a sign announcing the nearby town of Princeton. It set off an indistinct bell in my head, one of those moments when you react to something before your memory tells you why.

I had not quite resolved the question when the next sign several miles north answered it for me with jarring finality:

The Gil Hodges Memorial Bridge.

I slammed on the brakes, skidding a bit on loose gravel and coming to a halt just on the far side.

It wasn't much, a simple, concrete structure spanning the not-mighty White River in an area where coal had once ruled. The bridge was puny compared to the other one named after Gil Hodges—which connects the western chunk of New York's Rockaway peninsula to Brooklyn. His name was added to its more familiar Marine Parkway title in 1978, six years after he died of a heart attack on a Florida golf course, just shy of his forty-eighth birthday.

But this bridge *was* Gil Hodges—quiet, simple, strong, unadorned.

It was in the middle of nowhere—a pine forest framed the two-lane road with no signs of nearby life beyond the birds. It was a crisp, clear, windy October day, not unlike another October day decades earlier that began coming back to me in a rush.

It had already been a lovely morning. State Highway 57 shoots straight north out of Evansville. It quickly clears what pass for the suburbs of the small city and then becomes this quiet road, guiding a traveler by fertile fields of soybeans and corn, thick woods, and little else.

It was the right road for someone on the wrong roads a bit too much, the perfect respite from the homogenized sameness of interstate-airport-hotel "life." As a newspaper columnist with a yen for politics, this is familiar, favored territory because of its proximity to one of the most revealing stretches of real estate in America—the land on either side of the Ohio River. From Pittsburgh to Cairo, Illinois, where it meets the Mississippi, the Ohio defines what is called Middle America; every two years, the six states that touch it provide many of my best clues to where the country is headed.

I am a New Yorker by birth, childhood, and disposition still. Gil Hodges was my father's hero and he became my hero. At first, I assumed it was because he and my father were both from rural Indiana. Only later did I understand that my father—and eventually I—looked up to his enormous character, his abiding concern for others, his stoic response to adversity. It was very personal.

Gil Hodges was one of the stars on the Brooklyn Dodgers, a baseball team that after World War II personified the hard-luck struggler's lot; blazed amazing trails in race relations long before the rest of the country caught up; represented a huge chunk of New York with deep ties to the entire country; and then migrated west.

In addition to being one of the premier first basemen of his time, Hodges was also one of the stars on what for a great many years I had no difficulty identifying as the happiest day of my life—October 4, 1955, the only day in the seventy-odd years of the fabled and cursed franchise when the Dodgers ruled the world. I don't have to close my eyes; I can still see the solid single he hit cleanly into Yankee Stadium's left field that drove in Roy Campanella with the first Dodger run of the afternoon.

I can still see the long fly ball that he hit near the warning track in right-center field two innings later that for one thrilling instant looked like it might be a grand-slam home run. It was more than deep enough to drive in his pal and Ohio River valley neighbor, Pee Wee Reese, with the second and only other run of an excruciatingly tense game.

I can still see this tall, broad-shouldered man with a big, expressive face reaching and then reaching some more to take two famous throws at first base from his Kentucky friend that day— the first to complete an electrifying double play following a spectacular catch in the outfield that remains one of the memorable moments in one hundred years of World Series lore; the second to record the last out of the seventh game of the one Series Brooklyn won.

I can still see the Dodgers sprinting from their dugout, led by a courageous black man of legendary intensity named Jackie Robinson, to converge around the most improbable hero of all— a kid from upstate New York who had just turned twenty-three and had pitched a shutout at the New York Yankees with everything on the line, too young to understand or accept the long odds against him. For two hours and forty-four minutes, Johnny Podres had simply defied defeat.

And I can still see something else a few hours later, sitting on the stoop of a brownstone just off Atlantic Avenue in the heart of Brooklyn, a couple of steps above my father and mother, who were laughing and necking like teenagers while a parade of happy people pranced before them on the street.

That day on the bridge near Princeton, I had a few doughnuts and a milk with me, so I left my car by the side of the road and sat on the bridge for a while.

I have always associated my Dodgers with the World Series of 1955, and above all with the seventh and deciding game—the moment when they finally won a World Championship, finally defeated the hated New York Yankees, finally gave those of us who adored them the one (and, it would turn out, the only) World Series they managed to win after decades of usually daffy, maddeningly frustrating existence.

But my memories of that glorious day are bittersweet as well as joyous, painful as much as happy, sober as much as triumphant, quietly proud as much as tickled to death. They go well beyond baseball and the Brooklyn Dodgers.

In those days, baseball with its complicated but natural rhythms of pitch counts, innings, games, and seasons was such a shared experience across America that metaphors were not only common but also clear and unforced. Baseball and the Brooklyn Dodgers were major ingredients in the glue that held my little family together through tough times and happy times, a metaphor for hope, disappointment, triumph, and tragedy. On that one day in 1955, just before my tenth birthday, I had my first vague insight into how they all fit together—how effort is more important than result, why We is more important than I, and why the only things that truly matter are whether your word's any good and how you treat others.

The wise guy side of my journalistic persona always interrupts these reveries to remind me that romanticizing childhood memories, especially where a sporting event is involved, is just about the hokiest exercise in silly self-indulgence imaginable. In fact, there is nothing of my superficial memory that is special, much less unique. Where the Brooklyn Dodgers of 1955 are concerned, I was just one kid among roughly 3 million Dodger fans in New York City, an even tinier pebble in the ocean of people around the country in those days for whom the Dodgers were the epitome of deserving underdog-ism, just as the New York Yankees symbolized Roman Empire–like success and intimidating mastery.

In the twentieth century, sports on occasion reached legitimate, metaphorical heights—when Jack Johnson and Joe Louis reigned and when Seabiscuit raced during the depression, and earlier when onetime caddy Francis Ouimet took on the snotty establishment of golf at the democratizing breakthrough that was the U.S. Open in 1913. The fact that Dodgers–Yankees was multidimensional only added to its grand character.

On the bridge that day, it occurred to me that at some point in my life I might try at last to puzzle through all this—to see if my memory of that day and that astonishing seventh game stood up to examination, to understand the mixed emotions it evoked, and to see if the personal might find space in a larger picture of the Brooklyn Dodgers and their unique history. I have come, years later, to the conclusion that the Dodgers are well worth it and that my wise-guy side can go to hell.

That day and that game in 1955 turn out to be even more amazing and memorable than the snippets of memory that had remained with me. The game mocks the linear, shorthand summaries that have followed it for nearly fifty years—a brilliant 2–0 shutout thrown at the Yankees by a kid southpaw, a tight game saved by a spectacular catch in the sixth inning by another kid, a black man from Cuba. In truth, the game was nearly three hours of unrelenting torture and suspense, a roller-coaster ride mostly evocative of all the past years of disappointment until literally the final pitch. Each team came to bat nine times that afternoon, and the game and the Series could have gone either way during fully seven of them, not counting the Yankees' last, excruciatingly drawn-out at-bat. It is no accident of New York media myopia that this World Series and that game are on all the short lists of the most memorable games, strictly as baseball.

My memories should resonate with anyone for whom the Brooklyn Dodgers stand as a decent metaphor for life's battles against the odds and hard facts of history; they resonate twice as loudly because the only major-league team named after a neighborhood represented a special place that meant and still means melting pot, working families, and a rash pride in a unifying struggle that is mostly hard; and they resonate three times as loudly with the unique leitmotif of Dodger history, the fact that this is the organization that first clawed successfully at the walls of racial segregation that besmirched baseball's self-identification as the national pastime, long before civil rights was a powerful national movement, and even before Harry Truman ordered the desegregation of the country's armed forces.

After evolving in the 1880s, the Dodgers were down much more than they were up, a source of exasperation as much as love, and the inspiration for an annual defiant optimism immortalized by the cry after each disappointing season—Wait'll Next Year. They played for World Championships in only two of their first four decades—in 1916 and 1920—and lost each time. Between 1941 and 1953, they lost the World Series to the Yankees five times; in 1946, 1950, and 1951, they lost the National League pennant on the final day of the season.

The Dodgers are inextricably linked, their California migration notwithstanding, to a huge, noisy, diverse agglomeration of acreage called Brooklyn—two dozen sprawling neighborhoods of unique diversity. For more than three centuries, Brooklyn has been a destination as well as a gateway for tens of millions of Americans. The Dodgers make no sense without Brooklyn, and Brooklyn was their bridge to the rest of postwar America.

The famous chip on the shoulder remains an essential part of Brooklyn's character; true borough maniacs are proud to tell you that it was the place where the curveball, the seventh-inning stretch, and the box score all originated. Brooklyn's Dodgers complemented the borough's quirky personality. I still chuckle on my way there from La Guardia Airport when my car enters the borough via Williamsburg, where a sign at the border says: Welcome to Brooklyn. Believe the Hype!

There was so much more however, to the linkage between neighborhood and baseball team. Any one of the images conjured up just by saying the name Brooklyn Dodgers would not set it apart. This country is full of working family towns and neighborhoods, for which the local team is a rare source of unifying devotion and fun. The story of the hard-luck underdog is deeply etched in American myth and more than one American reality. The stories of diligent scrappers who overcome past failures and present odds to have a moment of pure joy at the expense of the direct source of so much of that woe is less common but hardly unique. And the long struggle to rid America of segregation and demonstrate that true integration can both work and inspire has its share of heroes.

But put them all together, one on top of the other, and the cumulative effect well beyond the boundaries of Brooklyn in 1955 was electric. It really was more than it seemed at the time, and even today it is a cut above a mere baseball story.

The Brooklyn Dodgers of 1955 are more complicated, but the impact of their trials and one triumph fit powerfully into the postwar period when America was already beginning to rush to suburbs and to move south and west. Several years ago, the superb writer Peter Golenbock compiled a fascinating survey of the Dodgers' three generations in Brooklyn via oral history interviews. One of them was with a man, Joel Oppenheimer, who grew up just above Manhattan in the tough town of Yonkers. He summarized most of it: "Dodger fans got beaten down so often that there was an essential humility and an understanding that Yankee fans never had. Yankee fans don't understand that the world is not a very nice place to live, that more bad things happen to you than good things. When you understand this, you appreciate the good things that do happen, and you're more apt to take it easy on the other guy who's having a rough time of it."

Add to this poignant observation the immense power of race (in this case an unusually positive tale of what is possible when racism is confronted by good people), and the fact that the 1955 Series and, above all, that thrilling seventh game get better the more closely they are examined, and a remarkable mosaic emerges. For baseball, the New York Yankees ruled the 1950s; in the larger context of the country in the 1950s, the Brooklyn Dodgers were America's Team.

It still resonates across the decades and across the country, a slice of life that managed to transcend its spot in time.

My own family fit neatly, if not always happily, into this Dodger picture. My mom worked as a secretary. My dad was a freelance writer who had great difficulty working after World War II left him partially disabled from jungle diseases in the

Pacific. We had a two-room rent-controlled apartment down by the East River and a rich, close life despite our hardships. I was aware from an early age that my parents were living through me, but it was encouragement far more than obsession. The reason I quickly latched onto their devotion to the Dodgers was that it was something we all shared that didn't have anything special to do with me.

Sorting all this out—from the game itself to the special aura that surrounded Brooklyn and the Dodgers of that long-ago time—is an exercise in both personal and larger history. I don't wish time had stopped forever at the moment the seventh game ended. I just wish the moment had lasted longer.

It amazes me how durable the memory is, and not just for me. It is equally amazing how durable the Dodgers have proved in our culture—in the movies and on television. A few years ago I bumped into a richly evocative example from the 1970s. By then nearly twenty full years had passed since the 1955 World Series, when the ABC television network had a prime-time special, a series of one-act sketches titled *Happy Endings*, coproduced by and starring the actor and comedian Alan King. The show featured the work of such well-known writers as Herb Gardner, of *A Thousand Clowns* and *I'm Not Rappaport* fame, and starred King and Art Carney, Dodger fans all.

In Gardner's sketch for the program, an elderly Jewish man, Samuel Margolis, is shown in a hospital bed wearing a baseball cap with Dodgers '55 printed on it, with several days' growth of beard on his face. He is hooked up to a heart-monitoring machine.

Sammy Margolis, his heart running out of gas, is trying to decide whether to have life-prolonging surgery or take a pass and let nature take its course. He has heard the urgent pleas of his physician respectfully but feels compelled to summarize the other side of the argument.

For emphasis, he gestures dismissively out the window, at contemporary life.

"Whatever they're doing I don't want to be party to it no more.

The times, these times, ain't my time. They took too much away without a snappy notion what to put instead. . . .

"You see the cap? Brooklyn Dodgers of '55. I do them honor. Nobody came to take their place. They took Ebbets Field away. You take the pyramids away from Egypt all you got is sand and rotten weather. Walter O'Malley, he sells them like shoes without ever discussing.

"What's left?

"Banks. You don't got teams now, MacDonald; you got Irving Trust plays Chemical Corn Exchange. The heart went with them and the city started to die. What's to root for? Without what to root the voice goes away.

"Duke Snider! He went away! A lifetime in the afternoon hollering 'I'm with ya, Duke; I'm with ya,' never dreaming for a moment he wasn't with me. Edwin Donald Snider, a person you *knew*, went to California, which doesn't even exist.

"They all went. The names, just say the names, you could sing them: Amoros, Gilliam, Campanella, Furillo, Hodges, Podres, gone, even the sound is gone. What's left? A cap, I got a cap, Dodgers '55, and sometimes I hear in the summer, on the wind, Red Barber's voice."

There must have been people watching who had no idea what Sammy Margolis was talking about, but the correct assumption at ABC was that a great many people knew exactly what he was talking about. The Brooklyn Dodgers survive—unlike, say, the St. Louis Browns or the Philadelphia Athletics—because they evoke themes that fit America like a Rawlings glove.

The enduring resonance of the Dodgers has been analyzed before and probably will be forever, but I had never thought of one element of it until it was mentioned to me by their starting pitcher that long-ago October afternoon, Johnny Podres. He is in his seventies now—a direct, interesting man. We had concluded a long talk about those days and that day in his home, still in upstate New York; I had run through the questions I had thought about ahead of time, but on an impulse I asked him why 1955 has lived on when other years and other events—some just as dramatic, some perhaps more so—have lived on solely as sports memories or not really survived at all. He smiled.

"One thing you have to keep in mind is what happened that day can never happen again. There will be other great seventh games, already have been. Someday someone will pitch another perfect game in the Series, someone will make another unassisted triple play, someone will hit another home run to win it all in extra innings. But the Brooklyn Dodgers will never win another championship. They are gone. The events of that day are frozen forever."

2

Apartment 2503

It was a Tuesday. October 4, 1955, was a more than decent autumn day—on the warm side, mostly sunny, breezy but not windy. The first thing I remember doing when I woke up that morning was looking out the window to check for the blue sky that meant the seventh game of the World Series was not yet threatened by the weather, just the Yankees.

The day's venue—Yankee Stadium—added to the element of threat. I used to go a few times a year, always with school friends whose parents had box seats. To my proudly prejudiced eyes it was a majestic palace that loomed forbiddingly as it came into view from the uptown subway. The images that stayed with me included the classical columns, the colossal upper deck in right field, and the immense expanse of center field stretching out to the faraway bleachers, decorated by the symbols of the team's perennial dominance—the stone monuments (on the field in those days) to Babe Ruth, Lou Gehrig, and Miller Huggins. The only thing I truly liked about the Stadium was the fact that if you sat near the field at the end of the game you could walk through the manicured green outfield to the exits after the game.

Ebbets Field was the perfect ying to Yankee Stadium's yang. To a nine-year-old it seemed anything but small, but it felt more hospitable. It was also famously grubby. Getting off the subway for the short walk to the ballpark in Brooklyn, there was homey brick instead of majestic columns to greet a visitor. The bathrooms were fewer, more crowded, and they stank. The crowd was much, much more diverse. Each ballpark offered short distances down the foul lines, but in Ebbets Field there was a signature forty-foot wall and fence in right field and an equally signature huge scoreboard in right-center. Above all, it felt familiar; in my family's typical perch in the left field bleachers, we always saw people we recognized from previous outings.

On that climactic day, the image of Yankee Stadium was hardly reassuring. The Dodgers had played sixteen World Series games there to that point and had only won five of them.

The World Series followed a much different routine in the days before television completely changed it. Into the early 1970s, the games were all played during the daytime, while most of America was at work or at school. People who were interested did their best to keep up, stopping in front of an electronics store to catch half an inning through the window, having a radio and an obliging boss or teacher; indeed, part of the fun of the World Series for ordinary people involved the logistics of simply following the games.

My family was lucky in this regard. Each autumn, my private school in midtown placed a large television set on the front of the stage in the gymnasium. There were regular activities in the afternoon for those who wanted them, but for the rare play-off and the annual World Series the set in the gym always beckoned. Many of my most crushing Dodger memories had unfolded in that gym—especially two bitter World Series defeats at the hands of the Yankees in 1952 and 1953.

Working at home when his health permitted, my father never missed a pitch, and my mother was fortunate to work at a baseball-friendly Wall Street law firm.

The family routine, however, began no differently than on any other school and work day. I was expecting another seventh game in the gymnasium amid a sea of little Yankee fans; I still remembered the lonely shame of the day in 1952 when a seventh game that was tied after five innings slowly slipped away.

The night before the seventh game in 1955 had been dominated by talk of a disastrous sixth game for the Dodgers, in which
they were crushed, 6–2; their travails were still in my thoughts
when I drifted off to sleep and still there when I got up at the
usual time the next morning. My mother always woke me at 6:15,
simply opening the door that connected the room where I slept to
the living room so I could hear the noise from the radio that
at that hour was always tuned to WNYC (the city-owned radio
station) and its early-morning diet of the classics and the news.
The open door meant I had fifteen minutes in the one-bathroom
ballet of our family life to get cleaned up and mostly dressed for
school before it was my mother's turn.

When I emerged, there was always a small glass of orange juice
waiting on the table, squeezed from the orange she picked up from
a street vendor on her walk home from the Lexington Avenue subway after work. Much less pleasant, there was also always a tea-
spoon next to it, along with a small bottle of foul-tasting cod-liver
oil—one of the few consequences of my mother's Norwegian heritage that I loathed. In lieu of matins in our odd routine, we always
recited in unison the hyperbolic station break on WNYC at the top
of the hour: "This is New York, the city of opportunity, where more
than eight million people live in peace and harmony and enjoy the
benefits of democracy."

Once the orange juice and cod-liver oil were downed, I was expected to turn off the radio, sit down at our piano (music was as
big a part of my life then as school and baseball), and do finger
exercises until my mother had dressed and made breakfast—
scales, arpeggios, chords, and selections from the technique books
that have punctuated every young musician's training. In an effort to give the morning exercises a little more life, my father had
encouraged me to finish with Bach; I could play his two- and
three-part inventions by then, and in contrast to the finger exercises they were at least melodic.

I don't remember it as drudgery, more just as part of my daily
routine. I was dimly aware that I was pretty good at my music,
and I applied myself diligently. There was no gun at my young

head, no expectations of a career that I was ever aware of; my parents talked to me about my music a lot, and even at the age of nine I was comfortably aware of their point that the only way to see what you could do with a gift was to give it a decent chance to develop. It was pressure, but the right kind.

Often as I practiced in the mornings, my father wouldn't stir from bed until breakfast. He would sleep in if he had stayed up late writing or, as was the case this morning, if he had been ill during the night. As I was finishing, however, I remember him padding toward the bathroom in his robe and then sitting at our new dining table, his chair just beyond the piano, waiting for my mother to serve him his hot drink—a hideous concoction called Postum, which was all he could take in the morning, caffeinated coffee or tea being much too rough on his ulcer-battered stomach.

The precision of my morning routine reflected two major facts of my childhood life—a lack of living space and a ridiculously but joyously crammed schedule. After World War II, very few working families enjoyed very much room while the housing shortage lasted. In my family's case, my father's illness and the financial straitjacket it produced meant that the tiny apartment was a fact of life. We lived in one of the many large buildings that were built in New York during the 1920s and which prospered nicely despite the allegedly onerous burden of rent control. Our neighborhood was called Tudor City, a collection of seven buildings off First Avenue between 41st and 43rd Streets, which were very desirable for families with children because 41st and 43rd Streets sloped up from Second Avenue and were linked by a bridge over 42nd Street, with small parks on each side. The result was that you could walk from 41st and Second all the way around to 43rd and Second without crossing a street; and the result of that, in a more innocent urban time, was that I could go outside to play by myself with my friends after my eighth birthday.

My mother had found the apartment while my father was away during the war, and after he came home they held on to it for dear life. It wasn't much, but after a basement studio in Greenwich Village and a walk-up in the Bay Ridge section of Brooklyn where they shared a bathroom with another family shortly after they married in 1935, it was more than tolerable. For me it was part sanctuary, part schoolroom, the place where we were a family.

Home was on the twenty-fifth floor of Woodstock Tower and faced north, with a decent sliver of the East River visible to the right. On a clear day, not so common in an era when coal was still being burned all over town, you could just make out the George Washington Bridge; along the river, we watched as the United Nations was built and were constantly drawn to the sidewalk in front of the building to watch big shots being driven down 42nd Street to the majestic building that was just five hundred yards from our front door—I remember a young Queen Elizabeth; Winston Churchill; and President Eisenhower, as well as the determined organizing work of my mother through the neighborhood Democratic Party club to make sure there were always a dozen or so people with unfriendly signs whenever they had word that Vice Pres. Richard Nixon would be at the UN. My mother and father differed politically only in degree: She was a Democrat; he was in the Liberal Party back when it was a real force in New York. She detested Nixon more than red-baiter Joe McCarthy, while my father reversed the order because he had so many blacklisted writer friends and sometimes fronted for them, turning in their articles and scripts as his own to the magazines and networks that refused to hire them. It was a matter of intense pride for both my parents that he never took the 10 percent cut people who fronted for others during that dark period usually did.

My mother could not stand Richard Nixon. It was part politics, part conviction that he was an opportunistic fraud, and eventually it became personal. Through someone at her Democratic clubhouse, she had volunteered as a part-time secretary for a well-known woman, Helen Gahagan Douglas, who had moved back east after getting crushed by a particularly vicious Nixon campaign for senator in California in 1950. All of Nixon's early campaigns after the war had sought to link liberalism with disloyalty as Cold War hysteria took hold; in 1950, Nixon had displayed some of Mrs. Douglas's political stands on cards that were colored pink to suggest how close she was to being communist Red. Mrs. Douglas was married to the actor Melvyn Douglas, and my mother did secretarial work for her on the occasional weeknight and weekend, sometimes bringing me along to the Douglas apartment, where the maid gave me cookies. One evening, my mother looked up from her work to see Eleanor Roosevelt standing in front of her; I could not have been seven, but I remember the two of them conversing and Mrs. Roosevelt asking me about school and patting me on the head.

Neither of my parents was a native New Yorker. Each had taken interesting paths there from the rural Midwest, part of a mass migration to the cities that had been going on for more than a generation by the time they began their treks. My father's began in central Indiana in 1909. The small town he emerged from lies in corn country a bit north of Indianapolis. It was from Frankfort that he departed in almost desperate haste, two years after his own father, a country doctor who worked around the clock, died at the age of just forty-four. Baseball was how my father's favorite Dodgers (Hoosiers Gil Hodges and Carl Erskine, along with Pee Wee Reese from the Kentucky side of the Ohio) made it to the big world beyond their towns. My father got out by his wits; the day he graduated from high school in 1926, he threw a dart blindfolded at his map of the United States, and he entered the University of New Mexico that fall. My mother emerged from as far north as you can go in Minnesota the following year, with a bit more purpose in her plans—junior college and then a job in Washington, D.C. Her parents were immigrants who had carved a life for themselves in America, but it was not a life that Anna Serena Selvog wanted. Like my father's loss of his own father, my mother's life had been touched by a tragedy—she lost the older sister she revered in a drowning accident—that strengthened her determination to strike out on her own. One thing my parents shared was a love of reading and learning that informed their dreams of a different life.

The Midwest connection was part of what originally attracted my parents to the Dodgers. My mother was every bit as rabid as my father (and, eventually) I were. Reflecting her heritage, she was more reserved than my romantic, quixotic father, but her quiet personality barely masked a mordant wit and a fiercely independent character that kept our family afloat. She had been a wife who went to the ball games with her new husband in the 1930s, but she rediscovered the Dodgers as *her* team hanging out at Ebbets Field during the war with girlfriends from work.

The Dodgers had been a part of my parents' offbeat life since before the war. The oddball character of the team during the 1930s, when they lost with amusing and zany originality, was a natural attraction for a young, slightly oddball couple, then living in an English basement on Bank Street in Greenwich Village during the depression. A game at Ebbets Field for them in the late 1930s was a big day out for not a lot of money.

Life was a scramble, but they were madly in love with each other and with New York. While my mother kept working as a secretary, my father slowly began carving a name for himself as a freelance writer and kept up his music by writing songs. In 1941, he and a partner had a big-time sixteen-week hit, "The Same Old Story" (I still have the 78 RPM record, with Billie Holiday singing and Teddy Wilson on the piano).

My father had fallen in love with music (he was a solid violin player, classical and jazz) and with writing by the time he entered the university in Albuquerque. Almost immediately, however, he got in mortal trouble with the university authorities by publishing a delightful article in the campus literary magazine about one of the town's more interesting prostitutes. He spent the next eight years roaming the country—often in the company of an equally free-spirited friend from Indiana who had a trust fund—playing in jazz bands, writing, and teaching himself by reading and rereading the classics voraciously.

My mom was a first-generation Scandinavian out of the small city of Warroad, Minnesota, alongside the Lake of the Woods. One of its principal employers is a factory that makes specialty hockey sticks for goalies. In her early years, she was as proficient in Norwegian and Chippewa as she was in English. Determined to make her own way, she got out via junior college, and her successful determination to master English landed her a secretarial job in Washington as the 1930s began.

They met because of my father's uncle. Herman Oliphant was an icon in my family—an Indiana boy who became a giant in the law and was named general counsel in Henry Morgenthau's Treasury Department as the New Deal began. He worked on the actual text of much of the decade's historic reform and economic security legislation and helped design much of the new regulatory framework before his death during Franklin Roosevelt's second term. He had become my father's second father, and one day in 1935 he played matchmaker with a young secretary he had taken a shine to—my mother.

My parents were married at City Hall in New York just weeks later. Herman Oliphant had hoped my mother would be a positive influence on his still somewhat wild nephew. My father's violin-playing days had just ended (thanks to a left wrist broken during a fight); my mother had just turned twenty-five. The timing, in short, was perfect.

The Dodgers fit neatly into their life. They were hopelessly addicted by the time the team, in 1941, won its first National League pennant since a brief glory spell in 1916 and 1920.

What followed the pennant in 1941 was a disaster that served as the perfect harbinger of what was to come—a unique series of ten crushing defeats that were almost triumphs that the Dodgers dealt themselves and their fans over the next thirteen years. The World Series that year also produced a play—catcher Mickey Owen's famous muff of a third strike pitch that would have been the final out of the fourth game—that is not only still discussed today but also was itself a harbinger of the agonizing plays that contributed critically to all of those heartbreaking losses.

Years later, my mother told me that listening to the Mickey Owen game on the radio at work that day in 1941 was her first memory of having cried in front of people who weren't family. The team, however, was reviving, and this was when the famous cry of the Dodger fan—Wait'll Next Year—actually rang true.

Pearl Harbor stopped their progress, as it did for millions of stunned and then angered Americans, my parents included. My father was thirty-two, but he enlisted immediately and with a group of writer friends somehow managed to get an idea past the War Department for a mass-circulation magazine to be published during the war for enlisted people. It was called *Yank Magazine*, and its volumes contain as good a raw history of the war as exists anywhere.

Rather than sit behind a desk, editing in New York, my father had gone to the war in the Pacific by the summer of 1942. At home, my mother followed a partner she knew from the Wall Street law firm into the U.S. Attorney's Office in New York that would be the focal point for most of the legal and criminal matters associated with the war effort. She worked long hours during the day and often at night, and among my treasures is a newspaper photograph that shows her taking a deposition from a would-be Nazi saboteur.

My father made much of the long island-hopping journey north toward Tokyo. He started in threatened Australia and was with several first waves—in New Guinea, the Solomons, Guadalcanal, the Philippines, Saipan, and Tinian. He came home with thousands of words of fabulous stories, a Bronze Star, and just about every jungle disease you could catch, the dreaded dengue fever included.

The tidal wave of creative energy that was unleashed after the war did not wash over the hundreds of thousands of young people disabled by it—most far worse than my father. For them, despite the nation's gratitude, the war never really ended but was replaced by a largely private struggle inside each family. My father's health deteriorated rapidly, to the extreme detriment of the writing life he was trying to live.

From the beginning, my life was a contradiction; the struggle my parents endured was omnipresent, but my childhood was also idyllic—a scholarship to private school, a perfect neighborhood that was self-contained as well as safe and nurturing on the edge of the Lower East Side, sports in my bones, language and music in my veins. To grow up in New York City was for me like working and living in an ocean of opportunities and choices, all of it made possible, under very rough conditions, by my parents.

Try as they did to mask them, the tensions involved in making ends meet out of a two-room apartment, where my father was often in great pain and rarely able to work, could still be sensed by a child. Not once can I recall feeling the slightest twinge of embarrassment at our condition, despite the daily contrasts with the world I saw up close around my private school. I loved being around my parents; there was a strongly perceived pressure to excel, but always at things I adored doing. If I had private wishes that didn't get articulated immediately, it was to help them, so that they would be happier.

More than anything, the stakes for us that Tuesday in 1955 were a chance, however improbable, to experience for however brief a time some moments of truly shared joy that were otherwise so elusive. As Dodger fans—awaiting as well as dreading the seventh game of the 1955 World Series—that hardly made us unique.

3

Scarlet

For me, 1955 was a memorable year even before the Dodgers' miracle unfolded that October. In addition to school and neighborhood and family, I was blessed by music in my life—singing and intense piano work. During the summer, I somehow got through the audition process at the Metropolitan Opera and was selected for the boys' chorus, a job I would hold until I was washed up with a useless baritone at thirteen. There are no words to describe the thrill of actually spending time on a stage with the likes of Maria Callas, Richard Tucker, and Rise Stevens; it was another world, where the most exacting kind of work mixed with the exhilaration of performance on a truly grand stage.

Many children work hard to please their parents, but what I truly longed for was good times that were about us, not me. That is the real hole the Dodgers filled in my life. Like any Dodger family, my father and mother filled me with the long, losing lore, taught me to keep a box score, and helped me find the smaller joys with which to battle annual disappointments—a metaphor I had no trouble grasping. So many of the genuine pleasures I saw them experience in those years involved the Dodgers, which only deepened the attraction.

Life was always busy and usually exciting in its variety and bustle, but it was also defined and confined by the reality inside that little apartment.

There were ten units on our floor, comprising a rent-controlled mosaic of New York life—including a young UN diplomat from Canada, a budding solo pianist, a war widow and secretary like my mother, another younger couple, and a music critic for *The New York Times*, who had been traumatized by his experiences as a medic during the war and was often in our apartment to monitor my progress and talk through his wartime experiences with my father.

Our apartment had an entrance hall maybe fifteen feet long, which I used for sliding practice by putting a pillow against the front door. The hall contained our one closet, which my mother had somehow divided into four compartments. It opened into a single room that faced north. To the left was what might charitably be called a kitchenette; it consisted of a small refrigerator of the size many people now keep in their offices. The counter had room for a sink and a two-burner hot plate on which all our cooking had to be done (meaning frying, boiling, pressure-cooking, but no baking and broiling, to my mother's intense frustration).

Against one wall was our aging Steinway upright; jutting out from the corner next to it was our only other valuable possession, a 21-inch RCA television set, which had been there since the preceding Christmas and was called Scarlet by my mother—a marvelous name that had nothing to do with color television, then in its commercial infancy, or with Ms. O'Hara from *Gone with the Wind*. In early December of 1954, I had come down with a slight case of scarlet fever that was quickly followed by double pneumonia, the only time in my life I was ever truly sick. In bed and bored out of mind, I was rescued within a few days by the arrival of a large box that turned out to be the television, sent by the father of one of my classmates who had me out regularly for companionship at the family's weekend home (to me it was more like a palace) at Port Washington on Long Island. The father was one of my first heroes I actually knew—then the president of NBC, the famously innovative Sylvester L. "Pat" Weaver, father of the *Today* and *Tonight* shows, pusher of the programming envelope during television's Golden Age until the business powers stopped him.

He was exceptionally kind and interested in my busy life, and his daughter was one of the first girls I actually liked (she was known as Susan then; today she is the actress Sigourney Weaver). When the holidays had ended and I had recovered enough to go back to school, my mother called Mr. Weaver's office to arrange for the set's return. She was told that either it would go to the Salvation Army or stay in the apartment; it stayed. In honor of my fortuitous illness, the set was quickly christened Scarlet.

The television was not the only big change that wonderful year. We also got rid of the apartment's major eyesore—one of those old pullout Murphy beds that came out of the wall opposite the windows—and in the process acquired our first real dining table for the vacated space. By coincidence, my parents had gone shopping in Greenwich Village two days before Game Seven and managed to find a secondhand relic they were able to fit into a Checker cab for the ride home. The result was not only a dining table (until then we ate on a card table that magically fit in that carefully stuffed closet) but also room above it for makeshift bookshelves for my father's most precious possessions, which had been arranged before that in stacks on the floor of the bedroom and on top of our two dressers. The place must have driven them to distraction, but I was too young and too small to notice. We talked about everything in that little apartment, with the glaring exception of the pain and frustration of my parents' struggle.

I have no childhood memory of my father wailing at the moon over his illnesses or his inability to work steadily; I never heard my mother vent any feelings about the double duty she performed without complaint. And yet I could see they had it tough. My father's pain was inescapably obvious; often, in the evenings, I watched my mother nod off early while trying to read. This is why singing professionally meant so much to me, not merely for the glamour and excitement but also for the chance to hand my pay to my mother after a performance. I didn't know how to express myself, but I knew that was often the grocery money. (Before I left for college she had replaced every penny.)

This is partly why baseball and the Dodgers meant so much to me. When there was a game—and especially when there was a World Series—all the excitement and hope and concentration involved all three of us to the obliteration of our cares. We shared the Dodgers; they were a metaphor and an oasis.

On that morning of the second seventh game of my conscious life, the team suffused the atmosphere of our apartment, mercifully.

The first words out of my father's mouth after he had occupied his regular post in the chair next to the piano were jarring. He said I looked terrible and was I feeling ill. I remember both being puzzled and insisting I felt fine, but my father would not relent. Did I feel flushed? Had I been coughing? Did I sleep all right? Did I feel at all nauseous?

By then, my mother was in the room, and after a few more of these confusing diagnostic questions she began to laugh, all the while being gently disapproving.

Then I got it. In typically overdramatic fashion, my wonderful father was encouraging me to feign illness. I was fully prepared to endure the inevitable seventh-game torture at school, but here was my father signaling that for this momentous, but frightening, final game of the World Series we could be together in the apartment, watching the action on Scarlet. It would be no less scary but a lot less lonely.

I laughed, too, as my father gestured to my mother to be still while he reached for the telephone to call my school. He transmitted the details of my unfortunate illness with appropriate solemnity and then put the phone down and winked broadly. My mother was happily in on the conspiracy and began divulging her own plans to experience the game. There was always a television set in her law firm's conference room and she wanted to watch, but that meant being around all the firm's partners, which meant Yankee fans. Nearly all the secretaries she knew were Dodger or New York Giants fans, so she expected to eventually migrate to the room where they took their coffee breaks, and imagine the game via the radio.

My father was feeling better that morning, so when we had finished eating we escorted my mother up 42nd Street to her subway stop. On the way back we stopped at the newsstand where we always stopped to buy the papers my parents allowed into the apartment—the *Times,* the *Herald Tribune,* and their favorite, the avowedly liberal *New York Post.* The guy selling papers, Tommy, was one of the neighborhood fixtures, a friendly guy in his twenties whose cousin was a fairly well-known and highly ranked lightweight boxer, Johnny Busso; he had once arranged seats for us at the old Madison Square Garden for one of his fights, much to my mother's horror.

The neighborhood was more a collection of these characters to me than a collection of buildings down by the East River. John Tomkins, who couldn't hear and couldn't speak, worked at the shoe store on 43rd Street and taught me sign language; Ray ran a candy store named after him around the corner on Third Avenue where kids like me bought bubblegum for a nickel in packages with five baseball cards and parents could get a bet down on the daily number; Huey Balboni jerked the sodas in the diner on 42nd and Second and then in the drugstore in Tudor City, always giving me two pumps of cherry syrup with my Coca-Cola; the day shift elevator operators in our building were actually named Tom and Jerry, the former formal and meticulous, the latter joyously loud and not always sober; and Louis Christopolous (he had lost a leg in Sicily) sold the fruit my mother bought on the way home from the subway, never failing to compliment her appearance with elaborate charm. I got to play with friends in luxurious apartments on Park Avenue and Fifth Avenue, but I was convinced I lived in heaven. It was self-contained, protective, friendly, a little odd, safe, fun, and a delightful mixture of the rigorous education that I got in my apartment and the introduction to the delights of diversity I got on the street.

My deal with my father that day was that I would finish my piano and some schoolwork in the morning and then we would devour the sports pages, make some lunch, and get ready as best we could for a game neither of us expected to turn out well. The sixth game had been such a swift, convincing, and deflating defeat, accentuated by the shellacking of one of my mother's favorites (Karl Spooner) and a knee injury to the team's star center fielder, Duke Snider. The sports pages oozed Yankee inevitability; the bookies made them 7–5 favorites. I was happy to be home from school but dreading the game.

By 1955 I knew what to expect. It was normal for the Golden Era Dodgers to win a pennant; they were almost as dominant in the National League as the Yankees were in the American and had won five pennants in the nine years after Jackie Robinson joined them. The heart of the batting order (Snider, Hodges, Campanella, outfielder Carl Furillo, and Robinson) would hit its customary ton of home runs, Don Newcombe would win twenty games, Carl Erskine would win eleven, and the journeymen and newcomers of the year, backed by superb relief pitching from Clem Labine and Ed Roebuck, would get enough others to clinch the pennant early. Like any young baseball fan, I knew my team backward and forward—from the left-handed hitting Snider's famous problems with left-handed pitchers, to the magical arm that made Furillo an outfielder base runners rarely tested, to the way Sandy Amoros wagged his bat just before swinging.

They were also accessible heroes. The Yankees' Mickey Mantle, even to his own fans, was distant glamour, almost a movie star. Even to me, the Dodgers weren't gods; they were people, easier to live and die with.

As it turned out, 1955 was the year I felt I almost lived at Ebbets Field. My father or my mother, or both, took me to at least a dozen games on their own, at which we always sat in the outfield bleachers. A special opportunity, though, came out of a rare break for my father. There was a man in our neighborhood, Saul Paul, whose brother, Gabe, was the general manager of the Cincinnati Reds—just then emerging as a slugging powerhouse, which would finally win a pennant in 1961. My father and Mr. Paul were casual friends from watching me and my neighborhood friends' progress from the sandbox to the sandlots, and out of their acquaintance came a magazine assignment for a profile of Gabe Paul. The article was what we call in the news business a feature story, and he must have loved it, because he invited us to be his guests that season whenever the Reds were in town. In those days, when eight teams in the National League played 154 games against each other, that meant 9 or 10 more games for us.

I had never sat in a box seat. For a nine-year-old to be so close to real major leaguers was beyond heaven, and these seats were in the first row behind the visitors' dugout on the third base side. The three of us made the pilgrimage to every game—days, nights, and weekends, including doubleheaders. One night, I watched in awe as Jackie Robinson scored all the way from first on an extra base hit; this close, he seemed five times as fast, and I remember being briefly startled when he took a wide turn around third and appeared to be running right at me. I could hear him breathe.

The next inning was for my mother. Her favorite Dodger was Roy Campanella; she called him Roly Poly in her Midwest twang and considered him cute. Someone on the Reds hit a foul ball far into the night sky, and when it came down into Campanella's huge mitt, he could not have been standing ten feet from us. It was the first time I ever saw my mother blush.

Part of the joy of life with the Dodgers was that it was intimate. In Ebbets Field, the feeling was akin to that on the sandlots; you were watching people you felt you knew very well, whose faults as well as skills were equally understood and appreciated. For most of the season in those years, the experience was almost blissful. To make it even more pleasurable in those years, the Dodgers were almost always either in the thick of the pennant race or way out in front.

Beginning in September, however, you learned the meaning of dread with this team as the World Series approached; you came to anticipate it. From my first baseball consciousness in 1950, I was evolving into the typical Dodger fan who knew hope but also knew history. The dread also had a rational component. The Dodgers matched the Yankees in power and speed; they were arguably even a little stronger. The Yankees, however, consistently had one or two more quality pitchers, usually the key in a short series, while the Dodgers were assumed to start out in trouble because their workhorse (Don Newcombe) was such a notorious autumnal disappointment after a spring and summer of overwork. As the World Series approached, the talk in our house and all over town was that the Dodgers needed a starter to win two of the games if their hitters were to be counted on to win two more for the championship. The problem was that none dared confidently predict who that pitcher might be.

For me, the World Series in 1955 began in my school's gymnasium. Somehow I had a scholarship at one of the city's fantastic private schools, Browning, the first true break in life for me after being born to parents who adored learning. In baseball terms, though, it was terrible, because the place was filled with kids from quite wealthy families who were nearly all Yankee fans. The only Dodger fan classmate I remember, and remember very fondly, was John Steinbeck's son—also the only fellow political leftie. Together we endured taunts about the Dodgers as well as those about Adlai Stevenson.

The taunts were especially strong as the World Series of 1955 began with two boilerplate nightmares at Yankee Stadium. Newcombe was ineffective, and the Yankees had two skilled and crafty left-handed starters that year—the famous Whitey Ford and the solid veteran Tommy Byrne, each of whom had been methodically masterful. Even a nine-year-old knew that fifty-two years into World Series history no team had yet come back to win after losing the first two games.

That made the Dodgers' victory, 8–3, in the first of three Ebbets Field games, in what was the sixth so-called Subway Series since the war, seem less significant. There had been a Dodger hitting eruption, to be sure, and this kid from upstate, Johnny Podres, had pitched a marvelous complete game on his twenty-third birthday. The timely hitting and clutch pitching carried over to the second victory in Brooklyn as well, a win made all the more satisfying because my parents and I enjoyed it together, with a family in the neighborhood; we laughed and yelled, so lost in the Dodger victory that no one remembered to keep score. The past, however, still hovered like a dark cloud over our happy Saturday.

Dread and history were forgotten, at least by me, for the final game in Brooklyn the next afternoon. It was the first World Series game I got to see in person. There was a nice lady who lived on our floor in 2509, a war widow who had no kids of her own and doted a bit on me. To this day, it grates on me that I cannot remember her name. We visited back and forth; my mother and she usually did their weekly shopping together and sometimes took in a movie. When my father was especially sick and my mother was with him in the hospital, this neighbor would often look after me in the evenings. ·

Bless her heart, she had two outfield bleacher seats to the fifth game from someone at work and asked my parents if she could take me. This was one subway ride I remember vividly. As always, we exited past one of the Ebbets Field environs' most colorful characters, a blind man who sold pencils. For years his routine had been to offer, for a nickel, to give the score before the game had even started; for thousands of the gullible, the answer never varied: "Nothin' to nothin'." When we walked up the ramp into the grandstand, the sight of the red, white, and blue bunting draped over all the railings was majestic; the fact that all thirty-six-thousand-plus seats and standing places were occupied only added to the thrill.

The game was a fan's delight. In the 5–3 Dodger victory, Duke Snider hit two home runs and Sandy Amoros one. For the Yankees, home runs were hit by reserve outfielder Bob Cerv and the only catcher of those days in Campanella's league, Yogi Berra. Five home runs in one World Series game, with three innings of clutch relief from Clem Labine on top of the four-plus he had pitched the day before to get the win. My parents had listened to the game on the radio at a friend's apartment, so I was quizzed on every detail when I burst through the door and babbled on long past dinner.

It was a doubly special evening and included the christening of our new dining table. It seemed a fittingly formal setting for my rambling, self-indulgent discourse on the game.

The dread had only been postponed, however, and the sixth game the next day made my mother particularly heartsick. With some girlfriends from work she had witnessed at the end of the previous season the debut of one of the true legends in the annals of Dodger tragedy. His name was Karl Spooner and he was a natural. The left-handed pitcher not only shut out the Giants but also struck out fifteen of them, and ended the season by shutting out the Pirates while striking out twelve of them. Spooner, another upstate New Yorker, became the personification of Wait'll Next Year. My mother claimed he was clearly a better prospect than another left-hander who had been on the team for two years, Johnny Podres, and she insisted Spooner's control was much better than that of the third kid left-hander then on the roster. He was nineteen, a Brooklyn boy, and a so-called bonus baby signed for twenty thousand dollars out of the University of Cincinnati, which meant he had to stay on the active squad for two years, which also meant he mostly rode the bench. His name was Sandy Koufax.

Spooner had a promising spring, but his arm and then his control started to go as 1955 wore on, and he only won eight games. Manager Walter Alston's decision to start Spooner in the sixth game was instantly second-guessed all over town, unanimously in my household. When Spooner proceeded to get shelled in the first inning, the I Told You Sos were deafening. What no one knew was that with his arm a wreck, he would never throw another pitch in the major leagues.

That evening, I mostly remember us grumbling about Alston's decision, a convenient means of avoiding the sinking feeling about the next day. What had already happened in five out of five World Series in just fourteen years seemed about to happen again.

What I remember even more sharply is that my father got very sick after supper. His major ailment then was a collection of continually bleeding ulcers that sometimes required a few days in the hospital and more bills to juggle. It was a particularly unpleasant night. I was never ashamed or embarrassed by my father's rough life; I was fiercely proud of his service in the war and in awe of my mother's quiet strength in holding us just above water. What I hated was the sadness he couldn't always hide.

On the night before the seventh game of the 1955 World Series there was not a molecule of hope in our apartment. Life with the Dodgers was so often a painfully real metaphor.

Little did we know.

4

Gil, Jackie, Pee Wee, and a Parable of Race

The game my father and I were getting ready to watch was not just another climactic seventh game.

As of that Tuesday morning, there had been twelve days in the previous fifty-two years when two teams had literally played for the World Series. Several of them had been marvelous melodramas, but by 1955 nothing held a candle to a Dodgers–Yankees seventh game because of the two teams' epic rivalry.

The Brooklyn Dodgers were as much a national team as the Yankees were; where the Yankees personified power and success, the Dodgers symbolized struggle, represented millions of dispersed Brooklyn émigrés, and wore their unique status among African-Americans proudly.

The sports pages of the day, of course, hyped the game with customary superficial excess and clichés. But after five Dodger–Yankee World Series—with the same outcome—traditional baseball banter could not do justice to what this almost annual, protean struggle between the two teams represented. Yankees–Dodgers had become a central element in a boisterous decade, with its racial undercurrent in a battle between an integrated team and a nearly all-white one, the contrast between power and heart, grand success and hard luck, optimism and reality. And it played out on a truly national stage. There were still only sixteen teams in the major leagues that year, not one south of Washington or west of St. Louis, so most of the country rooted avidly from a distance.

Since the World Series was first played in 1903, there have been other unforgettable games and unforgettable Series in strictly sports terms. People will argue as long as baseball survives (insoluble quarrel being a central part of the game's appeal) which should be called "the best." All involved dramatic seesaw tussles, as well as seventh games that put exclamation points after already magnificent struggles. Many saw the improbable triumphs of underdogs.

The war between the Ty Cobb Tigers and the Honus Wagner Pirates in 1909 comes to mind. So do the gritty St. Louis Cardinals of 1926 and 1946. So do the upstart Milwaukee Braves of 1957 and the Pittsburgh Pirates of 1960. So do the back-from-the-brink New York Yankees of 1958 and their younger successors four years later. So do the modern upstarts like the Pirates of 1971, the New York Mets of 1986, and the Minnesota Twins of 1987. So even do contemporary examples of the power of today's money to assemble teams almost overnight, like the Florida Marlins of 1997 and 2003 and the Arizona Diamondbacks of 2001. And so do victories that have the feel of justice, like the Red Sox sweep in 2004 after eighty-six years of frustration.

There have also been other moments of soaring drama, moments that have withstood time and television saturation: Willie Mays's over-the-shoulder catch a zillion miles from home plate in the Polo Grounds for the New York Giants in 1954; the one perfect game in Series history by Don Larsen against the Dodgers (who else?) in the fifth game of the 1956 Series; the seesaw sixth-game struggle between the Boston Red Sox and Cincinnati Reds won by the Red Sox on an extra-inning home run by Carlton Fisk in 1975; and the Mets' survival, an out away from elimination, on a fielding error by Red Sox first baseman Bill Buckner eleven years later in another third unforgettable sixth game.

These are baseball stories. Until 1955, however, only one World Series deserved a place in a larger story, and that was not clear until after it had ended. The conspiracy by several members of the Chicago White Sox to fix the 1919 World Series remains a metaphor for modern America grappling with the loss of innocence. The excesses of the Gilded Age and Industrial Revolution, the realization that modern technology and cities produced gigantic problems as well as progress, the disillusionment as an international order collapsed into the unspeakable carnage of World War I—all that, and then gangsters fixed the national game's showcase event. Whether or not the kid in Chicago ever said it, the heartbroken plea to the tragic hero "Shoeless" Joe Jackson, "Say it ain't so, Joe," survives.

The 1955 Series also went beyond sports, because of Brooklyn and what it represented and because of the Dodgers themselves and what they represented.

Above all, there was Brooklyn, a teeming collection of distinct neighborhoods on a unique scale, at once a destination and a gateway, with long, strong ties to hearts all over the country. Every World Series was a national event, but by the 1950s nothing engaged the country like the Brooklyn Dodgers and the New York Yankees. Their rivalry may not have had the white-hot intensity it had within New York's borders, but it divided the nation in a way Indians–Giants, Phillies–Yankees, Cardinals–Red Sox never could have.

The Dodgers also had a special collection of players—stoics and fierce competitors who raged against defeat; black men, not just Jackie Robinson, who heroically confronted America's original sin of racism; and quiet professionals whose consistent excellence raised the standards for performance on the team very high.

They had, for example, Gil Hodges.

There should not be a Gil Hodges Memorial Bridge, at least not yet anyway. He should be pushing eighty now, enjoying his grandchildren and looking back fondly on a career that included his time as one of the best first basemen of the post–World War II era, the manager who helped the lowly Washington Senators in their second, 1960s incarnation to respectability, and then the guy in charge when the Miracle Mets won it all in 1969. Instead, he died way too young, just two days shy of his forty-eighth birthday in 1972, the first of several Dodgers from that team to die too soon.

Gil Hodges was a star shortstop in high school, improbably enough because he was one big guy—an honest six feet, two inches tall, and weighing more than two hundred well-muscled pounds. It was the immensity of his hands that made a lasting impression on me the two times I actually met him, both during that amazing season of 1955. My nine-year-old hand disappeared entirely from view within his; it was said that when he spread his fingers, you could fit a ruler between his little finger and thumb. At Ebbets Field, I had managed through my father's connection with Gabe Paul to get on *Happy Felton's Knothole Gang*, the Dodgers' pregame show when television was still young. The host was an enormous, as in corpulent, man—part of the panoply of characters that dotted the team's history, including an oompah-pah band and a clown dressed as the storied Brooklyn "Bum." Felton introduced a few kids to a Dodger who played catch with them for a few minutes, offering pointers. Hodges tossed me a soft ground ball, which I fielded through my terror and threw back to him. He talked about stretching to the ball from first base instead of waiting for it and then put me in heaven by saying in his quiet voice, "Nice throw, kid."

Gil Hodges was beloved in Brooklyn, the person parents wanted their kids to emulate. He was not just quiet and well mannered; he also worked ceaselessly, hustled like a rookie, and never complained. It was the era when private lives stayed out of the newspapers unless they made the police blotter, but it turned out that Hodges really was all he seemed. Hodges came up to the major leagues late in 1943 as a catcher but in his only game that year played third base. After three years in the marines and a year in the minors, he was back in 1947, still catching part-time even as he was being transformed into a first baseman.

Two years later, he developed into an almost annual All-Star whose absence from baseball's Hall of Fame remains absurd. He hit with consistent power, and he fielded magnificently. One astonishing night in 1950 he joined the tiny list of men to hit four home runs in a game; and the grand-slam home run, the ultimate clutch hit, was his trademark—in his career, he hit fourteen, a National League record that stood until Willie McCovey broke it. In the field, his self-taught signature became a play that is called special for most but became routine for him—a double play that begins with the first baseman fielding the ball, throwing it to second for the force out, and then hustling to the first base bag to take the return throw.

For all his talent and character, though, Hodges was also famous for fading in the late stages of big seasons and in World Series play. In the 1952 World Series, another heartbreaker the Dodgers lost to the Yankees in seven games, he came to bat twenty-one times with not so much as a single to show for the effort.

There were no boos from a chip-on-the-shoulder populace famous for them, no recriminations in the mercenary front office or from fellow players—such was his reputation. Instead, Hodges's slump and how he might emerge from it were the talk of Brooklyn, all of it empathetic, almost tender. The next spring, however, after a winter of anguish, his slump continued through the first month of the season, and Hodges was actually benched.

The late Arthur Daley, who wrote the main sports column for *The New York Times* in these years with Pulitzer Prize–winning grace, memorialized an event that May. On a steamy hot Sunday, the Reverend Herbert Redmond was celebrating mass at a church in Brooklyn, when he startled his congregation thus: "It's far too hot for a sermon. Keep the Commandments and say a prayer for Gil Hodges." He started slugging again shortly thereafter.

Harold Henry Reese is a second Dodger who was adored in my family. He said after the Game—in which he was one of the critical fielding contributors, got a key hit, and scored the second run—that just before the last out he was hoping fervently that Yankee rookie Elston Howard would not hit the ball to him. After more than a dozen late-season crushing disappointments, he said he did not want to be the person who made an error that began another descent into failure.

It is astonishing that this meticulous, professional man would have such a fear. He was thirty-seven that day, playing opposite another of the excellent shortstops of the era, Phil Rizzuto. Alone among the Dodgers of 1955, Reese had been on the field for every one of the horrid chapters of the team's modern lore. He was at shortstop when the nightmare began as catcher Mickey Owen let the third strike get by him in 1941; and he was at shortstop ten years later when Bobby Thomson of the New York Giants hit the three-run home run that ended a play-off and the Dodgers' most maddening collapse of all. In between and thereafter, Reese played in each of the other might-have-beens that ended tight pennant races or dashed World Series hopes.

As far as my memory and research can tell, Pee Wee Reese contributed not one miscue, not one blown opportunity, to the entire saga it was his misfortune to witness. He was the epitome of the reliable professional, the obvious choice year after year to be the Dodgers' official captain.

That was not, however, what made him special in my family. What made him special was his role in helping end segregation in baseball and in making integration work.

The story was first told to me by my father as a parable of character. I could not have been more than six at the time, but it stuck with me. Years later, I discovered that the story was really two stories, almost identical except for where each occurred, and that they were preceded by an equally courageous act.

In 1947 general manager Branch Rickey acted on his historic decision to challenge segregation in baseball and bring a black man, Jackie Robinson, into the major leagues. Pee Wee Reese, more than anyone else in Brooklyn or baseball, for that matter, was the person who made this stunning decision work as day-to-day reality in the historic season of 1947.

My parents' affection for the Dodgers, and therefore eventually my own, exploded with the arrival of Jackie Robinson in 1947—a source of fierce pride, not just in Brooklyn but also among the politically liberal of the time, my parents being almost stereo-typical. Jackie Robinson was an authentic American hero. He sup-plied the Dodgers with a unique glow—internal pride on the team and in its neighborhood, and externally supplied by people all over the country, and by no means only African-Americans, who were inspired by the triumph over Hitler and fascism to imagine a more just society. Rickey's decision to select the former UCLA athlete and veteran as the "first" put a burden on Robinson's shoulders that is almost beyond imagination. He would have to compete at the major-league level, where only performance counts, and yet he would have to keep a pledge to Rickey that he would endure the inevitable slings and arrows of bigots for two years in silence.

The pressure on a man of his famously competitive spirit and pride was nearly unbearable. What is forgotten today is just how ugly it was after Robinson made his debut at first base (Gil Hodges caught that day) in a Brooklyn uniform at Ebbets Field on April 15, 1947, against the Boston Braves, before an official at-tendance of 26,623, more than half of them black.

The atmosphere in Brooklyn was warm, happy, and welcom-ing. But when the Dodgers hit the road the ugliness of racism was on display in all its disgusting elements—death threats, boycotts, beanballs and high spikes, and a cascade of foul language from the stands and from opposing team dugouts. The Democratic Party's longtime leader in the House of Representatives, Dick Gephardt, told me once that his first exposure to extreme profan-ity and vulgarity was as a boy sitting uncomfortably in the old Sportsman's Park in his native St. Louis with his father as Cardi-nal fans hurled insults at Jackie Robinson.

Indeed, before the season even began, Rickey had to quell a nascent rebellion among the Dodgers themselves. Led by one of their aging stars, popular outfielder Fred "Dixie" Walker, a peti-tion was circulated opposing Robinson's elevation to Brooklyn. Rickey isolated the ringleaders and Walker was gone after the season, but the person whose quiet opposition stopped the rebel-lion's momentum was Reese.

Before he died in the year 2000, Reese always spoke self-deprecatingly about his leadership. He had come from a border state, he noted, but had gained neither experience nor knowledge from being around people of color and shared some of the stereotypes of the day. He might also have had selfish motivation to oppose Robinson, who was originally signed by Brooklyn out of the Negro Leagues as a star shortstop.

Reese always insisted that he simply wanted to play baseball, that he was desperate to finally be on a championship team, and that after three years away for the war he needed to make money. Those comments, however, don't do justice to the guts it took to stand up to teammates and some personal friends. As a team leader, he shunned the petition and shamed its organizers.

But what Reese did after Robinson made his debut is inspiring. As name-calling escalated beyond even the rough stuff ballplayers reserve for one another, as the pitches thrown at Robinson grew in number and spiking and near-spiking incidents multiplied, there was a real question that first month whether bigots could make Robinson's presence unsustainable.

On the Dodgers' first road trip of the season, they came to the Ohio River town of Cincinnati to play the Reds. Just across the water from Kentucky, Cincinnati has always had a mean, racist streak in addition to its virtues, and fans and players alike on this occasion were particularly abusive toward Robinson, while the papers contained stories of explicit death threats.

Early in the game, the Dodger rookie grounded out to end an inning and waited around first base as his teammates came back into the field. On his way to shortstop, Reese stopped at first base and spent a long moment talking with Robinson after handing him his glove. As the taunts from the Reds' bench and the stands increased, Reese simply put his arm around Jackie Robinson and held it there. The message was a combination of "lay off" and "the team is with him." Some witnesses claimed a gasp from the crowd was audible; no matter, because the acceptance of Robinson (albeit with rough moments to come) is often dated from that simple, human gesture.

As if to prove it was no accident, it happened again, early the following season in Boston. With the Dodgers in town to play the Braves, the dugout and grandstand abuse this time had begun even during batting practice. Once again, Reese repeated the gesture, slowly walking to Robinson, putting his arm around him, and holding it there as they conversed. This is the incident Robinson himself recounts in his own autobiography.

Robinson's impact on the country in the 1940s and 1950s is impossible to exaggerate, as it was on Brooklyn and New York and on the special reputation the Dodgers enjoyed because of him. In Congress shortly after the war, it was considered a breakthrough to have a debate on a proposed federal law against lynching by mobs. The breakdown of segregation in baseball not only preceded President Truman's executive order desegregating the armed forces by a year; but Robinson's rookie year of 1947 preceded by eight years Rosa Parks's famous refusal to give up her seat on a bus in Montgomery, Alabama, the same year the fully integrated Dodgers won the Series, preceded by seventeen years the outlawing of segregation in public accommodations, and preceded by eighteen years the federal statute finally protecting the right to vote.

Like any important American story, the story of baseball is punctuated by race. In the case of the Dodgers, there was riveting national drama when Robinson made his debut in 1947, but the significance of race in understanding the significance of the Dodgers was not much noticed after that. In part this was because the Dodgers tended to downplay it, both for marketing reasons and because there was a judgment that the experiment was most likely to be successful in a low-key atmosphere. The truth, however, is that the team's special reputation is a principal reason they were an American, not merely local, phenomenon. Whites in the South largely despised them, but they were nationally respected for what they had done and in the case of African-Americans they were revered.

Deprived by war and segregation of his youngest playing years, Robinson displayed an inspiring competitive ferocity and restless energy during his ten years in the major leagues that transformed the game as no other player did until Willie Mays exploded on the scene after military service in 1954. Robinson was Rookie of the Year amid all the pressure of 1947. He was the league's stolen base champion in 1947 and 1949, the batting champion in 1949, and the Most Valuable Player in 1949 as well.

But it was his presence on the field that will forever remain with me. Even after it had been accepted that he was on the team and he had become a Dodger icon, there was a perceptible awed reaction when he was introduced. In competition he was ferocious. I watched him respond to a catcher's pickoff throw to first by sliding into second, and I saw him perform the more difficult feat of stealing third several times. The biggest thrill when Jackie Robinson played, however, was his unique moves when he reached third base. On virtually every pitch he would suddenly dart for home, stopping on a dime halfway there and scampering back to the bag; it drove seasoned pitchers to distraction. The reason it was so disconcerting was that everyone knew he was one of the few players who was fast enough and smart enough to steal home; he did it nineteen times in his career, once in the World Series.

That World Series was in fact the 1955 classic, and the play late in the first game remains one of the most controversial in Series history. It happened with the game on the line in the eighth inning and the Yankees leading 6–4. One run had already been scored and there were two outs. Robinson was on third by an act of his indomitable will: he had scampered all the way to second when his ground ball went off third baseman Gil McDougald's leg into short left field, and then dashed to third on a fly ball hit in front of him to left fielder Irv Noren.

With the count one ball and no strikes on pinch-hitter Frank Kellert, Robinson stunned everyone and broke for home just as Whitey Ford went into his windup. From the first-base side of the field, it appeared that Yogi Berra had tagged him out; but I found a picture in the Hall of Fame library in New York from the third-base side showing Robinson's foot on the plate and Berra's tag a tad high on his leg. Home plate umpire Bill Summers called Robinson safe, Berra went delightfully berserk, and the rest is history. It was vintage Jackie Robinson, but also possibly unnecessary, because the next batter hit a bloop single that would have scored him anyway.

For all Robinson's greatness and courage, the fact that he was just the first large tip of an even larger iceberg is sometimes forgotten. More for company than performance, a black pitcher named Dan Bankhead was briefly on the squad in 1947, though he would win nine games with Brooklyn in 1950.

In the year following Robinson's debut, however, desegregation became true integration as the Dodgers promoted a parade of All-Star-quality African-Americans. The premier catcher of the era, Roy Campanella, came up in 1948; a future Most Valuable Player, pitcher Don Newcombe, emerged the year after that; in 1951 the Dodgers showed the diligence of their outreach efforts by signing one of the top stars in baseball-crazy, pre-Castro Cuba, a fleet-footed outfielder named Edmundo "Sandy" Amoros; in 1952, pitcher Joe Black was Rookie of the Year, as stylish infielder Jim Gilliam was in 1953.

One day in the middle of the 1955 season, manager Walter Alston started a team that included Newcombe pitching, Campanella catching, Gilliam at second, Robinson at third, and Amoros in left—a majority. This happened at a time when three of the sixteen teams (the Philadelphia Phillies, Detroit Tigers and Boston Red Sox) were still segregated and the Yankees had only just succumbed by bringing up Elston Howard.

African-Americans may have been fixtures on the Brooklyn Dodgers, but their position in baseball was still marginal. The Boston Red Sox, the last organization to yield, would not desegregate for another four years.

The impact of Robinson and then the others on the national African-American community was almost as huge as the emergence of heavyweight champion Joe Louis in the 1930s. Many a time, the Dodger train would pull into a city late in the evening to find crowds of several hundred, nearly all black people, including scores of fathers with their sons, waiting for a glimpse of their hero.

Others went to great lengths, literally, to see him play. In 1955, Walter Riley was twenty-five and working for a hair-products company in Washington, D.C. Sensing that Robinson's career was nearly over, he and three friends were determined to get to New York.

For two months, they carefully accumulated some cash for gas money, tickets, and incidentals. Because one of them had a cousin with a house in Brooklyn they could avoid a hotel bill and splurge instead on four grandstand seats on the third-base side, closest to Robinson. They arrived at Ebbets Field early for batting practice before a Friday game, hoping but failing to get close enough to ask for an autograph. Fifty years later, and now running a car service, Riley fondly remembers betting his buddies five dollars that Robinson would steal a base. He did.

The Dodgers had a unique glow because they were the team that broke the color line; not only that, they had gone way beyond this to give a still-segregated and essentially racist society one of its few glimpses of equal opportunity itself. In the African-American community Jackie Robinson was beyond hero status; and in a growing part of white America that was embarrassed by overt racism a decade after World War II, Robinson's heroic achievement was a powerful symbol of hope that easily became affection for his integrated team. The hopes that were slowly kindled that afternoon in 1955 included the hope that the man who had inspired and helped change his country might have a World Series championship as part of his and his team's legacy.

The feelings were strong inside Robinson himself as he paced and yelled and kibitzed and fidgeted in the Dodger dugout before the game. It is sometimes forgotten, even by Dodger fanatics, that Robinson was unable to play in the seventh game in 1955. Already thirty-six years old and in his next-to-last season, he had badly injured an Achilles tendon while playing his heart out during the first six games. His skills might have been yielding to age, but not without a determined struggle on his part; he was the lion in winter that year.

In his revealing autobiography, *I Never Had It Made,* he wrote with characteristic directness: "It was one of the greatest thrills of my life to finally be on a World Series winner." Until the last out, however, he was a barely contained maniac in the dugout, his storied competitiveness forced into the unfamiliar channel of kibitzing.

The halting progress in professional sports and the military, however, was revolutionary compared to what was not happening in the rest of the country. That autumn saw the commencement of just the second school year under the Supreme Court's *Brown v. Board of Education* decision abolishing segregated public schools, and it had yet to be implemented anywhere. The public bus boycott in Montgomery, Alabama, that ushered in the modern civil rights revolution after the arrest of Rosa Parks would not begin until two months almost to the day after the seventh game.

That week, the major news in the country was the uncertain nature of President Dwight D. Eisenhower's recovery in Denver from his heart attack and the widespread speculation that he might not be able to seek a second term the following year. However, the papers were also filled with stories in the immediate aftermath of the routine acquittals of two white men in Mississippi for the horrific murder and lynching of an African-American teenager, Emmett Till. It was considered progress that there was revulsion in some parts of the country to the continuing terrorism against people of color, but the violence remained routine.

Most Americans were acceptingly indifferent to racism, and a great many all over the country were brought up to embrace it. I was so very lucky, born into a family of midwestern dreamers who signed petitions against segregation, marched in demonstrations, gave spare change to civil rights organizations, and raised me to dream their dream of confronting America's original sin. Through my music, I got to do choral work on the same stage with both Marian Anderson, a stunning woman with an unforgettably rich contralto voice (her long-delayed debut with the Metropolitan Opera at fifty-seven was the same year as mine at nine), and Paul Robeson (whose deep voice you could feel as well as hear, and whose formidable presence could be both intimidating and inspiring).

Through my father's music before the war I got to be in the presence of legends a few times in the years after the war. Billie Holiday and Teddy Wilson, among others, stopped by our apartment a few times to cheer him up when his health failed and to relive their recording of his hit song, which they always played when they visited. That inevitably meant I had to perform as well. A gentle man and a perfectionist, whose playing was both precise and lyrical, Mr. Wilson once approached quietly while I was butchering Bach and delicately put his index finger under my knuckles to lift my sagging bridge. In the decades that followed I have interviewed kings and presidents, but I can die happy just knowing I once sang "Summertime" in a two-room apartment with Billie Holiday to Teddy Wilson's lilting piano.

But I was a white kid living by the East River in Manhattan, largely isolated and ignorant of nonwhite culture, whose mind was only opened at first because my parents insisted on it. Jackie Robinson's story was a handy, inspirational allegory, and I was filled with its details, as well as the stories of the players who came after him.

My real education, though, was from John Tomkins. He must have been around thirty when I was five; he worked in a shoe repair shop on 43rd Street in my neighborhood and took the subway each evening home to Brooklyn. He could not hear and he could not speak; outside of teachers and my family's immediate circle he was the first grown-up I can remember who took an interest in me. And he taught me the basics of the baseball position I came to love the most—catcher.

The first thing I can recall about this stocky man with flashing eyes is that I was instructed to call him Mr. Tomkins, as my parents did, while everyone else who came into the store called him John. My first direct lesson in race relations, from my mother, was that the Mr. conferred deference and respect and that people used first names to people of color to signal alleged superiority.

The second thing I can recall is that Mr. Tomkins taught me to sign—a mixture back then of symbols and spelled-out words. I would sit where the people who were having their shoes shined sat and he would patiently drill me until I was reasonably proficient; I was so intent on learning that I barely noticed how relaxed and natural our relationship became. On many a Saturday and more than a few days after school in the neighborhood with my father, we would sit in those seats, hands and fingers flashing away, discussing the day's Dodger news and my progress in school.

On his lunch hours, Mr. Tomkins often ate in the parks where I played in pickup ball games or outside the store on 43rd Street where I learned stickball. He was a magician with the broom handles we played with and taught me how to swing at the tough pitches that came in low on one bounce, but my fondest memories are of him teaching me how to play catcher—how to concentrate on the ball, not the batter or the bat, so you could catch the ball without blinking after a swing, and how to block low pitches that bounced.

It was such a relaxed introduction to an African-American that as the actual state of race relations began to dawn on me I remember being surprised before I was disgusted.

My parents followed a more interesting path. My mother told me once that she considered herself lucky as a young girl in extreme northern Minnesota that several of her first friends were Chippewa and that she was naturally at ease in diverse company before she was introduced to the institutionalized bigotry of formal society.

The part of Indiana into which my father was born was, in his formative years, one of the centers of Ku Klux Klan activity at a time when the Klan was at the apex of its sinister national power. His great fortune was to be the son of a country doctor who revered education and culture and detested the Klan. My father told me often that the combination of his consuming grief at losing his dad when he was just fifteen in 1924 with his revulsion at the horrid racism all around him (lynchings and other murders were not unheard of nearby) was what compelled him to leave the area the instant he was handed his high school diploma.

After the war, Jackie Robinson thrilled both my parents and was responsible for the intensity of their love of the Dodgers, politically active as they were. I absorbed their passion in no time. Long before 1955, through conversation and the articles my father showed me when we visited the public library, I had learned the Robinson lore—from Branch Rickey's earthquake announcement to Robinson's astonishing willingness to endure the taunts and the assaults in silence for his first two seasons.

I also absorbed my father's pride in the baseball people who came, as he did, from the almost-South near the Ohio River and rose to the historic occasion. Even as a boy, I knew all about the former governor of Kentucky, A. B. "Happy" Chandler, who as baseball commissioner stared down the other fifteen club owners to permit Rickey's project to go forward, and the Dodgers from his part of the country—Carl Erskine, Gil Hodges, and above all Pee Wee Reese, whose generous character overcame backgrounds that more frequently produced bigots.

I especially remember one day when my father had prowled around the newspaper section while I was finishing a school project (I'm fairly certain it was in 1955) to assemble some articles about one of his favorite Dodgers, Fred "Dixie" Walker, the fabled "People's Cherce" in Brooklyn who was gone before I had achieved baseball consciousness. Walker had been one of the team's brightest stars, but he was a southerner (born in Georgia but by the time of his baseball career living in famously violent and virulent Birmingham, Alabama) deeply opposed to desegregation, and the organizer of the abortive clubhouse petition drive to keep Robinson off the team before the 1947 season started. Rather than accept Robinson's arrival, Walker asked to be traded and would have been gone early in the season had not Harold Patrick "Pete" Reiser had another of his collisions with an outfield wall, causing Branch Rickey to put his desire for winning the pennant ahead of his willingness to accommodate a conflicted ballplayer.

The articles painted a more nuanced picture of Walker than

do most cursory accounts of his story. The articles told not only how Walker made the best of an awkward situation that year but also how Robinson himself appreciated his good manners as well as his lockerroom batting tips and he understood that much of Walker's public posture stemmed in large part from intense pressure back home that directly threatened his hardware and sporting goods store. To help his white teammate with appearances, Robinson was even careful not to shake his hand in baseball's routine ritual of congratulations if Walker hit a home run with Robinson on base or on deck.

The first Robinson-induced trade had occurred almost immediately after he made his debut with the Dodgers in 1947. It involved another solid performer and popular player, Kirby Higbe, a fastball pitcher from South Carolina, and brought both Al Gionfriddo (who would make the history books with one play later that year) and one hundred thousand dollars to the Dodgers. It turned out, however, that Higbe had also been subjected to intense pressure from home and was both conflicted and embarrassed by his response to it. Indeed, despite his posture of opposition to Robinson, it had been Higbe during spring training who told Dodger officials about the petition drive before it could gather momentum. In his relentless instruction and conversation, my father explained how these stories showed the complexities of white people's behavior and that it took some study of the details of momentous stories like Jackie Robinson's to understand how difficult it was to confront the system of segregation.

It was also at the library that my father introduced me to the black press, especially to writers such as Sam Lacy and Wendell Smith, whose indefatigable advocacy had played such an important role in laying the groundwork for baseball's desegregation. It was from the black press that I first learned Branch Rickey had not been the first owner to try to break the color line, that it had been Bill Veeck Jr., and that Rickey had studied and learned from the flamboyant owner's mistakes. A ceaseless promoter (when he owned the old St. Louis Browns, his team once fielded a midget pinch-hitter), Veeck sought in 1943 to purchase the Philadelphia

Phillies and fill it with the best available players from the Negro Leagues. His disclosure of his intentions ahead of time, however, enabled the baseball establishment to have the National League take over the financially moribund team and sell it to a local lumber baron for half the price Veeck had offered. It was this chicanery that taught Rickey to keep his own plans to break the color line secret until the last minute.

The blocking of Veeck was stage-managed by baseball's dictatorial commissioner, Kenesaw Mountain Landis, the judge who had been named the sport's only boss in the wake of the Black Sox scandal a generation earlier. It was implemented by the league president, Ford Frick (later Chandler's successor as commissioner). Landis's uncompromising attitude toward gambling was matched by his determined vigor in keeping the business's whites-only status inviolate. It was through accounts of Landis's racism in the black press that I first learned of the tortured lengths the white mind went to in order to justify the unjustifiable. Landis repeatedly denied that there was any ban on black players (how could the "national pastime" be officially racist?), and he, the owners, and white society in general and the establishment press in particular presented a patently absurd picture of custom and the same questions about talent and ambition that have dogged every effort to advance civil rights.

In my family the Landis name was dirt. I particularly remember my father arguing once that Shoeless Joe Jackson's sins in taking the criminals' money in 1919 but double-crossing them by playing hard anyway should have been forgiven eventually. My father said that Landis instead should have blocked the elevation to the Hall of Fame in the 1930s of one of its most famous hitting stars from before the turn of the century, Adrian Constantine "Cap" Anson. It was Anson who was more responsible than any other individual for the imposition of segregation. His actions took place at the same time reactionary forces were imposing brutal restrictions on black people throughout America, but especially in the South, as the hopeful developments after the Civil War were halted with the abrupt end to Reconstruction.

A first baseman and manager for the old Chicago White Stockings of the original and all-white National League, Anson was from Iowa. He used his star power in an ugly campaign to exclude African-American players after he objected vehemently to having to play on the field against them in preseason games with teams from other leagues. It was largely as a result of his public and private agitation after the 1887 season that a "gentlemen's agreement" among owners erected the barrier. It would stand for the fifty-eight years that passed between the dropping of the last black player from the Newark team in the old International League (a catcher named Moses Fleetwood Walker) and the day Jackie Robinson took the field for the Dodgers' top farm team in Montreal in 1946.

The articles in the black press at the library were also the source of my first, primitive understanding of the gigantic impact Jackie Robinson had as a hero among black people. Poring over material my father found from Robinson's rookie season, I can remember newspapers filled with advertisements of welcome placed by black-owned businesses in National League cities. The papers were also filled with accounts of thousands of families who flocked to the ballpark, most in their Sunday best and many in tears, to see and applaud history even as white fans on the other side of ballparks were spitting out abuse. The papers also contained the stories, remarkably similar, of the hundreds of men who would show up at train stations to greet the Dodgers upon their arrival, often late in the evening, and usually with their young sons in tow—just to get a glimpse.

"It was the dawn of a new day," a Washington pal, Vernon Jordan, explained to me decades later about his first impressions as a boy in Atlanta. "We grew up in awe of the accomplishments of Jesse Owens in track and Joe Louis in boxing, but very few people had a chance to see them perform. This was spectacularly different, partly because it was baseball, the national sport at the time, and not an activity for one individual but one where you were part of a team—at first a white team."

Vernon Jordan is both a major figure from the postsegregation civil rights movement of the late 1960s and 1970s and eventually a genuine pillar of the Washington legal, business, and political establishment. He followed the late Whitney Young into the presidency of the Urban League, endured a tortuous recovery from a would-be assassin's bullet in Indiana, and then rose to prominence as a power broker and business figure. He was twelve years old during Jackie Robinson's rookie season.

Two years later, Jordan witnessed history as the Dodgers broke spring training camp in Florida and headed north for the regular season—stopping in Robinson's native Georgia to finally integrate professional baseball in the state. The inaugural game was in Macon against the Class B Peaches on April 7, whereupon the team moved on for three games in Atlanta against the premier franchise in the old Southern Association, the Crackers (that really was their name). There is a delightful account of what followed in Jordan's revealing autobiography, *Vernon Can Read!*, but when we talked I begged him for more details.

As a reward for his children's attendance at church, Vernon Jordan Sr. had precious tickets for himself, his namesake, and his other son, Windsor. On what was Palm Sunday he met them at Atlanta's long-gone Ponce de León Park after the two boys had been dispatched to Sunshine's Department Store to get khaki pants and white shirts so they would look their best on a historic day.

At the segregated stadium, they had to walk through a small gate down the first-base line under a sign that said: Colored Patrons. Robinson and Roy Campanella (Don Newcombe was not yet with the team for his rookie season) had stayed separately at the Royal Hotel, which catered to people of color, while the rest of the Dodger entourage enjoyed the comforts of the Henry Grady on famous Peachtree Street. Inside the stadium, segregation—whites in the grandstand, blacks in the outfield bleachers—was rigid.

On that day, more than twenty-five thousand people (including several busloads from Robinson's hometown, Cairo, in South Georgia) showed up to see the final game, nearly double the park's capacity and a substantial majority of them African-American—this despite a week of ugly threats of violence from the Klan and its Georgia Grand Dragon, some fool doctor named Samuel Green. To accommodate the nonwhite throng and take their ticket money, Cracker owner Earl Mann had a rope stretched across the relatively deep part of the outfield grass (any ball that bounced beyond the rope was a ground-rule double). At least five thousand people were turned away even after that accommodation; there were large numbers of black fans on the railroad tracks that looked down on the field and still more on top of buildings behind them. Right behind the rope in left-center field stood the three thrilled Jordans.

"There was tremendous excitement because this was history," Jordan recalled for me, "but there was a distinctly racial tinge to it. We cheered every time Jackie Robinson came to the plate, but you could also hear the loud boos and taunts coming from the grandstand. The first time he came up, white fans actually threw two black cats onto the field."

Robinson made an out in his first appearance against George Diehl (who had played parts of two seasons during the war for the Boston Braves). The second time up, Jordan said, Robinson singled to left field, stole second, and scampered to third on a short fly to right. Once on third, he began his patented intimidation—darting off the bag to take his lead, then pretending to sprint home as Diehl went into his windup, only to halt abruptly just before he threw. The Atlanta catcher that day was one of the most popular Crackers ever, Ralph "Country" Brown, a Georgia boy who never made it to the major leagues and normally played in the outfield. He must have relaxed as Robinson came to a halt, because without looking in his direction Brown casually tossed the ball back to the mound.

At precisely that instant, of course, Robinson stole home. Jordan remembers the brief delay while the crowd labored to figure out if what it had just seen had really happened, followed by a roar that he can still hear in his head.

"We blacks were cheering as if he had won something for us," Jordan wrote in his memoir. "And, of course, he had."

The family's thrills on that historic day had not ended. The

Dodgers' backup catcher, Bruce Edwards (who had lost his starting job to Campanella the year before), hit an automatic beyond-the-rope line double right at them. Jordan's father disappeared in the pile of bodies scrambling for the baseball and emerged holding it high. Windsor Jordan is the keeper of the family treasure to this day.

From that time behind the rope line in the outfield as a boy witnessing history Jordan's journey took him to a favored place among the mourners at Jackie Robinson's achingly sad funeral at New York City's Riverside Church in 1972.

"It is literally impossible to overstate what he meant to me, to all of us, to the country," Jordan told me. "It is as instructive and inspiring a story of courage as you can find. For the sake of perspective, it is possible to see how major-league baseball can be isolated from the rest of the country's social and economic problems that were hardly being addressed at all, because it was a sport.

"But what Jackie Robinson and the Brooklyn Dodgers did turned out to be one of the first clues—and it was easily the most visible and powerful one—that the system of segregation was beginning to come apart. His place in the story is crucial. He made us all Dodger fans; there was a special glow around them wherever they went because of what they represented and what he had done."

To better understand the New York of my childhood, the setting in which Jackie Robinson (and then all the other black ballplayers on this integrated team) played half their games, Jordon urged me to see his mentor in life and faith—Rev. Gardner Calvin Taylor.

Reverend Taylor, in his eighties when we talked in his spacious home just off Eastern Parkway in Crown Heights, arrived in Brooklyn from his native South to minister shortly after Robinson arrived to play baseball. He remembers well the thrill and significance of the breakthrough.

"We were so starved for attentions and recognition," he said in a soft, reflective voice. "This was almost another emancipation to see this amazing thing happen, especially to see it happen when it happened, when hardly anything else good was occurring. Jackie Robinson, to the entire country and not simply to those of us here in Brooklyn or those in baseball, was one of the very few glimpses there were then of black leadership and accomplishment in a white world."

Reverend Taylor—theologian, civic leader, civil rights leader, prominent Kings County Democratic Party official—quickly became part of the emerging leadership in New York that made change possible and then pushed it hard when doors started to open. After a lifetime of service, his Presidential Medal of Freedom (from President Clinton in 2000) hangs in his front hallway. Until his retirement in 1990, his base—which he expanded exponentially—was the Concord Baptist Church of Christ, where he hosted Martin Luther King Jr. (his family and Dr. King's in Georgia were acquainted) in the early days of his national leadership.

To his credit, Branch Rickey reached out to this evolving structure that Taylor helped lead for both help and advice as he labored to make sure Robinson succeeded and was welcome in Brooklyn and to expand on the first year's success. New York was not the Louisiana of Reverend Taylor's youth, but as I told him my own experiences and the importance of John Tomkins to my formative years, he smiled.

"At that time, the best word to describe the situation in New York was *ambiguous*," he said. "It was a time of great ferment as we began to plan for change. To most of us, there was no question we had escaped a much more rigid system in the South. There was mobility on the subway and the buses.

"It is also true, though, that there were many stores in New York where we were not welcome. Residence was strictly, and I mean strictly, segregated. And opportunity was severely restricted; apart from the professions within our community, only menial jobs were available with very, very few exceptions. At Ebbets Field, nearly all of us sat in the outfield bleachers. In government, there were as yet no opportunities at all. In the city system when I got to

New York, the highest-ranking position was a make-work job created in the office of the Brooklyn borough president.

"And yet things were starting to happen, and Robinson's arrival was an enormous catalyst. It helped that Brooklyn itself was for that time the most tolerant and diverse place in America. The key, no question about it, was the large Jewish population, which operated throughout this period as our collective social conscience. It was such that it was not considered appropriate here to oppose the arrival of Robinson and the additional steps to integrate the Dodgers that were taken after 1947."

Back then, the storied alliance for civil rights between the black and Jewish communities was on vivid display to anyone who visited Ebbets Field. The first Yiddish word I remember hearing was *Yonkel*, shouted happily from grandstand and bleachers alike, which translated as "Jakov" in Hebrew, or "Jack."

It is clear now, but wasn't back then, that each step the Dodgers took involved hard work by numerous individuals on the team and in the city and no step was taken without careful consideration and debate.

As Reverend Taylor put it, "Each time someone was added, there was discussion of whether there would be a backlash, whether the Dodgers were moving too quickly ahead of their time. This was not entirely a matter of older leaders trying to restrain younger leaders; we all worried about this. Remember, we wanted this to work; we were not just seeking to make a statement. And yet, each time the issue of race arose, the consensus was that while there might be a need for care, there was certainly room on the team for one more black player."

Few people were more intimately involved with these decisions than Emil J. "Buzzie" Bavasi, the young Dodger front-office man—a Larry MacPhail hire in 1939—whom Rickey used to check out Robinson before the final decision to bring him up to the Dodgers after the start of the 1947 season. Bavasi told Rickey that Robinson's reputation was rock-solid after observing the way the players' wives in Montreal deferred to his wife, Rachel. Bavasi was the general manager in 1955, five years into a job he would perform with great skill until Walter O'Malley fired him in 1968 to make room for his son, Peter. I visited Bavasi at his home in La Jolla, California, high up Soledad Mountain with a spectacular view of the Pacific Ocean. Bavasi had gone on to develop the San Diego Padres franchise and retired as the part-owner he had tried to become with the Dodgers. Well into his eighties, his eyes twinkle with memories of slick deals and roguish maneuvers as well as brilliant coups. It was he who sprang the shocking trade of Robinson to the Giants after the 1956 season, a deal that fortunately never went through when Robinson retired. Bavasi built four World Series-winning Dodgers teams—1955, 1959, 1963, and 1965; under Peter O'Malley, they won two.

Bavasi's father came to this country at the age of seven from Marseilles, eventually becoming one of New York's most successful newspaper distributors. Buzzie grew up comfortably in the suburbs and graduated from DePauw University in Indiana, where he was the school catcher for three years. His baseball connection, helpful in landing his first job, was a friendship with Ford Frick's son. After paying his dues in the Dodgers' farm system in Georgia, Bavasi spent the war with the army, which helped prepare him for the special role in baseball that was ahead of him.

"I was in the 350th Mountain Division," he told me. "We fought from Naples up to the Austrian border and it was rough going. I particularly remember an occasion when a squad of black kids took a very bad beating one day; they must have lost fifteen out of twenty guys, and I remember thinking how ridiculous it was that they were treated in America the way they were when they were fighting and dying for their country just like everybody else."

In 1946, Branch Rickey gave Bavasi and another famous Dodger boss what turned out to be a critical job—running the farm team in Nashua, New Hampshire, where Roy Campanella and Don Newcombe began their careers. Buzzie Bavisi was the team's overall boss, and Walter Alston was the manager. Both established stars in the Negro Leagues, Campanella and Newcombe were sent to New Hampshire (while Jackie Robinson went to

Montreal) because it was the only team further down in the system that would accept them.

"I doubt there were ten black people in Nashua at the time, and I worried about it long and hard before the season, going around and meeting with local businesspeople, including the newspaper," Bavasi recalled. "I shouldn't have bothered. Everyone up there was fantastic."

Signed immediately after the barrier-breaking announcement of Robinson's contract at the end of 1945, the two players were being prepared for special roles—Campanella playing a leadership position on the field as a catcher and Newcombe preparing to throw fastballs at white players with bats in their hands.

Jackie Robinson was born in tiny Cairo, Georgia, and came of age in Pasadena, just next to Los Angeles. The two superstars who followed him to the Dodgers were more traditional city kids. Newcombe was raised in tough neighborhoods of Newark, New Jersey. Campanella grew up in Philadelphia, and the racism they each confronted was especially virulent in the great catcher's case because he was born to a Sicilian father and an African-American mother.

If Bavasi was excited about being part of history, Alston was typically stoic. As he put it in his memoir, "I recall that I took the pioneer assignment in stride. I take no particular credit for this acceptance of the new status quo. I was not being charitable or altruistic. I simply had a job to do and accepted it without question."

Together, Bavasi and Alston proved a successful team. One time when he was thrown out of a game by an umpire, Alston casually designated Campanella to take his place. On another occasion, after a particularly ugly day of racial epithets from another team (not surprisingly, the Red Sox farm team from Lynn, Massachusetts), the two young men appeared at the visiting team's bus after the game and challenged its manager and anyone else to fight. No one answered.

In Brooklyn, Bavasi agreed with Reverend Taylor from the team's perspective. Bavasi said the question of adding black players after the first few years was always carefully considered, if not always with the loftiest of motives. On at least three occasions, the Dodgers missed the chance to sign players who went on to have a major impact on the league.

The first was Sam Jethroe, a swift and solid-hitting outfielder for the Cleveland Buckeyes in the Negro Leagues. The Dodgers had signed him after Robinson's first season as a Dodger, and Jethroe went on to dominate the International League with Montreal in 1948 and 1949 (when he stole eighty-nine bases). That winter, however, Rickey sold Jethroe and another player to the Boston Braves for $255,000. He was Rookie of the Year the following season at the age of thirty-two. He could have filled the left field opening that plagued Brooklyn for years after the beloved Pete Reiser's injuries.

Rickey's famous parsimony also cost the team the chance to sign Monte Irvin, a famous slugger with the old Newark Eagles (the Negro Leagues team that began in Brooklyn in 1935 by taking the name of the local paper and was founded by a numbers racket boss, Abe Manley, and his wife, Effa, who ran the franchise where Don Newcombe first played). Effa Manley was angry and vocal about the major-league teams that raided her league, and insisted on compensation for players. Had Rickey been willing to part with five thousand dollars, he could have signed Irvin, who eventually came up with the Giants and is now in the Hall of Fame.

The most revealing story, however, involved a teenager from Puerto Rico with a rifle for an arm and a famously quick bat, who grew up listening to Dodger games on the radio and idolized Carl Furillo. Roberto Clemente was signed for ten thousand dollars in 1954 by Dodger scout Al Campanis (the man who signed Sandy Amoros, among others) and played that year in Montreal. As Clemente was what was known as an "amateur free agent," with a bonus of more than four thousand dollars, the league rules required (in order to restrict big-spending owners) that either he be on the Dodger roster the following year or another team could draft him.

"O'Malley said flatly that winter he didn't want any more colored guys on the team," Bavasi told me. "It was complicated, but it was a combination of what he thought the fans would accept, what he thought the team could handle, and the fact that he got heat from some of his partners who worried that the more integrated the Dodgers became, the more pressure they felt to hire blacks in their own businesses."

Bavasi said that Jackie Robinson himself expressed misgivings about Clemente. There had already been tension on the team when eroding skills and the arrival of Gilliam prompted the Dodgers to demote popular third baseman Billy Cox to part-time status while a gradually slowing Robinson moved over from second base to replace him. In the case of Clemente, Bavasi said Robinson was concerned that if the Dodgers activated him, he would take the roster position of George "Shotgun" Shuba—a journeyman outfielder and pinch-hitter who was popular, white, and once Robinson's 1946 teammate on the Montreal Royals.

Bavasi said Branch Rickey—by then at the end of his career running the Pittsburgh Pirates—had been willing to let the Dodgers keep Clemente, but bad blood with O'Malley prevented a formal deal. Rickey drafted the future Hall of Fame player in the first round and Clemente was gone to the Pirates.

For all the intrigue, however, the fact was that the Brooklyn Dodgers in 1955 were a team with a national following based in no small part on the fact that not only had the team broken the segregation barrier, it had also shattered it.

I was only nine, but all this history, including my own and my parents', was pounded into my bones as we completed our morning routines that long-ago Tuesday. Long before the first pitch, a huge national following as diverse as Brooklyn itself had begun to hope (again) for something that transcended victory in a baseball game.

5

Two Pitchers

I was on my own for the long morning after my father and I dropped my mother off at Grand Central Station for her subway ride to work. After my father bought the papers, we split up. He was headed farther downtown to the office of the agent who produced many of his magazine assignments. Miss Strassman was an elegantly dressed woman with jet-black hair who was loyally devoted to my father despite the fact that his failing health made him one of her least productive clients.

Alone, I walked the rest of the way back down 42nd Street to our building. If this was a weekend I would have been in the park in a flash to play ball before the game started. Arrangements never had to made ahead of time; there were always enough kids around for a game. But this was a weekday, and it never occurred to me, "sick" or not, not to take the elevator upstairs to our apartment and finish practicing the piano and completing my schoolwork. I was in the fifth grade that year, and my teacher, William Kenney, was an exacting instructor who could be a warm, witty mentor unless you failed to do your work. He lived in Queens and was a die-hard Giant fan, which made us adversaries during the baseball season but allies in Yankee hatred every autumn.

I have no memory of the late morning, except a mental picture of my father's return home—the signal that it was time to make sandwiches and devour the sports pages, which we mostly did in silence. That day, they made much of the obvious classic clash between the Dodgers' very young left-hander, Johnny Podres, and the Yankees' veteran left-hander, Tommy Byrne, the kid who had dominated the Yankees and put the Dodgers back on track in Game Three and the experienced professional who had methodically shut them down in Game Two. Logic as well as atmospherics, not to mention the bookies' odds, dictated that the veteran was more likely to repeat than the kid.

The newspapers' preoccupation was both traditional and appropriate. Baseball is a team game comprised of individual actions, and no individual is more important on any given day than the pitcher. The Yankees and Dodgers may have been stocked with some of the best and best-known players of their day that day—Mantle-Berra-Martin-Rizzuto versus Robinson-Snider-Hodges-Campanella—but the nature of the game would be established by two of the lesser-knowns. It is a team game, but the pitcher on his own on his mound is one of its enduring symbols.

As it was, one of the oldest of melodramatic story lines—talented youth versus talented experience—was itself the product of two very human and equally hoary narratives, the gritty rise to success and the comeback from adversity. What is more, Podres and Byrne were in position to face each other because of the pivotal role played by the same man—Podres's first Brooklyn manager, Charlie Dressen. It was Dressen who had first taught Podres as a minor leaguer three years before how to throw the pitch that made him an effective major leaguer—the changeup. And it had been Dressen shortly after that, dismissed from the Dodgers and managing on the West Coast, who had spotted the comeback potential in Tommy Byrne after his career in the major leagues had seemed to come to a sad stop.

It made perfect sense that someone like Byrne was one of the starters in the seventh game. But although Johnny Podres was hardly the first kid to be in the spotlight at a climactic contest, he didn't quite fit for such an epic moment in an epic rivalry. He had finished his third season with the Dodgers, but he was not part of Dodger lore, not really known or appreciated. Hard-core Dodger fans, my family included, would have felt less uncomfortable on this terrifying day if Carl Erskine's arm had not gone sore on him. Podres's performance in Game Three was beside the point; this was it, but the Dodgers were going with a guy who'd been hurt much of the season and never made much of an impression.

Once again, little did we know. Above all, we didn't know Johnny Podres. Come to think of it, we didn't know Tommy Byrne, either.

It is an oft-noted fact that relatively few of the people who played that seventh game in 1955 are still alive. Fate, as it turns out, has been much kinder to the pitchers than to the hitters. Podres and Byrne, two very different people who arrived at their celebrated meeting by taking very different paths, are two of the exceptions—alive, in fairly decent health, full of memories of interesting lives and of that day, which they have long since come to terms with as the inevitable public reference point of their careers. I sought them both out at their homes in New York and North Carolina on the assumption that they were the best narrators of their paths to Yankee Stadium on that October afternoon and that they would be the best people to set the stage for the Tommy Byrne curveball that opened the game. I was not disappointed.

Nearly fifty years later, standing in the parking area of a Mobil station just off Interstate 87 in the upstate New York town of Queensbury, I noticed the black car coming my way when it was about a quarter of a mile away. I don't know anything about cars, but this was a nice one, perhaps a bit out of place in a middle-class community like Queensbury, which lies north of Albany and just north of horse-racing heaven in Saratoga, just south of the working family vacation area around the southern shores of Lake George, in the foothills of the Adirondacks. It is also barely an hour's drive south of the small onetime mining town of Witherbee, where the hero of the 1955 Series was raised.

The car, a Cadillac DeVille, pulled into the parking area where I had been pacing earlier, and there was no doubt whose it was from the license plate—MVP55. As it stopped in front of me, I saw a solidly built man behind the wheel, wearing a Philadelphia Phillies cap. When Johnny Podres turned to face me, smiled broadly, and stuck out his hand, what I recognized instantly was the eyes—deep-set above a serious nose, not wide or sparkling, but dark and intense, eyes that could concentrate to the point of fixation.

When we had talked on the phone after I had arrived in the area, he had insisted on meeting me at the gas station to guide me to his house. It was no more than two miles away, but there were enough turns to convince me I probably would have gotten lost on my own. Podres's gesture was typically considerate, made matter-of-factly: I would go to this gas station; he would meet me there; he would lead me from there. He was warm but to the point; there were no extra words.

His two-story white house is on the corner of a quiet street of well-kept family homes, not a gated community of McMansions, where today's professional ballplayers are likely to be found. On the day we talked, he was planning to meet his son later at Saratoga. Johnny Podres loved the ponies as a player, and he loves them in retirement. He and his boy own a pacer that Podres races at county and state fairs during the summer; he was fresh off a victory in Massachusetts.

Podres's retirement is anything but lavish. He had a successful postplaying career as a pitching coach, working with the Minnesota Twin teams in the 1980s that won two World Series and then with the Phillies, where he helped develop a young pitcher named Curt Schilling and with whom he still consults. The day I met Podres was a few days before the annual induction ceremonies at baseball's Hall of Fame in Cooperstown, a couple of hours' drive to the west. He was planning to go over to one of the souvenir shops on the town's main street to, as he put it, make a few extra bucks signing autographs.

He ushered me into an ordered living room dominated by a

long couch and a large leather lounging chair, where he sat, leaning back so the footrest came out. On the way into the room, the wall in the hallway is filled with his plaques, but until you look closely and see his award as the Most Valuable Player of the 1955 World Series, it could be the trophy wall of any modestly successful athlete.

The fact is, Johnny Podres came up the hard way. It was his grandfather who came to this country from Poland, settling in Schenectady. His dad, who died young, worked in the iron mines of upstate New York. He and Podres's mom (still vigorous in her nineties, dividing her time between friends and family in Witherbee and nearby Mineville in the summer and her son's home during the winter) had five children, Johnny Podres being the eldest.

It was a baseball family. Podres was taught the game from the age of four by his father, a pitcher who played what was known as town ball—guys from a community who worked regular jobs all week and played on Sunday for the few dollars the team had left over after expenses. It was called semipro baseball, but even the *semi* was an exaggeration. In addition to playing ball all the way through school, young Johnny Podres was playing town ball in the area by his sophomore year, often pitching against his dad.

As it happened, the principal at Podres's high school knew somebody who knew a major-league scout, who arranged two tryouts for Podres in the summer of 1950. The first, with the Phillies at the old Shibe Park in Philadelphia, brought him no offer. His second shot was at Ebbets Field, where he remembers throwing along the first-base line in front of the Dodger dugout for at most a half hour. Upstairs in the office, Podres also remembers the booming voice of Branch Rickey, then in the final weeks of his astonishing tenure. After the season, another aching Dodger disappointment that slipped away on the last day to a young Philadelphia Phillies team immortalized as the Whiz Kids, Rickey sold his 25 percent share of the team to master maneuverer Walter O'Malley and departed for his final gig with the Pittsburgh Pirates.

"Don't let that kid get away," the voice bellowed. Podres signed with the Dodgers for a $5,200 bonus and a minor-league contract paying $160 a month. In retrospect, he wishes he had negotiated for a somewhat smaller bonus and a somewhat larger salary. But it was more money than he had ever imagined existed, and he bought some new clothes and a blue Oldsmobile.

At spring training, he came face-to-face with the reality of trying to break into professional baseball—more than five hundred fellow prospects vying for minor-league jobs. Podres got a good assignment—Class B at Newport News, Virginia, under a former Chicago Cub pitcher and well-regarded teacher, Clay Bryant. He did not perform well, however, and after going 0–2 the first month of the season found himself further down the chain in Hazard, Kentucky.

Not for the last time in his career, however, Podres responded to having his back against a wall. He won twenty-one games, two more in the league play-off, and won a shot with the Dodgers themselves the following spring.

"I was warming up one day, throwing the fastballs and curves I threw, when Charlie Dressen walked by and said, I can still hear him, 'Hey son, you got a changeup?' I didn't know what the hell a changeup was."

Neither did I, so Podres picked up a baseball on the coffee table in front of me and held it in his left hand.

"Try to imagine that first joint on your fingers is like a lifeless stub, but squeeze the ball hard in your palm while you're throwing normally. It slows it down. I learned it quickly and Charlie Dressen fell in love with me. Before spring training was over he told me I had made the team."

In those early days of the Cold War, however, it wasn't as simple as that for a young player. There was nothing unusual about players being drafted into the armed services (Don Newcombe himself was away at the time), and Podres was classified 1A, ready to go. Baseball's rules were like those governing every employer, meaning that people who were drafted were entitled to their same job back when they got out of the service. For Podres, that meant that if he came all the way up to the Dodgers that spring, he might get drafted, go away for two years, and then try to keep his job in the major leagues after all that time away. It was second nature for a child of the depression to have job security firmly on his mind. The smarter move was to start the season with the Dodgers' AAA club in Montreal; if he was drafted, served, and then came back there, he would have a better chance to reacquire his skills and then move up to the parent team. The Dodger management agreed with Podres. In 1952, a promising rookie pitcher would have been a nice addition to the staff, but the team still enjoyed the productive services of a solid veteran and one of the most popular players in Brooklyn, Elwin Charles "Preacher" Roe.

Podres had a solid year on the Royals (where the top pitcher that year was still another young left-hander named Tommy Lasorda), but playing pro ball was beginning to take a toll on his back and pitching shoulder. It wasn't career threatening, but it was enough to make him ineligible at that point for the military draft, always a weird bureaucratic maze that passed on more than a few young men who had conditions (like bad backs, flat feet, and marginally poor eyesight) that didn't affect their ability to do their jobs or, truth be told, to be in combat.

The next year, Podres made the Dodgers in spring training.

As in his debut in the minors at Newport News, Podres struggled at first and got little help from Dressen in his first two pitching assignments—against Giant ace Sal Maglie and then against the Phillies' future Hall of Famer Robin Roberts. Podres was 0–2 before his first major-league victory, against the Phillies—a game in which he was relieved at the end by Carl Erskine, who was normally a starter. The struggling continued, however, and by the early summer Podres was looking at the real possibility of a trip back to Montreal.

In the 1950s, one of the minor rites of the Dodgers–Yankees rivalry was an exhibition game near the middle of the season, a charity affair known as the Mayor's Trophy Game. The teams didn't play their stars for the entire game and second-line pitchers were typically used, but fans paid attention and in 1953 so did Johnny Podres, the starting pitcher. Aware that his future might be on the line, he once again came through with a dominating performance, in which he struck out thirteen Yankee hitters.

His job was safe, but Podres's progression as a major-league pitcher was nonetheless slow, if steady. His rookie season record on the pennant-winning team (in many respects a more intimidating group than the Dodgers of 1955) was 9–4, with a respectable 4.23 earned-run average. It was enough to earn him the starting assignment in the pivotal fifth game of the 1953 World Series at Ebbets Field, with the Series deadlocked at two games apiece.

He only made it through the second out of the third inning, after which the Yankees had six runs on the way to an 11–7 victory. As Podres delights in pointing out, however, the score doesn't tell the real story of a kid just barely twenty-one years old who gave a decent account of himself.

In the first inning, Podres had given up a home run to Yankee left fielder Gene Woodling, whose fly ball made it into the left field stands, a run the Dodgers got back in the second. In the third, Podres had gotten two outs with one man on when Yankee first baseman Joe Collins hit a ground ball off Gil Hodges's normally near-perfect glove for an error, scoring a run. Podres then hit right fielder Hank Bauer and walked Yogi Berra to load the bases, at which point Dressen yanked him in favor of Russ Meyer (a Whiz Kid with the pennant-winning Phillies three years before).

What followed was a memorable event in World Series history—a grand-slam home run by Mickey Mantle that landed in the left field stands' upper deck. If Hodges had fielded Collins's ground ball none of those runs would have scored.

The next year, Podres was an even more respectable 11–7, with more than 150 innings under his belt, but it was in the championship season of 1955 that he appeared to be on the way to stardom.

After a spring training dominated by doubts about aging hitters and untested pitchers, an injured Roy Campanella, an aging Jackie Robinson, and a Don Newcombe still rusty from two years in the military, the Dodgers simply ran away with the pennant. They won their first ten games, breaking the modern (as in twentieth-century) record, and, after two losses to the Giants, proceeded to break the record again by reeling off eleven straight. The last one was a masterful performance by Newcombe, who pitched a one-hitter against the Cubs but thanks to a double play faced only twenty-seven hitters to get twenty-seven outs. The team in effect never looked back and ended up clinching the pennant against the second-place Milwaukee Braves on September 8, earlier than any National League pennant had ever been clinched, breaking the mark set by Brooklyn two years before.

Most descriptions of Podres's 1955 performance completely miss the point, focusing on either his 9–10 record or his two bouts with injury. As Podres himself will tell all who inquire, he had won seven games by June, though two of his three losses just happened to be the ones that ended the two record-breaking winning streaks. The trouble started late that month, when he pitched into extra innings against the St. Louis Cardinals and felt a twinge in his pitching shoulder that became a pain so severe he often couldn't sleep; that cost him his effectiveness for the rest of the summer. Then, in early September, he was standing near home plate before a game, hitting fly balls to the outfielders as pitchers often do during warm-ups; behind him, the Dodgers' crew began pushing the large batting cage on wheels for its long journey to a gate in center field.

The crew didn't see Podres and he didn't see the crew. The result was that the side of the cage hit the pitcher squarely and painfully in the ribs. Two more weeks were lost. At the end of the season, when the Dodgers were making their final decision on who would make the roster for the World Series, Podres was given a relief assignment against the Pittsburgh Pirates. At the time, the choice for the final pitching spot had come down to Podres and still another promising left-hander in the Dodger system, Kenny Lehman, who was then with Montreal. Once again with his back to a wall, Podres responded by retiring all twelve batters he faced and his spot on the roster was secure.

The Dodgers' day-to-day chief executive at the time, Buzzie

Bavasi, told me he remembers Podres in his office shortly before the decision was made, talking animatedly about the situation.

"He asked me if I wanted to win the World Series or not," Bavasi recalled. "The kid was a real horse player and he had a burning desire to win. His dad had worked in the iron mines upstate and he never wanted to have to go back there."

In the sports pages before the World Series began, and even before he pitched in the third game, Podres was at most an afterthought in the listing of Dodger pitchers, usually with the adjective *sore-armed* in front of his name.

"What I suppose people didn't realize, though I certainly did, was that I had a rested arm, a fresh arm," Podres told me.

The biggest day of his baseball life is mostly a blur to him now, not because his memory is the slightest bit dulled (at seventy-one he's as sharp as a tack) but because his concentration on simply throwing the ball to Roy Campanella's glove was so intense.

Podres told me that his confidence stemmed from a conviction that his presumed disadvantage—youth and inexperience—was in fact his advantage. The Dodger veterans for the most part were famously preoccupied with the multitude of disappointments of the previous decade. Podres was not. His one World Series, though a disappointment, was anything but an obsession. He said he was excited and nervous before the game, but not scared. What he didn't say was what others have said for years: he was also brash.

He recalls nothing special about the morning of October 4 beyond visiting briefly with two of his uncles and his father, who had driven down from Witherbee for the proudest moment of his hard life. Before the game, he was warmed up by the Dodgers' bullpen catcher, Dixie Howell, who came out of the Louisville area like his teammate Pee Wee Reese. *Bullpen catcher* was a fancy term for third-string catcher, behind Campanella's usual backup, Al (Rube) Walker, but Howell was a diligent contributor in the third of what would be eight years in the major leagues. He had only gotten into sixteen games in 1955, but the pitchers swore by him. A good bullpen catcher can make a huge difference in preparing a pitcher for a game, especially a young one. He eases the pitcher into top speed, varies his pitches so that each is ready for use in the game, spots the ones he is having trouble with, and nudges him back into command of them. Dixie Howell was very good at what he did.

Podres has never had trouble remembering one moment, sitting on the bench next to Howell in the visitors' dugout after warming up, while the Yankees' mellifluous-voiced public-address man, Bob Shepherd, was announcing the starting lineups, and he recalled it for me as if to illustrate his mood.

"I knew Mickey Mantle was hurt bad and couldn't play the outfield and I knew Hank Bauer [the Yankees' right fielder] had a bum leg. As Shepherd went through the names, I just turned to Dixie and said, 'That lineup can't beat me today.'"

Earlier, on the team bus driving over to the Stadium from Brooklyn, Duke Snider remembers an excited Podres as among the last players to board the bus, circulating in the aisle, repeating over and over again, "Just get me one run today. That's all I need. Just one."

He did it so often, the more relaxed veterans started kidding him by occasionally asking him with mock seriousness how many runs he needed. Podres didn't joke back; he just kept repeating—one, just one.

Podres has no memory of his manager, Walter Alston, a quiet, stoic man, circulating in the clubhouse, telling players as he had told them before the Dodgers began their comeback in the third game in Brooklyn that he thought they were the better team, trying to counter the pervasive sense of jinx that affected players and fans alike; there is, however, a rare picture of him doing just that right in front of a seated Podres. He has only slight memories of his pregame clubhouse chat alone with Roy Campanella but is quite clear about what the strong-willed catcher had established as the strategy for the game.

At Ebbets Field, Podres had varied the speed of his pitches the entire game, as befits a relatively tiny ballpark where mistakes tend to be called home runs. He told me he threw his changeup at least twenty times during the game and also varied the speed of his curve.

At Yankee Stadium, Campanella had something else in mind because of the way shadows slowly creep toward home plate there during a day game. In the early innings both pitcher and batter are bathed in sunlight, but by the middle of a game shadows gradually come between them, giving the pitcher an advantage as his ball travels from the bright to the darker light at roughly ninety miles an hour. One of the many aphorisms attributed to the Yankees' great catcher Yogi Berra, one that he really uttered, was his observation that in the Stadium "it gets late here early."

For the seventh game, Campanella's idea was for Podres to show the Yankees his changeup early, to throw it just enough in the early innings to keep the hitters from sitting back and waiting for fast pitches, to hope that his control of the pitch was as sharp as it was during Game Three in Brooklyn to make it effective. Once the shadows arrived, however, Campanella wanted the hard stuff for as long as Podres's strength lasted.

More than his sketchy pregame memories or the details of his career and season to that point, what I got out of conversation with Podres—even after all the intervening years—was a clear sense of his intense determination. He had acquired a bit of a reputation as a young player as a rambunctious person who loved the horses and other aspects of the fast life, perhaps a bit much for his own good. What came through to me to round out his portrait was a will of the iron his dad used to mine. When we parted, his ability to pitch in crucial games—where his career or his team's season was on the line—was much less of a mystery.

On the other side of the field warming up that day was an experienced pitcher who is the perfect bookend for the kid Walter Alston started. Off his record that year, Tommy Byrne was as natural a choice by the legendary Casey Stengel to pitch the second game of the Series, which he won, as he was to pitch the seventh. Through the years, as descriptions of him declined toward shorthand, the common adjectives have been *veteran, stylish,* and *crafty.*

I had heard as I began working on the game's story that Byrne was a much more interesting character and that getting him away from stick-figured caricature was as important to the actual drama as understanding more about Johnny Podres.

That was an understatement. The tall man who greeted me in his driveway was eighty-four years old, still spry despite heart trouble, with a firm handshake and a delightful wry wit. He lives near where he went to college in Wake Forest, North Carolina. After baseball, he had a very successful business career in real estate and development and was mayor of Wake Forest twice, and an active supporter of the public school system. His wife, Mary Sue, to whom he was devoted and who passed away late in 2002, was every bit as well-known locally as he was, having played a leadership role at the end of the 1960s in promoting the peaceful and successful desegregation of the area's schools. Byrne lives today in a house built next to a golf course he developed in the early 1960s and eventually sold. As we walked into the house, he stopped in the garage and pointed out a golf cart casually parked amid the clutter. It had a Rolls-Royce hood ornament in the front and was decorated all around in Yankee pinstripes. It took a while, but my eyes gradually strayed to the number 7 in the back. It had been Mickey Mantle's golf cart; Byrne had picked it up at a charity auction years before, and though his heart trouble has limited his golf time, the cart is still used. Eventually, Byrne said, he will give it to the Hall of Fame.

As he walked me around the memory-filled home, two pictures among the many on his walls caught my eye. One was a blown-up version of the traditional posed pregame photograph of the opposing pitchers that long-ago day, autographed by both men. Byrne never knew Podres well, he said, but they have crossed paths occasionally over the years, always on friendly terms;

Byrne remains astonished at Podres's gutsy performance in both games in 1955 and was pleased after inquiring to hear that his long-ago opponent was enjoying life. The other picture was taken with Byrne's wife, sitting on a camel in front of the famous pyramids in Giza. Following the World Series in 1955, the Yankees had gone on what was then known as a goodwill tour of Japan, playing exhibitions against local and all-star teams; when the tour ended, Byrne took his wife the rest of the way around the world, a tiny reminder of what an enormous sum of money fifty-seven hundred dollars (the losers' share that year) was in 1955.

Like Podres, Byrne came from next to nothing. Unlike Podres, Byrne made it to the mound for that climactic game after a remarkable comeback from a years-long wildness streak that typically ended careers.

Thomas Joseph Byrne is from Baltimore, the youngest of four boys, all raised by their mother after their parents separated. He came by his baseball inspiration early. At the age of five, he was taken by his mom to the old ballpark where the then-minor-league Baltimore Orioles played. She was the acquaintance of another Baltimorean who had made it to the major leagues—Wilson Lloyd (Chick) Fewster, who was a reserve infielder with the post–World War I New York Yankees, who were in town that day for an exhibition.

At the ballpark, Fewster introduced the young Byrne to the most famous left-hander of them all, also the product of a broken home in Baltimore—Babe Ruth. Ruth signed his name to a baseball and gave it to the awed boy; the handwriting has faded over the years, but the ball remains with Byrne's other mementos in his home. Byrne's first brush with greatness stayed with him as he learned baseball; at that time, every left-handed kid in Baltimore had visions of Babe Ruth dancing in his head. Much later, when Byrne had made it to the Yankees, he told the then-retired superstar about their long-ago encounter. After that, until cancer got him in 1948, Ruth always made it a point to use Tommy Byrne's glove—he called it a pud—whenever he appeared in one of the Old-Timers' Games the team put on each year.

Byrne was a star pitcher in a tough league, playing for Baltimore City College High School, with well over three thousand
students; it was an environment well-known to professional and
college recruiters. He could have signed out of high school in
1939 with the Detroit Tigers, but he wanted to go to college.

The offers weren't long in coming, primarily channeled
through the owner of a local sporting goods operation that sold
uniforms all over the country. In North Carolina, Duke offered a
full scholarship that came with the small string of a job in the
cafeteria; Wake Forest offered the scholarship without the cafeteria job, so Byrne went there to major in mathematics.

It was no small adjustment for a city kid, a devout Catholic, to
head off to what was then a small Baptist college town. However,
virtually adopted by his coach's family and warmly embraced by
the area he would call home for the rest of his life, Byrne flowered.

The professional contract came after his junior year, a ten-
thousand-dollar bonus from the Yankees that came with a job at
their top farm team, in Newark. Byrne did not neglect his studies,
though; taking classes over the next three winters, he earned his
degree just before entering the navy and World War II in 1943.

He had made his debut with the Yankees earlier in the year, appearing in eleven games and winning two. He was fast, he was
smart, but he was also wild from the start.

In the war, he was a gunnery officer on a destroyer (the USS
Ordronaux) that saw action in both the Atlantic and Pacific The-
aters ("for that work my aim was much better"). Byrne's ship was
primarily an escort vessel, helping protect convoys from the constant danger of submarine attack. It was in on more than one kill
and was part of the massive armada off the coast of France on
D day. Byrne is especially proud of one mission, in the group of
escort vessels guarding President Roosevelt as he steamed toward
Yalta in the Crimea for his historic summit with Stalin and
Churchill near the end of the war and of his life.

Byrne returned to the Yankees in time for the 1946 season. His
moments in the sun were delayed, but they came as he was near-

ing his thirtieth birthday. He won eight games in 1948, fifteen in 1949 (a Yankee pennant year and the first of their still-astonishing five consecutive World Championship seasons), and fifteen more in 1950. Byrne was chosen to start the pivotal third game of the 1949 World Series at Ebbets Field against Ralph Branca; he lasted into the fourth inning, yielding a run on two hits, but loading the bases before he was pulled for Joe Page, one of the five-game Series's stars.

In addition to his pitching, Byrne was famous for his ability to hit, which few pitchers could do consistently (one of the more notable exceptions was the Dodgers' star, Don Newcombe, but Byrne was just as good). From high school through his time with Newark he was a high-average batter with power. Ultimately, he hit fourteen home runs as a major leaguer, including two grand slams hit with two outs in the ninth inning to win ball games as a pinch-hitter.

He also hit when it counted in the World Series. In 1949, he kept the first run-producing Yankee rally going in Game Three with a sharp single to center field that sent Yankee right fielder Cliff "Tiger" Mapes to third base. In the second game of the Series in 1955, Byrne did more than pitch a complete game victory. In the Yankee half of the fourth inning, with the Dodgers having scored first, he drove in what turned out to be the game's winning runs off Brooklyn starter Billy Loes. Coming up to bat with the bases loaded and two outs, Byrne sent another sharp single into center field to score both Elston Howard and Jerry Coleman—runs 3 and 4 in a game the Yankees won 4–2.

Back in 1949, however, Byrne's wildness became legendary and ultimately intolerable. In his time, he had the dubious distinction of leading the league in hit batters an astonishing five times. He walked a league-leading 179 hitters in 1949, a league-leading 160 more in 1950, and a league-leading 150 more in 1951, when the despairing Yankees traded him to the lowly St. Louis Browns for a journeyman pitcher (Frank "Stubby" Overmire) and tossed in twenty-five thousand dollars to sweeten the pot. That was the beginning of a three-year slide. The Browns then traded Byrne to the Chicago White Sox along with light-hitting shortstop Joseph "Oats" DeMaestri, for the answer to a trivia question, an equally light-hitting shortstop from Cuba named Willie Miranda, and journeyman outfielder Hank Edwards; the White Sox sold his contract for just twenty thousand dollars to the Washington Senators, who after the 1953 season sold him to a Pacific Coast League team, the Seattle Rainiers, which did not have an affiliation agreement with a major-league team.

Tommy Byrne, however, neither died nor faded away. He simply learned to pitch better.

"Pitching is God-given talent above all," he told me. "If you have speed at the major-league level the ball moves so much when you throw it hard and probably eighty percent of your pitches are fastballs and hard curves. Control is something different; it's a frame of mind, a very different type of desire than just using your talent and throwing as hard as you can."

As a youngster, Byrne relied on his talent, and it took him to the New York Yankees and to the All-Star Game. As he got older, however, it wasn't enough; it never is. Making the transition from what is called a thrower to a pitcher is one of the keys to a long career in the major leagues, and not every pitcher can do it. Byrne told me he was still struggling with the transition, playing winter ball in Venezuela after the 1953 season, when he began working harder on his own changeup and learned the slider—a vicious pitch so-called because, as he put it, the pitcher reduces the friction of his fingers on the ball as he throws, making it "slide" off them, as opposed to quickly releasing it. It can look like a perfectly normal and inviting pitch as it comes toward home plate, until the bottom falls out of it at the last moment. He recalls winning thirteen games that winter.

"I had gone as far as I could on my talent, throwing hard and trying for strikeouts," Byrne said. "I figured it was time to change. I decided I was going to make the hitters hit the ball and let my fielders field it."

He had also acquired a reputation, in addition to his wildness, for being playfully mischievous in ways that distracted hitters. He was no longer relying on speed to get hitters out. He was living by his wits now, and he is a delightfully witty man.

From the mound he began talking occasionally to the hitters he was facing. Usually he would playfully call out the next pitch he was going to throw, alerts that were sometimes true, sometimes false. This kind of behavior is quite common with catchers but genuinely rare in pitchers. Byrne also sometimes added an extra hitch to his fluid pitching motion, casually flipping the ball in the air and catching it in his pitching hand, just before drawing his arm back to throw the ball.

"I remember the first time I did it," Byrne said of his mound conversation with a wry smile more suited to his adopted North Carolina than to urban Baltimore. "The Yankees had shipped me to St. Louis and I was ahead of them one day when Hank Bauer [New York's hard-hitting right fielder] came up. I yelled that a slider was coming. I did it a second time, and then a third, where-upon Hank hit a home run. I used to talk to hitters who tended to hit me well—like Al Rosen [the Cleveland Indians' All-Star third baseman] and Ted Williams. It was fun, but I noticed that it sometimes unnerved them."

In Game Two of the 1955 Series, he shouted at Duke Snider at least twice, though the results were mixed; Snider, famous for his inability to hit left-handed pitching, actually knocked in one of the two Dodger runs.

In 1954, without a major-league deal, Byrne hooked on with Seattle. After four months, he had won twenty games, and his name began once again to circulate among major-league general managers—George Weiss of the Yankees included. At the time, the Yankees were in a pitching transition not unlike the Dodgers'. The pitchers who had played central roles for the team in the 1940s and early '50s were retired—Joe Page, Allie Reynolds, Vic Raschi, and Ed Lopat in particular. That year, the first after the famous five-Series streak that the team failed to win a pennant, the Yankees were bringing in kids, and the prospect of an experienced pitcher back on top of his game was obviously enticing.

In the West Coast league that year, 1954, Charlie Dressen was managing in Oakland after the Dodgers dropped him following the World Series disasters of 1952 and '53. After seeing Byrne pitch, Dressen told his buddy Casey Stengel on the telephone one day that the left-hander had come all the way back and that the Yankees were nuts if they didn't pick him up. Stengel immediately went to George Weiss, and Tommy Byrne was a Yankee again.

After all that had happened four years before, the onetime wildest regular pitcher in the league could not be confident of his place on the team; he would have to prove himself all over again. He started the 1955 season without a clear role, but his big break came early when one of Stengel's promising young pitchers—Bob Grim—developed arm trouble and Byrne got a spot in the starting rotation that he never relinquished. He won one more game that year—sixteen in all—than he ever had before and was one of the mainstays of the staff, along with a hard-throwing right-handed rookie, Bob Turley, and the team's masterful left-handed starter, Whitey Ford.

Against the Dodgers, Byrne was trying to do what Johnny Podres was trying to do—keep the ball away from the most powerful hitters. Like Podres, Byrne was also trying to make use of the opportunities Yankee Stadium offered to a pitcher. Instead of the afternoon shadows between the pitcher's mound and home plate—an advantage to someone with a good fastball—Byrne was trying to take advantage of the famous ballpark's depth from left-center to right-center field and avoid giving hitters a chance to pull the ball down the Stadium's notoriously short foul lines—in those days, 301 feet in left, 298 in a right field built to accommodate Babe Ruth.

Podres was trying to show the Yankees his changeup just enough to keep the hitters off balance, to keep them from waiting for fastballs. Byrne, without the speed of his youth, had to vary speed and locations all the time, hoping for ground balls and flies hit toward the deep outfield. With Mickey Mantle hurt, Podres's greatest concern was putting men on base when the Yankees' dangerous catcher Yogi Berra was at bat. Byrne told me that it was Berra's counterpart, Roy Campanella, who was his greatest concern with men on base. One of the seventh game's ironies is that Berra had two chances that day to blow the game open with men on base and couldn't do it, while Campanella made his major contributions when the bases were empty and when he bunted.

That irony is not lost on Tommy Byrne, an educated man who survived a rough childhood as much by his wits as by his athletic ability. Fifty years later, what happened that one day lives on in the rounded perspective of a full life of accomplishment and happiness. The fact that the game day picture of Podres and Byrne is in his living room suggests he is aware that one day that game will dominate the single-element obituary that is regularly written about baseball players of long ago. His only regret is that he didn't get a chance to finish a game he pitched more than well enough to win. In his pleasant community in North Carolina, however, the place that nurtured a young college kid so many years before, The Game is but a blip, a piece of trivia.

On the day of the climactic game, the sports pages were full of kid versus veteran clichés, as have been the accounts ever since. I was hoping for more depth. The event had been so enormous a moment of my childhood that I wanted the protagonists to be worthy of the ultimate drama they dominated. Were they ever.

THE TORTURE BEGINS

I had begun to notice after my father came home from his trip downtown that he was unusually quiet. He neither engaged me in detailed pregame analysis nor inquired about my schoolwork or my piano as we ate our lunch and traded newspapers. For us, this was most unusual; normally we babbled incessantly about anything and everything. On this day, however, my father was quiet and therefore so was I. The first thing I remember him saying as one o'clock in the afternoon neared was that he thought it was time for me to "wake up Scarlet."

I trudged dutifully over to the television, pulled out the power button, and then engaged in the 1950s ritual of playing with the rabbit-eared antenna on top of the set until the picture was as clear as the blue sky over Yankee Stadium,

Before the seventh game, Johnny Podres and Tommy Byrne warmed up right on the field, throwing from makeshift mounds in foul territory close to the stands and not hiding in the walled-off bullpens of today—Podres near the third-base line in front of the Dodger dugout, Byrne on the opposite side. During the season, if you got to a ballpark early, this was a chance for a kid with a ticket in the cheap seats to come down toward the field and get so close to a major-league pitcher he could hear the whir of the pitched ball and the thud when it hit the catcher's mitt. I had done it countless times.

The only time there was ceremony at a World Series in those simpler days was before the first game. The players were introduced and lined up along the baselines; there was a band, usually assembled in the outfield to play the national anthem while a flag was raised. After that, except for the bunting draped over the front railings and the packed houses, the games were essentially hoopla-free.

As the Yankees took the field, my father and I took our own positions. I was on the couch, which was called a davenport then, an early example of modern (and cheap) furniture with a sleek black Scandinavian design. It was wide and comfortable, with large foam rubber cushions. I had arranged one of our bright red pillows against the wooden armrest so I was lying on it with my legs straight out. I had never been superstitious about sports events or anything else until that moment. For some reason, as I stretched out, I left my legs separated; when the Yankees were at bat I crossed my ankles.

My father was seated at the new dining table, with an ashtray and his cigarettes in front of him. Like Franklin D. Roosevelt, he used a holder, one he had bought when he first got to Australia at the beginning of the war. I didn't notice right away, but as the game progressed, this equally nonsuperstitious man was smoking when the Dodgers were up and seated with his arms folded when they were in the field.

One of the absurd delights of superstition is the assumption that one individual's magic can suffice unchallenged by another's. As it turned out, the Dodgers themselves—that season and that special day—had a serious one going.

Some time during the summer, a buttermilk cake arrived in the Dodger clubhouse from Frank Kellert's family in Oklahoma. After it was shared, the team went on a winning streak. Later in the season, during a Dodger slump, he asked his family for another one, after which the Dodgers caught fire again. For each game of the 1955 World Series, there were buttermilk cakes from the Kellert clan in the clubhouse. In his delightful memoir, Carl Erskine has preserved the recipe.

While the umpires, Dodger captain Pee Wee Reese, and Yankee manager Casey Stengel were having the ritual meeting at home plate, my father pulled the phone from the freshly fashioned bookshelves in the wall next to the table and called my mother at work. I couldn't hear what he said as I concentrated on the television set, but their conversation could not have lasted more than a minute.

In addition to our unspoken reliance on superstition, something else was different that day. Ordinarily, when my little family watched or listened to a ball game, we took turns keeping score on one of the yellow legal-sized pads my father used when he worked. On this day, neither of us made a move to get out a pad and neither of us said anything about it.

We also didn't speak after the Yankees took the field, which was odd. My father was a chatterbox, but this day he was silent. Like most nine-year-old kids, I took my cues from my father, so I didn't say anything, either. He seemed serious, intent, so I did my best to follow suit. It felt perfect to be alone with him. I easily could have been with my schoolmates, screaming at the set in the gym; I could easily have been with a friend at his apartment. This was special.

In the room, the only sound was the baritone, Alabama-formed voice of Mel Allen, the Yankees' famous broadcaster who would be doing the play-by-play for the first half of the game. My parents favored the cooler, less-cluttered style of people who transmitted information as well as a clear sense of what was going on. In our household, Red Barber was God and the first voice that brought Dodger baseball to my ears, but by 1955 he was gone to the greener (as in money) pastures of the Yankees and our allegiance had passed to a young man from the Bronx whom Barber had trained in his inimitable fashion to be more informative and witty than melodramatic. His name was Vin Scully.

In those days, the World Series on television was only four years old as a national event. I didn't realize it at the time, but 1955 was the first World Series to be broadcast by NBC in color, a fact of nearly no significance to the still black-and-white country. The corporate sponsor was Gillette—"to look sharp every time you shave"—and the broadcasters were from the teams that were playing. The fact that Mel Allen was beginning the game meant Vin Scully would be with us on the television set starting in the last half of the fifth inning. I had mentioned this happy fact to my father while we were having lunch, only to be reminded that Scully had also been broadcasting at the end of another game that had ended the World Series, the depressing Game Six of the 1953 debacle.

After the Yankees took the field and Byrne walked slowly to the pitcher's mound to make his final warm-up pitches, I have distinct memories of a quiet crowd and of staring at the Yankee pitcher who had been so dominant just days before. Tommy Byrne had a fluid pitching motion and, very much like his more famous left-handed pitching partner that year (Whitey Ford), never seemed to be very fast or overpowering. When he was doing well, he just seemed to methodically get people out.

As an experienced Dodger fan I knew to pay close attention whenever the top of their batting order was up. The opening trio of Jim (Junior) Gilliam, Reese, and Snider was notoriously run producing. The Dodgers had led the National League that year in runs scored by a huge margin—more than a hundred runs—and the combination of Gilliam as the leadoff man, Reese as the versatile second man, and Snider as the first power hitter to bat had scored more than a third of them. Reese and Snider were of course well-established stars, but it was Gilliam who had become a critical spark plug for the Dodgers and was, moreover, a vivid example of how deep the team's commitment to integration had become.

James William Gilliam, a slender, gifted athlete from Nashville, was twenty-seven years old that day. He was known as Junior back then, a residue of his status in the late 1940s as the youngest member of the Baltimore Elite Giants in the Negro National League. He had been mentored in infield play (second base was his original position) by one of the best shortstops of the 1940s, Thomas Butts, whose nickname, Pee Wee, was for Gilliam prophetic. He was fast, able to play in the infield as well as the outfield, and had come into the major leagues two years before as one of the last of the players to emerge from the Negro Leagues, which had begun to fade almost from the moment Jackie Robinson became a Dodger.

The team that Branch Rickey assembled after World War II was not merely designed to break the infamous "color line" that had imprisoned the sport like the rest of America in segregation. It was designed to obliterate it. Rickey's plan provides a vivid illustration of the important distinction between desegregation (ending the whites-only restriction) and integration (bringing African-Americans into the game as equals).

As with the rest of society, this required a measure of what was eventually called affirmative action to jump-start the process. Then, as now, the issue is not the phony concepts of qualification or reverse discrimination; what was involved was making a special effort to recruit nonwhite talent, because the traditional system was inherently incapable of producing it. In the early 1950s, the Dodgers were still buying players from the Negro Leagues, which in a desperate attempt to stay alive financially were selling them off. In the wake of Walter O'Malley's takeover of the team from Rickey, one of the executives who remained under the new regime was Lafayette Fresco Thompson, a legend who ran the team's productive farm system.

The year after Rickey left, Thompson was going after a top

pitcher on the Elite Giants, Leroy Farrell, then in the military. The sale price was supposed to be ten thousand dollars, but in an effort to get a bargain for his penny-pinching boss, Thompson persuaded the Elite Giants to add two young players to the deal. As it turned out, Farrell never made the team.

One of the throw-in players was Joe Black, a pitcher with a wicked fastball, who developed quickly into the Rookie of the Year in 1952, a critical cog in the Dodgers' pennant-winning season.

The other was Junior Gilliam, who blossomed into the Rookie of the Year in 1953. (The National League's relatively more aggressive pursuit of African-Americans paid off quickly; five of the first six Rookies of the Year were African-Americans, including Robinson in 1947, Don Newcombe in '49, Sam Jethroe of the Boston Braves in 1950, and Willie Mays of the New York Giants in '51; only Alvin Dark, who won in 1948 with the Braves, was white.)

By 1955, Gilliam was firmly ensconced as the Dodgers' switch-hitting leadoff man, but his initial role as the team's second baseman had changed. That year he also played more than forty games in the outfield, usually in left field when the opponent was a left-hander, as he was that famous day. With Jackie Robinson usually playing third base by then, this gave the Dodgers an opportunity to use a solid young player—Don Zimmer, then completing his first full year with the team—as the backup second baseman.

Gilliam did nothing spectacularly but everything well. He had the patience at the plate to walk often, he hit decently, and on base he was a legitimate threat to steal or play run-and-hit with the batter behind him, Pee Wee Reese, who was also a talented bunter. That was why we were paying especially close attention as the game began; if Gilliam could get on base, dangerous hitters were coming up with a chance to bring him home.

We were not simply paying close attention, however. We were already in the early stages of Dodger agony, hoping to the point of prayer that this might be The Day, but without confidence. I had a habit by then that has always stayed with me of tensing my stomach muscles and pursing my lips in a moment of anticipation and tension. I was concentrating on Scarlet's black-and-white picture so much that I was aware of nothing else in the room as the game began. Mel Allen was obviously saying something on the air, but my memory is of no sound at all, just that big picture that included a thin man walking toward home plate with a bat.

Gilliam, hitting right-handed, dug in, and the smooth Byrne wind-up began. The pitch to Gilliam was a tantalizing slow curveball. It started high from the first-base side of the mound and then seemed to steadily break in and down to him. But Gilliam timed it well, swung hard, and the ball got past Byrne before he could even reach for it. I sat upright on the couch because my first sense of the ball was that it was headed straight up the middle into center field for a single.

Within a split second, however, it was clear the ball had gone almost dead as soon as it hit the ground and was bouncing slowly on the infield grass behind the mound. In an instant, Phil Rizzuto came running into the picture from shortstop. He fielded the ball cleanly after a perfect hop into his outstretched glove and threw Gilliam out at first by three steps. As quickly as I had tensed and sat up, I sank back into the couch cushion.

The next two outs came quickly: Pee Wee Reese on an easy fly ball to Bob Cerv in center field; Duke Snider on a routine ground ball to Billy Martin at second. Tommy Byrne, after shutting the Dodgers down in Game Two at the Stadium, looked just as dangerous as he walked back to the Yankee dugout.

Because Johnny Podres had pitched so magnificently in the pivotal third game at Ebbets Field, I don't recall feeling scared because he was the pitcher on this day, just disappointed that neither Erskine nor Newcombe was available. To a kid of nine, twenty-three did not seem young. After Karl Spooner's disastrous start the day before, what I remember is hoping that the Dodgers would keep the game close in the early innings, that the Yankees wouldn't score first or have a big first inning. I had no experience with triumph; I just wanted the Dodgers to keep having a chance.

The Yankees were difficult to follow during the World Series that year. With Mickey Mantle nursing a badly injured leg, Stengel shuffled his other outfielders in and out of games and shuffled his batting order repeatedly, with a different one for each of the first five games. After the sudden outburst of hitting in Game Six, however, he stood pat for the final game. The meant a professional every bit as seasoned as Pee Wee Reese, shortstop Phil Rizzuto, would lead off, followed by the hustling, intense second baseman, Billy Martin, and then another solid pro in third baseman Gil McDougald.

Podres's pitching motion was more herky-jerky than Byrne's; he kicked high and reached way back with his pitching arm before he threw; he threw so hard that he sometimes stumbled off the mound. Rizzuto had difficulty getting around on Podres's fastball and sent a foul ball into the air near home plate. Campanella caught it easily. Billy Martin swung in front of a changeup and pulled it, but the ball went way up in the air down the third-base line; Gilliam dashed over from his left-field position and got under it easily, just in fair territory. Gil McDougald was clearly uncomfortable at the plate his first time up to face Podres's varying speeds; he took a called third strike to end the short inning.

At the outset, at least, Podres was following the Campanella plan methodically. He had already assuaged my worst fears before I had had much of an opportunity to experience them. I cannot remember anything about Johnny Podres of consequence before that World Series. I was aware of him, I was aware that he was good, I had seen him pitch, but on a team that season that had Don Newcombe and Carl Erskine, nothing had stuck with me. The first time I had truly concentrated on Podres was when he threw a heroic game at the Yankees in the Game Three across the river that the Dodgers had to win, but everything I had heard before the seventh game began was about how the pitching matchup favored the Yankees and Tommy Byrne. I was consumed at the outset of the game with the fear of a first-inning Yankee explosion, but the inning was so methodical, so routine, that I relaxed—mistakenly.

The second inning was different, more tense, with more plays like Junior Gilliam's leadoff ground ball that made one stiffen and then relax as something that appeared one instant like a turning point turned routine in another. With one out in the Dodgers' half of the inning (a Campanella ground ball to Martin), the team's veteran right fielder, Carl Furillo, sent a shot out to left field. For another instant I was off the cushion, until it was clear that the ball was not hit quite far enough and the Yankees' first and only African-American player, rookie Elston Howard, caught it on the dirt track in front of the seats. Perhaps a bit ruffled by the close call, Byrne proceeded to walk my hero, Gil Hodges, in his first time at bat, but the inning ended quickly when Don Hoak (Jackie Robinson's replacement at third base in his second year with the team) grounded out, also to Martin. It was almost a serious threat, the first introduction to the agonizing reality of a low-scoring game with the World Series on the line.

The Yankees provided a second in their half of the inning. The first man up, Yogi Berra, made me flinch by sending a line drive into center field, but it was almost directly at Duke Snider. I had no sooner relaxed while Hank Bauer grounded out, however, than Podres threw a soft pitch on the outside part of the plate to Bill Skowron. The youngest of the three Yankee first basemen pounced on the pitch and hit it viciously on one bounce into the right field seats for a double. There was no time to react to the play: one instant the pitch was at the plate; the next it was in the seats.

For the first time in the game, there was someone on base in a position to score the first run on a single. Worse, the Yankee coming up was not merely Mickey Mantle's replacement in center field that day. He was Bob Cerv, a consistent hitter who had batted .341 in his part-time role that year and had hit a home run while I watched in horror and in person in Game Five.

Podres's first pitch to him in this clutch situation was slightly outside and low, and Cerv made the mistake of swinging at it. The result was a delightfully easy ground ball to Reese at shortstop. Once again: sudden tension, sudden release. For the first time in the game I remember making eye contact with my father; he was looking intently at me, but he didn't speak, so neither did I. It was perhaps an unusual way to be experiencing the decisive game of a World Series, but looking back, I have always focused on its intimacy. It wasn't every young boy who got to play hooky that day and be alone with his father and the Brooklyn Dodgers.

When Tommy Byrne and Whitey Ford were at their best, the pitches changed speed and locations with almost monotonous regularity and more often than not the batters hit ground balls or popped up. The balls they hit hard tended to go to the deepest parts of Yankee Stadium where outfielders could run them down. What was most maddening was that Ford and Byrne got into trouble so rarely that they mostly denied an opposing fan the opportunity to hope. They were understated performers, with smooth pitching mechanics that made their dominance seem routine, almost businesslike.

In Ford's case, however, businesslike doesn't quite do justice to his mastery in busting the rules about doctoring the baseball. He was never caught, but Dodger fans everywhere were pleased to learn eventually that all his catchers, as well as Ford himself, played with specially sharpened belt buckles; in addition, Ford had an edge sharpened on the back side of his wedding ring. So-called "cut" baseballs interfere with the air currents over them and break very sharply. Ford was also the developer of what was called a "gunk" ball—which was wetted with a mixture of legal resin and illegal baby oil and turpentine from his cap.

In Game Seven, Byrne got through the first third of the contest without a serious scratch on him. In the third inning, we had barely settled down to watch the Dodgers hit when there were two quick outs: Gil McDougald threw out Don Zimmer, and Billy Martin threw out Johnny Podres, routine ground balls to third and second.

The only faint sign that Byrne was the least bit human came when he walked Gilliam with two outs. Gilliam was a swift and smart base runner (he had fifteen stolen bases that year), but among Byrne's many gifts was an excellent pickoff move to first base, so the Dodger left fielder played it safe and took only a short lead. There was another of those momentary surges of tension when Reese hit Byrne's third pitch on a hard, straight line toward center field, but the ball was right at Bob Cerv, and the inning was quickly over.

Johnny Podres was pitching just as effectively. Except for his mistake to Bill Skowron the inning before, Podres had been dominant. As I crossed my ankles, the dominance continued. His pitching speed was unpredictable, the changeup had made several strategic appearances already, and he had his control above all.

In the Yankee half of the third inning, Elston Howard sent a lazy fly ball to Snider in center field to lead off, and Tommy Byrne looked at a third strike.

With two quick outs, I was one of those baseball fans who foolishly considered an inning like that basically over. It consistently amazed me when the Dodgers rallied with two men out, and it was especially demoralizing when the opposing team scored in that situation.

The Yankee threat developed quickly. Phil Rizzuto walked on four straight pitches; no exciting, full-count, pitcher–batter drama, just four quick balls and he was at first base. Billy Martin then went with an outside pitch (much as Skowron had the inning before) and sent a line drive into right field that was clearly going to be a single the instant it left his bat.

Dodger fans were conditioned not to panic at such moments. The team had baseball's best right fielder in Carl Furillo, a veteran (he was thirty-three at the time) from a small town near Reading, Pennsylvania. Known as Skoonj around Brooklyn (short for *scungilli*, the snail from the ocean that is a special treat in marinara sauce), he was an intense ballplayer with a vicious streak whom the Brooklyn fans loved for his skill at playing the caroms off the wall in Ebbets Field and for a throwing arm that was awesome to behold. I can recall one game where he played shallow, fielded a sharply hit ball on one hop, and threw the batter out at first base. Martin's single came to the charging Furillo on the second hop in shallow right field, and there was no question that Rizzuto would dare try to run to third base and challenge Furillo's famous arm.

However, the play meant that there were now two Yankees on base, with Gil McDougald coming to bat. A versatile, consistent professional, McDougald played third, second, and short during his ten-year career, and he was a dangerous hitter with men on base, as capable of a single as of a home run (he hit seven in eight World Series). Podres has no memory of getting especially tense at this point. What he remembers is being careful, following Campanella's signals to keep the ball just barely in the strike zone, never down the middle of the plate. Obviously, however, Podres was being a bit too careful, because in short order the count on McDougald was three balls and one strike.

Podres was one pitch away from loading the bases for the most dangerous Yankee hitter other than Mantle—Yogi Berra.

For the first time in the game, one of the managers came out of the dugout for one of baseball's rituals—the slow walk to the pitcher's mound. Like most Dodger fans, my father could not stand Walter Alston, then in his second year as Charlie Dressen's replacement. My father could not stand Alston's nondescript blandness, for one thing. For another, he hated baseball owners in general and the Dodgers' owner, Walter O'Malley, with a purple passion exceeded only by his loathing for the Yankees' Del Webb. Anybody who presented himself as an owner's employee was a stooge to my father, and Alston's lack of a public persona—his nickname was Smokey—made him a natural target for abuse in a New York environment that rewarded flair. There was also the small matter that Alston's Dodgers had lost the pennant to the hated Giants in his rookie year, 1954.

As always, the truth turned out to be much more complicated and interesting. Alston's job was by definition nearly impossible—pleasing a penny-pinching owner and managing a diverse collection of established superstars and kids on their way up. He was diligent and stolid, but he also had a keen baseball mind. Already his image was changing in this World Series; several of the Dodger players with whom he had tangled all year to establish his authority, notably Jackie Robinson, had praised his demeanor after the second loss in Yankee Stadium, when he told the team that he believed they could still win the Series because he believed they were the better team.

Podres today has no memory of his manager's first visit to the mound. At the time, however, Podres and Campanella said that

Alston's message simply reinforced Campanella's signs and targets: keep the ball down.

The next pitch to McDougald appeared to be in keeping with Campanella's instructions: no more than knee-high on the inside part of the plate and another of his changeups. McDougald appeared to time it well, however, and swung hard.

Major League Baseball and NBC, to their shame as the game's custodians, have not kept film or tape of the entire game. To refresh my memory, I was able to get my hands on perhaps forty minutes of the action, fortunately including all of the important plays. On this one, there was no question that McDougald had not hit the ball squarely but had grazed the top of it.

Some subsequent descriptions of the crucial play say that the ball was "chopped," but the film does not show any high bounces and the ball was not hammered into the ground near home plate. Instead, it could be described as a slow ground ball that bounced no more than three times before reaching the vicinity of third base. From the moment it hit the ground it had all the trappings of a bases-loading infield single.

The Dodgers' third baseman that day was Don Hoak, the substitute for injured Jackie Robinson, playing a position made famous in Brooklyn after World War II by a slick fielder with a rocket for an arm, Billy Cox. To the displeasure of many fans, and of an embittered Cox, he had been traded after the 1954 season for his final year in the major leagues with the Baltimore Orioles, along with another veteran and Dodger fans favorite, Preacher Roe, who never played again.

Hoak was also a slick fielder, but in just his second major-league season he had not yet become the solid player he would be for nine more years (he was the regular on the Pittsburgh Pirates team that beat the Yankees in 1960).

Playing at medium depth behind the third-base bag, Hoak was in position to charge the slow-bouncing ball, with more than a decent chance to nip McDougald at first. Hoak would, however, have had to react the instant the ball was hit.

Instead, he barely moved. By the time he was almost even with the third-base bag, the most he could have done was fielded the ball. McDougald, who ran decently, was going to be safe at first for certain.

From his position leading off second, Rizzuto did what every ballplayer is trained to do on base with two outs when someone hits the ball—he ran. The film, however, shows him beginning his slide into third from well off the bag. It was a long, long slide.

And then the most amazing thing happened.

Rizzuto's left foot was no more than two feet from third base when the ball bounced off his left thigh. I remember being confused for an instant, but there was nothing confused about the reaction of the third-base umpire, Lee Ballanfant. Trotting toward the bag and Rizzuto, he pointed his right index finger at the Yankee shortstop and then jerked his hand back, thumb outstretched—out! Hoak darted into foul territory to retrieve the ball as the other Dodger players ran off the field.

Phil Rizzuto simply remained seated on third base, stunned. It was unfairly ignominious. This was as classy a Yankee as there was, and he had just made the most humiliating out imaginable.

It would be wrong to second-guess the slide, however; in retrospect, and supported by the film, it was the correct move on his part. Normally, base runners will do anything to dodge a ball hit near them—jump, contort themselves. In this case, however, Rizzuto's sliding took away the chance that Hoak might field the ball and step on third base for the force out that would end the inning.

The risk, of course, was that the ball would hit Rizzuto before he reached the base. Rizzuto—who that day set a World Series record by playing in his fifty-second (and, as it turned out) final game—almost made it. McDougald was awarded the third Yankee hit of the young game, but it was a meaningless, and only technical, single.

From the dining table my father continued to say nothing. But when I looked over at him, his eyes were twinkling and his eyebrows were moving up and down in exaggerated enthusiasm. Within a second, the telephone rang for the first time that afternoon. My father listened, spoke quietly a couple of times, and then hung up.

It was my mother, he informed me. I wish I could re-create this conversation, but all I remember is words to the effect that it was about time we got a break against the Yankees. The only words I can recall him saying into the phone were, "Hang in there."

My mother had slipped into her office—a cubicle, really—which adjoined her boss's cavernous playpen. He was a partner at Cahill, Gordon, Reindell and Ohl, specializing in the arcane minutiae of franchise law—then a burgeoning business that was expanding from its origins in automobile dealerships to auto parts stores and, increasingly, to what we still thought of as hamburger joints but which would eventually be called fast-food restaurants. It was already very, very lucrative and her boss was something of a pioneer in the mechanics of putting these distribution deals together.

He was a very nice but wooden man (Princeton, I think), and my mother was proud of her ability to translate his memoranda and legal briefs into concise English. Whenever she took me to the office when she had to work on weekends or holidays, he was invariably kind to me, as well as to my mother.

Once a year, we would get on the Long Island Railroad train and visit his family in Garden City for dinner. He had two daughters about my age, and as I got older we used to laugh on the way back at how they treated me—as a weird specimen from some dangerous jungle where fear lurked on every street corner and poor urchins like me scavenged for food. I was just as culturally confused by these communities that were becoming known as suburbs, wondering why anyone would live so far away from opera and baseball.

At this point in the game, my mother was still watching it on the television set in the firm's conference room. I could imagine her trying to maintain her composure in the staid atmosphere among blue and gray suits and Yankee fans, stealing glances with her fellow secretaries and Dodger fans. The only thing missing in our apartment that unforgettable day was her.

6

Getting By

She was pretty as a picture, with large expressive eyes and long curly dirty-blond hair that in those days reached her shoulders. Like my father, she wasn't tall; by 1955 I was well on my way to her five feet, four inches. Her voice was soft. I could hear the Midwest in it easily, but she had a singsong inflexion that gave away her Norwegian heritage as well. She was simple, unadorned, dressed conservatively, and maintained a reserve most of the time that made her high-pitched giggle when she laughed especially entertaining. Her direct manner came with immense inner strength and a highly developed sense of order. Life around her was often chaotic and never easy; she made it work with sheer willpower.

Opposites attracted in my household. My father had black hair, combed back, constantly twinkling eyes, a relatively stocky build, and a deep baritone. He was emotional, florid in his language, and had no sense of order whatsoever. He misplaced his slippers, his notebooks, his wallet. His energy was almost entirely creative, rarely practical. Largely self-taught, he remains the most literate, best-read person I have ever met. My favorite memory that links the two of them involved his daily trips down the hall to the elevator before going out; my father bemoaned the fact that his mind was idle and that he was bored simply standing there waiting for the elevator to take him down twenty-five floors, so my mother typed out dozens of three-by-five cards containing morsels of Proust or Tolstoy or Voltaire so he could use the time better.

My first clear memories as a child paint the mixed, happy-tough picture of our lives. I was three when my father's efforts to work steadily as a freelance writer began to falter because of his health. He published articles regularly at first and had an agent who was a fixture in our apartment. My father's output began to diminish after a couple of years, however, as the ulcers left from his jungle infections began to bleed. He would feel better periodically and think he was recovering, only to fall ill again with increasing severity and pain. By 1949 one of his kidneys had begun to malfunction and then to fail, requiring what was then a very dangerous operation.

My very first memory is of me and my mother standing at the end of 43rd Street, looking down at First Avenue and the area that was slowly becoming the UN. My father was on the east side of the avenue, getting ready to board the bus that would take him uptown to New York Hospital for the operation that would remove his kidney. We are waving at him, he is waving back, and my mother is crying.

My second memory is about a month later. I am standing in the little hallway of our apartment with a woman on our floor who was watching me that day (the same lady who would magically produce the bleacher seats for Game Five in 1955). The door opens and my father returns from the hospital with my mother. I remember being shown the scar, a set of railroad tracks that went all the way across his lower back.

The other three memories are about my life, clearly reflecting my parents' hopes for me even as they struggled. These memories clashed with the first two—then and always.

The first is of the kindergarten room at the private school on the Upper East Side to which my father had taken me to be interviewed and examined for possible admission to a rarefied world to which I had had no exposure at all to that point. I was not yet five. After I grew up, this process became better known as hyper-ambitious parents with money hired consultants, gave money, and performed unethical favors at work to manipulate the system on their children's behalf. All I remember is being uncomfortable. Somehow my parents had arranged for this examination and somehow there was a scholarship on the line (my parents could not have paid one week's tuition), though I was shielded from that fact until I had nearly finished grammar school.

I am alone with a much older woman, who would that fall become my first teacher, Doris Allen. I have no memory of anything she said and no memory of anything I said. I just remember this dark room and my being alone in it with the forbidding figure of Miss Allen. She was administering a simple test orally, making statements to me that I was supposed to label true or false. All I remember is the one, the only one, I got wrong, I suppose reflecting my sense of high stakes. She told me that squirrels laid eggs, and unadulterated city kid that I was at that point, I remember pronouncing the statement true and being more surprised than disappointed to discover my error.

The second memory is of an incident shortly after my examination. My mother had gone back to work when I was about three after my father's illness made it impossible for him to support us anymore. During the day, I was left at a "nursery school" (the term *day care* was still decades away from the language) run by a church on First Avenue. What I remember is coming down the stairs one day and encountering my father at the bottom, there to inform me of my admission to the Browning School for Boys. I don't remember at all how I felt, but I can still see the happiness on his face.

The third memory is my first of the role of music in my young life. It is this same period, and some couple is in our apartment to have supper. I am in the second room alone, while my father is at the piano. He is playing single notes, and from the bedroom I am calling out their identity—A-sharp, B-flat, E. I hated being shown off in this fashion, but I was too far removed from the age of successful defiance to resist.

This scene, I was often reminded, was a reenactment of the moment when my father first realized that musical ability lurked inside me. He no longer played the violin, but he was at the piano constantly—for jazz and for Bach. He had written no more songs after the war, but the piano was a haven for him, and while he was entirely self-taught, he was more than good. Just as he had taught me my letters at three, he had also sat me down at the piano to teach me the notes and to make stabs at them with my index finger at musically appropriate moments. One day, according to the family legend, he was playing a single note repeatedly out of concern that the piano needed tuning; playing idly in the other room, I supposedly identified it. Curious, my father played a few more, and my life changed.

He didn't push me, rule my life ruthlessly, or hover relentlessly. It was more like a gentle, loving nudge, always supplied in the interest of developing potential and having choices in life and, more important, always supplied with love and support. My mother never questioned any of this, but through her hard work she managed to make everything associated with a young boy's probably much too busy life go more smoothly.

In my childhood, there was only one moment of rebellion. I was not exactly the world's best baseball player, but I held my own in my neighborhood and at school, and behind the plate the fact that I had never blinked when a batter swung while I was catching opened the door to a position I loved to play because the entire game was in front of me. By the eighth grade, I was catching for the varsity team, because although I was not much more than a slap hitter, I could throw runners out stealing.

When my father found out I was catching he was furious, telling me in the sharpest of terms that one foul ball off my throwing hand would make the piano impossible, perhaps reflecting what one stupid punch had done to his budding violin career. It was the only time when I got the direct sense he was thinking career for me, and I was equally furious and adamant that he had no right to tell me what position I couldn't play in baseball. It was hardly normal to be going to school, being a kid, playing the piano two hours a day, and working at the Metropolitan Opera. I was desperate to fit in and determined never to tell my coach and my friends that I couldn't catch because of my music.

At first, my father taught me piano himself. Since he had taught himself, he was aware of his limitations, especially in technique. After I started grammar school, he cajoled the music teacher there into taking me on more formally. My father's zeal didn't stop there; down the hall in our building lived a young concert pianist from British Columbia, Gordon Manley—a very tall, thin man with wavy black hair and a deep, booming laugh that belied a touching sensitivity. He was struggling for a toehold in the competitive New York world, traveling occasionally for concerts in his native country and by then twice in Europe. He lived in a studio, half-filled by a nine-foot Steinway that he (and, eventually, I) almost always played with a cloth damper across the interior wires for the benefit of the neighbors, though nothing could rival the sound in the dark hallway when Mr. Manley let loose. He had no time for pupils, but he made time for me, and my mother cooked many a meal for him and ironed his shirts. He taught me, more than anything, how to perform, how to toss off inhibitions. I lived for my lessons with him once a week, and his presence just down the hall, and therefore the potential for disapproval, kept my practicing almost always serious.

As I tried to learn what being serious about something really meant, I found the atmosphere mostly exciting, if exacting. I felt surrounded by caring people, more nurtured than instructed.

To make life more complicated, it was also my fate to have just the right voice range and strength for a boy soprano. This was first noticed by the mother of one of my friends at our church Christ Church Methodist near my school on Park Avenue—who worked at one of the city's largest talent agencies. Early on, I started singing in church choirs that paid money—my first job was at the age of seven—and soon thereafter was invited to the annual tryouts for the Metropolitan Opera's boys chorus. Once again, it was a nudge, not a push, from home—the suggestion that it might be fun.

It was. Opera for me was not fancy audiences in glamorous settings, getting kissed by Renata Tebaldi or patted on the head by Maria Callas. It was an exhilarating combination of rigorous discipline in rehearsal followed by the unrestrained exuberance of performance. I couldn't get enough of it.

In those pre–Lincoln Center days, the Metropolitan was in a huge barn of a building on Seventh Avenue a few blocks south of Times Square. We workers entered by a nondescript stage door, punched a time card as if it were a factory, and then walked through a maze of backstage pathways to the elevator that led to the practice and chorus dressing rooms we shared with the ballet dancers who had parts in many a performance or were used as extras.

It was not all work. The backstage routine, as at any theater, included serious stretches of inactivity; on occasion I did schoolwork, but mostly I joined one of backstage life's time-honored rituals—poker games. With stagehands, some of the other boys, and extras, it was strictly penny ante, but the pennies tended to add up. The games were an odd thrill for me because they were my first excursion into secret activity my parents would have vehemently objected to. Before a performance, I was careful to remove from my piggy bank fifty pennies (never more), which I managed to get out of the apartment unnoticed for my entire career.

The chorus was rarely onstage for long stretches. There was a great deal of downtime, not all of it wasted learning poker. Backstage, the Metropolitan was a fascinating obstacle course of stored scenery and other clutter, and there were several ladders that led to catwalks and other perches high above the stage. I discovered that with my diminutive size it was easy to climb unnoticed and watch a performance from these spots; I spent many an evening enthralled as some of the most famous singers in the world performed below me and an occasional fellow stowaway. I had been in the opera and looked down on it long before I ever saw a performance from the audience.

As I became more conscious of my parents' struggles and my father's illness, my too-young mind had trouble with the mixture of my own accomplishments and their troubles. Nothing I did growing up could satisfy a yearning that things be normal, that they not have it so tough, that my father not be so sick all the time. All I ever wanted was for them to be happier, and to be able to help. The money I earned singing was only partial satisfaction of my yearning, but it gave me a large chunk of what I craved.

So did the Brooklyn Dodgers. When we went to a game, two of us or all three of us, we were a family; we were together. What I did in my bustling life was forgotten; what they did to get by was forgotten. We were just enjoying something we had in common. A trip across the river could be on a whim—my favorite was an impromptu afternoon journey in 1955 to cheer me up after my parakeet, Jocko (after a National League umpire named Jocko Conlon), drowned in a glass of water that morning; it turned out to be the day Sandy Koufax made his major-league debut. It could also be carefully planned, like monthly excursions to the left-field bleachers for a Ladies Day game, at which my mother was always carefully dressed in skirt, blouse, and heels. It could be a simple evening in front of the radio or, beginning in 1955 the television, taking turns keeping careful score on the yellow pads; in our household, if my schoolwork was done, if there was no performance at the opera, I was always permitted to stay up until the game was over, even the "late" ones from Chicago, Milwaukee (where the Boston Braves had moved in 1953, starting a trend that would eventually involve the Dodgers), and St. Louis. For those precious hours the world outside mercifully withdrew while we shared something that brought enormous pleasure to each of us.

7

The Good (and Bad) Old Days

Before me, the Dodgers had belonged to my parents. Their stories are not stereotypical journeys as Dodger families' stories go. My parents do, however, fit every decent metaphor ever coined about what it meant to pull for this unique baseball team. They had talent, brains, good looks; they had come from very little far away; they struggled, they sometimes succeeded, they often fell down; but they always got up, always worked hard, they were cheerfully perseverant, full of love, and they came to love their Brooklyn Dodgers.

They did not set out for New York with the Dodgers on their minds. They gently, almost accidentally, bumped into them in their search for an inexpensive diversion. It was, moreover, an acquired taste, not a natural one. My father was a typical Indiana boy in at least one major respect; he was a devout basketball fan in a state that worshipped the game even in its infancy in the early 1920s. The coach at his high school, a man well known to students of the game, was the young Everett Case, who thirty years later would lead North Carolina State to a national prominence. My father in his last two years in high school covered Case and his team for the local paper.

In the extreme north of Minnesota, my mother also had a sports passion, which she tried without much success to transplant into me at the old Madison Square Garden, to which she had a steady supply of ticket offers from her law firm superiors. It was hockey, whose fast, intricate skating patterns fascinated her and mostly confused me until much later in life.

My parents were participants in the huge migration that took place during the first half of the twentieth century from rural to urban life. It was in New York, as newlyweds, that they discovered baseball.

My father's birthplace was a tiny farming community called Forrest in central Indiana, east of Gil Hodges, north of Pee Wee Reese, south of Carl Erskine. His mom was from a farm in Wisconsin; his dad was a local boy and country doctor who had been in the Spanish-American War as a medic. They had met in Chicago, where he made extra money as a freshly trained physician treating hangovers and other guest ailments at the old Palmer House, where his bride-to-be worked on the switchboard.

My father's birth in 1909 ended my grandmother's childbearing career (he weighed more than twelve pounds and took too much out with him), but his memories of childhood were idyllic. His dad took him on many of his endless rounds with first a horse and cart and then a Model T; he got to hear the stories of Civil War veterans in the Old Soldiers' Home. He worshipped his father, as did a struggling community that could rarely afford his often-donated services.

My grandfather's death, after moving to the nearby town of Frankfort, devastated my teenage father; I don't think he ever recovered from the shock. His mom had gotten him started in music (she played the organ at the local funeral home and a local church), and he had written his first songs in high school. His dad had also sparked an interest in learning. Writing came easily to my father and, also in high school, he worked for the local paper, covering the Frankfort High School sports teams (called the Hot Dogs, of course). But he was inwardly miserable and sensed that his one chance was to leave, which is why he threw the dart at his map of the United States. New Mexico was the perfect choice—utterly, magnificently different. He plunged into studies, fraternity life (Sigma Chi), music, and writing. With some pals, he started the university's first literary magazine.

And then everything fell apart again. One of his best pieces in the magazine was a long profile about a young woman of more than a little education who worked as a prostitute in Albuquerque. It was not sensationalized but, with the romantic enthusiasm that always marked his work, described her life, her impressions of professors and students alike, and her hopes and dreams.

The shit, of course, hit the fan immediately. The administration expelled him on the spot for a grave offense against taste and morals, and only the publicized intercession of a new organization called the American Civil Liberties Union changed his expulsion into permission to withdraw. He was not yet twenty and adrift again.

His next opportunity came quickly—via a casual acquaintance from Indiana who had inherited too much money from an inventor-manufacturer in Muncie. These two misfits (they argued forever about who was Don Quixote and who was Sancho Panza) then set off in search of whatever in Nevada and California. For my father, it turned out to be his music. His violin playing was becoming seriously proficient, and the money from playing sets with jazz bands was enough to keep him fed and in study with accomplished professionals first in San Francisco and then in Los Angeles.

And then a stupid punch in a bar ended his dream; the damage to his left wrist was permanent. It was 1935 and he was once more adrift. The one remaining relative to whom he was devoted was his uncle, Herman, who had become a highly regarded law professor and then entered the New Deal as the general counsel to Franklin D. Roosevelt's Treasury secretary, Henry Morgenthau. Herman Oliphant was one of those round-the-clock New Dealers with a storied "passion for anonymity" who helped shape the historic administration's domestic policies. He was a true believer, once labeled by *The New York Times'* conservative columnist

Arthur Krock as one of the country's more dangerous individuals—
a badge of distinction in my family. Nor was he the only Oliphant
to make it out of turn-of-the-century Indiana. A third member of
the family, a cousin with the classically Indiana name of Elmer Q.
Oliphant, was a college football giant, a famous All-American runner and dropkicker for Purdue and then Army just before the twenties. Uncle Elmer, however, soon gravitated toward the insurance
business and, worse from my father's perspective, into the Republican Party. He finally wrote Elmer off completely when in 1952
he showed up on a committee self-titled Football Greats for
Eisenhower-Nixon. But my father worshipped his uncle Herman,
who in turn took a near-paternal interest in his welfare. When he
visited Washington in the early autumn of '35, his uncle must have
thought that settling down would be the wisest course for his brilliant but vagabond nephew, which is why he introduced him to one
of the secretaries in his office—my mother. They flipped for each
other, this romantic who had never really fallen in love and this reserved product of a Scandinavian emigrant family whose imposing
reserve never totally masked an adventuresome spirit and an en-
gaging, understated wit. They were at the Foley Square courthouse
in New York with a marriage license on November 1. For her, it
was the culmination of a very long, also difficult journey.

Anna Serena Selvog was raised in the community of Warroad,
Minnesota, way, way north on the Lake of the Woods across from
Canada, in a largely Lutheran culture that frowned severely on
fun. She had four brothers and an older sister (Edla), whom she
idolized. Years later, she said it was the unspeakable trauma of
her sister's death in a drowning accident that nudged her into the
dream of leaving to make her way in the cities she had only read
about in school.

Her way out was through the northern Minnesota city of Virginia after high school and secretarial training in what was at the
time a junior college. Her English, back then and forever after,
was meticulous, precise, and she loved to read. The city she focused on was Washington, D.C., where she arrived before she was

twenty-one, finding work in the Navy and War Departments before landing at the Treasury and finding roommates for a sunny
apartment on Sixteenth Street.

We don't get to choose our parents and we don't get to choose
when we get conceived, but I've often wondered what would have
happened if I had come along immediately after my mother and
father got married. As they struggled to make their way, my presence would quite likely have precluded military service for my
thirty-something father and would quite likely have precluded
round-the-clock work for the Justice Department by my mother.
There would probably have been another kid; my mother had already picked the name for a girl—Christina, after her mother.

As things were, however, they got to be young and in love, first
in the Bay Ridge section of Brooklyn (my mother often worshipped in a small Norwegian church there that was a magnet for
sailors in the bustling port community) and then on Bank Street
in Greenwich Village.

For struggling newlyweds in the 1930s, diversion was often a
walk, the parks, a visit to a museum. There was no car, no vacation, no continual dining out, almost no theater or concerts. The
ballpark was a more affordable diversion, and they soon began
haunting Ebbets Field. My father told me that, compared to Yankee Stadium or the Polo Grounds, the atmosphere was more fun,
the view from the cheap seats was better, and Brooklyn offered
more variety, if not better baseball.

It was a different era. New York basically belonged in those
days to the Giants under manager and former star first baseman
Bill Terry and to the Yankees under Joe McCarthy. The Dodgers
simply stank as they flirted almost annually with bankruptcy as
well as the National League cellar. Their miserable condition, fortunately, was leavened by an entertaining, creative, often endearing approach to losing—epitomized by a series of improbable
misfortunes and daffy goofs that formed a unique lore, the source

of their second nickname, always said with affection—The Bums. These stories were passed on to me, as they were to all serious Dodger fans, at a very young age, and they became an indelible part of my baseball consciousness. They constituted part of the prism through which the seventh game in 1955 looked like an insurmountable challenge.

As I learned the history, the World Series of 1920 was crucial to the Dodgers' reputation and self-image. The team was actually quite good during the young century's second decade, winning the pennant in both 1916 and four years later under the leadership of a large, odd character named Wilbert Robinson (the team name famously changed often in those years and was the Robins under his tutelage, which lasted until the Dodgers became the name for good in 1932).

Their loss in the '16 series to the Boston Red Sox, who had an astonishingly good young pitcher who could also swing the bat (his name was Babe Ruth), is excused by the familiar reason that the better team won, four games to one. The Dodger team had a future Hall of Famer in outfielder Zack Wheat and a delightfully eccentric young outfielder from Missouri named Casey Stengel who would be running the Yankees thirty-nine years later and who managed the Dodgers in the 1930s when my parents became fans. But the Red Sox had Ruth, who in Game Two pitched one of the great games in World Series history, going fourteen innings to outlast Sherry Smith, 2–1.

Four years later, however, the Dodgers had an excellent chance against a Cleveland Indians team that just barely won the American League pennant after eight Chicago White Sox players (the immortal Shoeless Joe Jackson among them) were suspended as the story of their having been paid to fix the 1919 Series broke the following September.

Cleveland, however, was the winner, greatly helped by three plays in Game Five that had never happened before, one of which has never happened again in a World Series. With the Series tied, Cleveland right fielder Elmer Smith hit the first grand slam in World Series history off Brooklyn spitballer Burleigh Grimes in

the first inning, and three innings later Cleveland pitcher Jim
Bagby hit the first home run ever by a pitcher, a three-run shot to
deepest center field—both feats all the more remarkable in an age
of relatively few home runs.

The Dodgers, however, attempted a comeback, putting two
runners, Pete Kilduff and Otto Miller, on base with no one out in
the fifth. The next batter, relief pitcher Clarence Mitchell, hit a
hard line drive toward right field that appeared to be beyond the
reach of the second baseman, a twenty-six-year-old native of the
Cleveland area, Bill Wambsganss.

With both runners on the move, however, Wambsganss went as
high as his nearly six-foot body would take him into the air and
somehow caught the ball. Within a Dodgers' breaking heartbeat,
he then stepped on second to force the departed Kilduff and then
tagged Miller as he approached him on the base path. More than
eighty years later, there has never been another unassisted triple
play in the World Series.

As if on cue, the disappointment of 1920 soon turned into a
long downward slide, though the Dodgers were at least enjoyable
losers. Casey Stengel was an important source of the antics, having once gone to bat with a small bird under his hat, which he
tipped mischievously before standing in to hit, turning a chorus
of boos into laughter. Tex Rickards, the beloved malapropist
(called Ricketts in Brooklyn) who manned the public-address system all the way to the team's departure for Los Angeles, once told
the customers who loved half-stripping and folding their gar-
ments over the box seat railings on hot days, "Ladies and gentlemen, the umpires request that the fans in the left-field boxes will
kindly remove their clothes"; on another occasion, he announced
that "a little boy has been found lost."

Among a parade of pitchers with odd names none stood out
more than Clyde "Pea Ridge" Day, who celebrated his occasional
strikeout with the hog calls of his native Arkansas. Wilbert Robinson himself added to the legend. Shortly after setting up a Bone-
head Club complete with five-dollar fines for stupid plays, he
abandoned his campaign after he turned in his official lineup

card to the umpires one day with Al Lopez listed as his catcher and then promptly made him ineligible by sending Ernie Lombardi out to play the position. Another time, Robinson had walked briskly to the home-plate conference and handed the umpire crew chief his dry-cleaning ticket.

The most lovable metaphor, however, was an outfielder from Buffalo, Floyd Caves "Babe" Herman, who could hit a ton (in his best season, 1930, he had thirty-five home runs and drove in 130 runs) but was a wretched fielder and an inattentive base runner. One of the famed team executives who helped build the powerhouses of the late thirties, forties, fifties, and sixties—a former infielder from Alabama named Lafayette Fresco Thompson—recalled how against the Giants one day at the Polo Grounds in the ninth inning, with one out, Herman caught a fly ball, put the ball in his pocket, and ran into the clubhouse while the tying runs scored, thinking there were three outs. He was also the start of perhaps the most famous Daffy Dodger play of them all in a game against the Boston Braves in 1926. With the bases loaded and one out, Herman hit a smash into right field that looked like a double at least.

One run scored. The man on second (Dazzy Vance) stopped at third, joined shortly by the runner from first (Chick Fewster, the same man who when he was a Yankee had introduced Tommy Byrne to Babe Ruth); they were in turn joined by an oblivious Babe Herman. For the record, the men tagged out after the Braves third baseman recovered from his shock in this unique and uniquely Dodger play were Fewster and Herman. Henceforth, the joke became that when someone told you the Dodgers had three men on base, you were supposed to ask, "Which base?"

My parents, like so many depression-era Dodger fans, made the best of those madcap years. Brooklyn was still the only urban neighborhood in the country with its own major league team, and the Dodgers were beloved, if not always respected. By the latter half of the decade, though, the lack of success on the field was accompanied by a gusher of red ink and debt on the business side that was threatening to take the team under. In 1938, the telephones had been disconnected for nonpayment of the bill, and the Dodgers were drowning in unpaid obligations in excess of $1 million, at least half of which was owed to the venerable Brooklyn Trust Company, a debt that would eventually attract the full-time attention of a young lawyer for the bank, a native with an engineering background named Walter O'Malley.

First, however, the Dodgers had to stabilize their organization, rent by feuding among the heirs of their original owner and builder, Charles Ebbets, and his business partners, Edward and Stephen McKeever. In 1937, the owners sought help from the then–National League president, and later baseball commissioner, Ford Frick. He in turn consulted the league's most dynamic boss, one Branch Rickey, who had built the successful St. Louis Cardinals of the Gashouse Gang years. Rickey immediately suggested a friend of twenty years named Leland Stanford (after the Gilded Age West Coast railroad king) MacPhail.

Larry MacPhail, born to wealth, a mercurial and rarely sober genius, came to Brooklyn in 1937 having quit as general manager of the Cincinnati Reds after a fistfight with its owner, Powell Crosley, for whom the team's old ballpark was named. With the Reds, also on Rickey's recommendation, MacPhail had rebuilt the team, staged the first night baseball game, and hired a suave radioman from Mississippi named Walter "Red" Barber.

In Brooklyn, MacPhail spent money to make money. Ebbets Field got a facelift and better plumbing, the latter improvement persuading my mother to have one beer during the games because she at last felt comfortable going to the once-wretched bathrooms. Red Barber followed the physical improvements, and then came a network of scouts and then more money to sign better players. For a manager, MacPhail chose one of the spark plugs of the St. Louis team, none other than Leo Durocher. Five of his moves set the stage for the Dodgers who would dominate the league in the forties and fifties.

Two were in his management group—Fresco Thompson and a young man fresh out of college, E. J. "Buzzie" Bavasi.

The other three were players. In 1939, MacPhail paid the

then-enormous sum of seventy-five thousand dollars for a highly touted young shortstop playing in the minors in Louisville, near his home. Harold "Pee Wee" Reese made the team the following year.

Harold Patrick Reiser appears to have cost MacPhail a great deal less than that to lure or (depending on your point of view) steal from the Cardinal organization. The lore is that Pete Reiser cost MacPhail a hundred dollars. If so, it was the greatest bargain of all time, because Pistol Pete was arguably the greatest talent to ever wear a Dodger uniform—an outfielder who combined all of the magical skills that distinguished the three New York outfield stars of the 1950s: Duke Snider, Willie Mays, and Mickey Mantle.

Reiser could hit for average and hit for power; he was blazing fast and he fielded fearlessly in the outfield. In his first full season in 1941, at the age of twenty-two, he led the league in batting (an amazing .348 average), slugging percentage, doubles, triples, and runs batted in (117). Tragedy awaited him and a legion of Brooklyn fans, but I heard my father say many times that in that one season Pete Reiser was the most exciting, most complete baseball player he ever saw.

The Dodgers also nurtured another promising young outfielder who was playing near his hometown in Reading, Pennsylvania. Carl Furillo could also hit consistently with power, but what made him a precious asset was the slingshot he had for a right arm. His ability to throw was so impressive that he briefly experimented with pitching, discovering that he was incurably wild. His young manager in Reading, Fresco Thompson, persuaded him to stick to the outfield, and Furillo made the Dodgers' top minor-league squad in Montreal before going off to war.

For the short term, MacPhail was breathtaking in the speed of his acquisitions, picking up the nucleus of a contending team—Billy Herman, Dixie Walker, Waite Hoyt, Hugh Casey, Joe Medwick, Kirby Higbe, and Dolph Camilli. One of MacPhail's last acquisitions, from Rickey's Cardinals for the princely sum of sixty thousand dollars in 1940, was a solid catcher respected for his defensive skills, Mickey Owen.

To me in the 1950s, these were names, statistics, and stories. To my parents, they were a winning team that finished third in 1939, second in 1940, and nipped the Cardinals by two games for the pennant in 1941, winning one hundred games. Lured by success, the renovated ballpark, and Red Barber's sweet voice, the crowds swelled. My parents started attending regularly. My mother's job was working out, and my father had his first true hit song, was selling arrangements to bands around town, and had begun writing magazine articles as well. They had struggled, but they were beginning to make it, and when they talked of the baseball, the nights out, the plans they had, the remembered happiness was poignant. They had begun to talk about having a kid.

That last autumn of America's innocence began with a perfect World Series pairing for the 1941 World Series. For the first time, the Dodgers' opponent was the Yankees, who had won one more game during the season. That was the year their young center fielder, Joe DiMaggio, hit safely in fifty-six straight games, while the young left fielder of the second-place Boston Red Sox, Ted Williams, was hitting .406 for the season—performances that have never since been equaled.

There had been five previous Subway Series between the Yankees and Giants, and the expectations for the first one that would cross the East River were high. Games One and Two, moreover, lived up to them—tight one-run affairs that the teams split.

The first taste of the fourteen years to come in the Dodger saga came in Game Three at Ebbets Field. For six innings there was an exciting pitching duel between Marius Russo of the Yankees and Dodger veteran Freddie Fitzsimmons, by then an aging, rotund starter with a devilish knuckleball. Shades of 1920 returned in the seventh inning, with the opposing pitcher delivering the key blow again. This time it was a line drive off Russo's bat that struck Fat Freddie flush on his left kneecap, shattering it, but arriving in Pee Wee Reese's glove on the fly for a truly weird out. Fitzsimmons, however, was out of the game, and in relief Hugh Casey couldn't keep the Yankees from scoring two runs in the eighth to win the game.

The more famous disaster happened the next day. Hugh Casey relieved again and did what he couldn't do the day before, hold a lead through eight innings and give the Dodgers a chance to even the Series by getting just three more outs. Casey got two of them quickly but went to a full count on the Yankees' dangerous right fielder, Tommy Henrich.

The 3–2 pitch broke sharply in on the left-handed hitter, who swung and missed for strike three and the ball game's apparent end. Unfortunately, the ball glanced off Mickey Owen's glove and rolled all the way to the barrier behind home plate. Sitting close by was a young Buzzie Bavasi, who told me more than sixty years later that he could have jumped on the field, picked up the ball and thrown it to Dolph Camilli at first base for the out. As it was, by the time Owen retrieved his passed ball error, Henrich was safe on first.

Casey insisted until he went to his grave ten years later (upset over marital troubles, he killed himself) that the pitch was a curveball. Several Dodgers insisted just as vehemently over the years that it was a spitball that caught Owen by surprise. Casey's inning, at any rate, then disintegrated—a single by DiMaggio, a double by Charlie Keller, a walk to Bill Dickey, another double by Joe Gordon, and the Yankees had four runs, the game, and, after an anticlimactic next day, the Series.

My father told me once that it was only in retrospect that the Dodgers' ensuing history of bitter disappointments in high-pressure situations could be said to have begun the moment Mickey Owen's glove failed to follow Casey's pitch. He remembered it as a bitter disappointment more in line with the wacky stuff that had endeared the Dodgers to him and my mother in the first place. There had been so many odd plays like that passed ball. It helped explain why people who had either experienced the Dodgers over time or knew all the stories could be so pleasantly surprised when Phil Rizzuto (like Reese, he played in his first World Series in 1941) slid into that ground ball at a crucial moment fourteen years later.

The frustrating conclusion to the 1941 World Series did not

1955

WORLD SERIES

BASEBALL

SCORE CARD

BROOKLYN

DODGERS

V S

NEW YORK

YANKS

EBBETS FIELD ·····— YANKEE STADIUM

The cover of the paper scorecard sold for a nickel on the street outside
Yankee Stadium on the day of the seventh game of the World Series
in 1955. *(Photo courtesy of Thomas Oliphant)*

BROOKLYN DODGERS

BROOKLYN DODGERS

		1	2	3	4	5	6	7	8	9	10	AB	R	H	RBI	A	E
19	Gilliam, LF, 2B	6-3	W			4-3		2-6		9							
1	Reese, SS	8		8				K									
4	Snider, CF	4-3			K		E-3		K								
39	Campanella, C		4-3				5-23	7									
15 Amoros, LF / FURILLO RF	14 Hodges, 1B		7		6-3		W	8									
14	Hodges, 1B						8		3								
6 Furillo, RF / HOAK 3B			4-3	5-3													
42 Robinson, 3B / ZIMMER 2B				6-3		K	3-1		W								
17 Erskine, P					4-3		5		4-3	8							
36 Newcome, P																	
30 Loes, P												2	5				

45 Podres, P.	12 Kellert, IF	10 Walker, C	22 Herman, C
	23 Zimmer, IF	54 Howell, C	31 Pitler, C
34 Meyer, P	43 Hoak, IF		33 Beckor, C
37 Roebuck, P	8 Shuba, OF	32 Koufax, P	44 Bessent, P
48 Spooner, P		41 Labine, P	24 Alston, Mgr.

NEW YORK YANKEES

Yankees

		1	2	3	4	5	6	7	8	9	10	AB	R	H	PO	A	E
RIZZUTO SS 9 Bauer, R.F.	2	W-5	5-3														
MARTIN 12 McDougald, 3B	7				W	9											
McDOUGALD 8 Berra, C	K		HIT	1-6-3													
BERRA C 7 Mantle, C.F.		8		7	9												
BAUER RF 15 Collins, 1B		4-3	9	6-3	K												
SKOWRON 25 Noren, L.F.			4-3		6-3	1-3											
CERV CF 42 Coleman, S. S.	6-3	5		6-3	7												
HOWARD LF 1 Martin 2B		8	7		6-3												
16 Ford P	K	K	6														
23 Byrne P GRIM MANTLE (6)																	
19 Turley P TURLEY																	

3 Crosetti Coach	28 Morgan, P.	37 Stengel, Mgr.	51 Leja, I.F.
6 Carey, I.F.	29 Silvera, C.	39 Wiesler, P.	53 Kucks, P.
10 Rizzuto, S.S.	31 Turner, Coach	40 Carroll, I.F.	55 Grim, P.
17 Richardson, I.F.	33 Dickey, Coach	41 Cerv, O.F.	14 Skowron, I.F.
18 Larsen, P.	36 Robinson, I.F.	47 Sturdivant, P.	32 Howard, L.F.

The box score kept that day by then-Army Lt. Gary Hymel, including the paid attendance he penciled in the upper right when announced during the seventh inning. *(Photo courtesy of Thomas Oliphant)*

The infant daughter, Amy, of then-Army Lt. Gary Hymel, in uniform and about to lick the famous scorecard shortly after the Dodgers won the World Series. *(Photo courtesy of Thomas Oliphant)*

My father, with his grandfather, near Frankfort, Indiana, in 1919. *(Photo courtesy of Thomas Oliphant)*

The author's father, on the right, and a buddy flank Filipino war hero and diplomat Carlos P. Romulo shortly after Liberation Day in 1944.

(Photo courtesy of Thomas Oliphant)

My father, age five, in his baseball uniform next to his Indiana home.
(Photo courtesy of Thomas Oliphant)

My mother, Anna, in 1941, the first year the Dodgers lost to the Yankees.
She joined the U.S. Attorney's Office in New York in time for
World War II. *(Photo courtesy of Thomas Oliphant)*

Mother and child on the terrace of the tiny Oliphant apartment near the East River in Manhattan, 1946. *(Photo courtesy of Thomas Oliphant)*

Father and son, on the same day in 1946, the year the Dodgers lost a playoff for the pennant to the St. Louis Cardinals.
(Photo courtesy of Thomas Oliphant)

Father and son in the Tudor City park where baseball thrived, in the spring of the magical year of 1955. *(Photo courtesy of Thomas Oliphant)*

The fifth-grade class at the Browning School for boys in the fall of 1955. The author is in the top row, second from the right.
(Photo courtesy of Thomas Oliphant)

The first edition of *Yank* magazine, shortly after World War II began. It was pulled off the presses because of the unfortunate juxtaposition of the FDR headline and the picture of the author's father holding a fistful of cash. *(Photo courtesy of Thomas Oliphant)*

For fifty years, the same still newspaper and wire-service photographs of Game Seven have been shown over and over again. This book has digitized some of the remaining film clips of the game to show the players and the most important plays from different angles. It offers a more fresh, if grainier, perspective.

Manager Walter Alston (24) with the Dodgers just before Game Seven. Johnny Podres is seated in front with arm on leg, in front of Gil Hodges.
(Major League Productions)

The protagonists, Tommy Byrne of the Yankees and Brooklyn's Johnny Podres, on the sidelines before warming up.
(Major League Productions)

Johnny Podres warms up, just before telling bull-pen catcher Dixie Howell that the Yankee lineup can't beat him and teammates that he just needed one run to win. *(Major League Productions)*

Tommy Byrne warms up—in those days, right on the field.
(Major League Productions)

Phil Rizzuto, killing a rally, slides into Gil MacDougald's hit as Dodger Don Hoak prepares to field it. *(Major League Productions)*

The ball hits Phil Rizzuto's left leg, barely a foot from the third-base bag, in the third inning. *(Major League Productions)*

Umpire Lee Ballanfant runs into view to call Phil Rizzuto out as ball goes past Don Hoak's right shoulder. *(Major League Productions)*

The play over, the rally killed, a stunned Rizzuto tarries on the bag. *(Major League Productions)*

The patented Tommy Byrne flip in full view, just before delivering a key pitch to Roy Campanella in the fourth inning. *(Major League Productions)*

Roy Campanella's smooth swing that produced the most important double in Brooklyn Dodger history. *(Major League Productions)*

Gil Hodges's swing produces the most important single in Dodger history, driving in Roy Campanella with the first run. *(Major League Productions)*

The famous Duke Snider bunt in the sixth inning that created the second Dodger scoring threat. *(Major League Productions)*

The equally important Roy Campanella bunt, as the next batter, that put Dodgers on second and third with one out. *(Major League Productions)*

Gil Hodges starts for first, just after hitting a Bob Grim pitch for the most important sacrifice fly in Dodger history, driving in Pee Wee Reese with the second run. *(Major League Productions)*

Dodgers meeting on the mound: Walt Alston joining Johnny Podres and
Roy Campanella, just before Yogi Berra came up in the Yankee's sixth
with two men on and nobody out. *(Major League Productions)*

Yogi Berra punches at Johnny Podres's high, outside pitch to start the
most famous double play in Dodger history. *(Major League Productions)*

Moments after Yogi Berra connects, Sandy Amoros goes into full sprint
toward the left-field corner. His dash began at least twenty-five yards
further toward center field. *(Major League Productions)*

The Catch. Sandy Amoros's left leg is already in motion for his pivot to make perfect relay to Pee Wee Reese behind third base.
(Major League Productions)

At the moment of the catch, Yankee Billy Martin is at left, stopped between second and third, but Gil MacDougald (arrow) has already rounded second from first—trapped. *(Major League Productions)*

Glove hand raised, Pee Wee Reese prepares to take Amoros's relay, in perfect position to make pivot and long throw across diamond to complete the double play. *(Major League Productions)*

Yankee Hank Bauer swings and misses on Johnny Podres's fastball, shown in Campanella's glove, striking out to end a serious Yankee threat in the bottom of the eighth inning. *(Major League Productions)*

Completely fooled, Elston Howard taps final-out ground ball to Pee Wee Reese at short. Howard's bat is shown way in front of his body on last change-up from Johnny Podres. *(Major League Productions)*

Champions at last! Don Newcombe (in jacket) is first Dodger from bench to reach Don Hoak, Johnny Podres, and Roy Campanella after third out. Junior Gilliam is at right, as Jackie Robinson (arms extended) arrives from dugout. *(Major League Productions)*

merely end another baseball season. Two months later, the Japanese attacked Pearl Harbor.

World war interrupted my parents' ascent, as it did the life of the entire country, and there was nothing unusual about their response. They were central casting Greatest Generationists, never really thinking much about whether to respond after Pearl Harbor, but talking between themselves primarily about how to respond. My mother never hesitated in following one of her bosses at the law firm to his job as U.S. Attorney for the Southern District of New York, one of the nerve centers of jurisprudential activity during the war, including famous espionage and sabotage cases. Hers was a white-collar Rosie the Riveter life, with volunteer work on the side and a husband overseas to fret about. Her boss, Matthew Correa, was a somewhat remote, formal man but was extremely solicitous toward my mother during their long stretch of service together. He made sure she was always invited to fancy receptions, where the food and drink were special and free, and was careful to inquire continually about the news from my father.

After Pearl Harbor, my father and his buddies were plotting within days how to win War Department approval for their idea of a mass circulation magazine aimed at enlisted men. Within three months, he had been through basic training at Fort Dix, New Jersey, at the age of nearly thirty-three, and by the summer of 1942 was an army staff sergeant on a troop ship bound for Australia, from which he began three years of island-hopping through hell. When he returned after joining the first waves ashore at Saipan and Tinian (the islands whose capture made the strategic bombing of Japan itself possible), my mother got pregnant almost at once, a statement about the future that would become collectively known as the Baby Boom. I know that I completed them; what they didn't know was how much I wished they could have enjoyed life more and been more comfortable.

In addition to the daily frustrations and the deeper disappointments of my father's ill health, my mother did not escape trouble, either. Shortly after my father lost his kidney, ovarian tumors necessitated a hysterectomy for my mother, ending her dreams of a daughter to name after her mother. What I remember most about my mother's illness is that there was a woman from her office or our building in our apartment every night for the two weeks she was in the hospital and the week she recovered at home, helping my father and me with supper and laundry. He tried his best and my mother was strong when she wasn't heroic, but for all the excitements of my own life, there was a heavy atmosphere around the apartment that never quite lifted.

My happiest moments were not at school or in the music world. They were at our weekly dinners at the Automat on Third Avenue, the occasional play or movie, and above all with the Dodgers. It was not difficult to identify with a baseball team that had enormous talent and a famously adoring following nationwide and that also struggled gamely through disappointment after disappointment. In fact, it was natural.

8

One Run

Those who followed baseball closely in the 1950s knew to pay special attention whenever Roy Campanella walked slowly up to bat, as he did in the fourth inning of Game Seven, swinging two Louisville Sluggers above his powerful shoulders as power hitters did in the years before weighted bat rings. Campanella waved the bats in the air as if they were made of balsa wood. His start in the major leagues had been delayed until he was twenty-seven years old because of segregation; he was thirty-four the day of The Game, but he was as dangerous as ever, still at the top of his remarkable ability, and coming off a Most Valuable Player season (his third).

Sitting in his living room nearly fifty years later, Tommy Byrne told me that Campanella was the Dodger hitter who most concerned him that day, especially leading off or with men on base. If you let him, Byrne said, the Dodger catcher would try to pull the ball down the short left-field lines in both Ebbets Field and Yankee Stadium, which meant that the best chance to get him out was to keep the ball low and away from his power. Better yet, it was important to get the people batting in front of him out.

Byrne met that test as the fourth inning began, striking out Duke Snider, a notoriously poor batter against left-handers. That brought Campanella to the plate for the second time. The previous season, 1954, had been his first nightmare as a Dodger. After years of taking direct hits from foul balls and the brunt of collisions with runners trying to score, the toll on his left hand became too great. He was in surgery once during the 1954 season to set a break and once more after the season ended. As the 1955 campaign began, Campanella was new manager Walter Alston's most significant question mark and there were even trade rumors in the newspapers.

The catcher's conditioning, his will, and his talent, however, were more than sufficient for another great year (as it turned out, his last as a superstar). Campanella ended up with thirty-two home runs, 107 runs batted in, and a full season expertly handling a pitching staff liberally sprinkled with kids and rookies. He was already one of the hitting stars through the first six games of the Series, with two home runs, three doubles, and four runs scored.

As Byrne knew, Campanella was an intelligent as well as opportunistic power hitter, and he was hot.

For this at-bat, Byrne went to one of his distracting tricks—casually flipping the ball in the air and catching it just before delivering his pitch to the plate. The ball came in a bit high, slightly on the inside part of home plate. Campanella was not in the least distracted. Reacting to the unexpected opportunity, Campanella almost pounced on the ball; his swing was very hard, very fast, brutal.

From my couch I can see Byrne throwing the ball, and the next instant the ball is on a sharp line toward the left-field corner; there was no time to wonder if it was fair or foul, no time to wonder if it would get past McDougald at third base. One instant the ball was in Byrne's hand; the next instant it was in the corner, fair—a baseball moment remarkably similar to Bill Skowron's double in the second inning.

There was not a shadow of a doubt that the hit was going to be a double. Campanella did not hesitate as he rounded first base at full speed and headed toward second. There was also not a shadow of a doubt that he was going to be safe.

In left field, Yankee rookie Elston Howard made no mad dash toward the ball. It had landed on a line just in front of the dirt track that looped around the outfield in front of the wall, and then rolled along it. To add insult to the double's obvious injury, the ball took a little hop over Howard's glove and rolled between his legs, forcing him to turn around to pick it up.

For the first time in the game, the Dodgers were threatening. Carl Furillo was next at bat, the man who had flied deep to Howard in the second inning. Byrne was more careful this time. Furillo was fooled by an off-speed pitch and hit a ground ball toward Rizzuto at shortstop.

But because Furillo was fooled, he hit the ball off the end of his bat, making the ball travel very slowly to the left side of the infield. Campanella sensed the opportunity and took off immediately for third. Normally, baseball players are taught not to try to advance on a ground ball hit in front of them, but this one was hit so slowly, forcing Rizzuto to charge and field it on the grass, that he had no realistic play at third. Furillo was out by a mile, but Campanella was safe at third with two men out.

Just as the Yankee threat in the third had brought Walter Alston to the mound, the Dodgers' response brought Casey Stengel out of the dugout. First base was open. One of the premier Dodger hitters and my personal idol, Gil Hodges, was coming up; the issue was whether to pitch to Hodges or walk him intentionally (Don Hoak, in the game for his glove, not his bat, was up next); and if the decision was to pitch to Hodges, the question was how.

According to Byrne, there was no argument about Stengel's instinct to pitch to Hodges or Byrne's feeling that he had a good chance of tempting Hodges with off-speed pitches on his fists inside or away from his power and that if by being careful he walked the slugger, so what? Don Hoak would later have some solid hitting years in Cincinnati and Pittsburgh, but this was only his second season of half-time duty in the major leagues and he had barely hit .240.

Pitching to Hodges was a real risk. The quiet, solid Dodger was dogged by his past—miserable in the '49 Series and then the nightmarish, 0 for 21 in '52—but he had rebounded smartly in 1953 and already had six hits, a home run, and three runs batted in 1955. This was a big decision that reeked of rash. I recall nothing of the brief meeting at the mound and have no memory of being either pleased that Hodges would get a chance to hit or insulted that the Yankees were pitching to him because they thought they could get him out.

With my hero, I always had the same sensation whether he was making a play in the field or hitting—a warm, relaxing, confident feeling. On the surface, Hodges was a rare athlete who combined grace and power. His build was large and muscled, but there was no swagger to his style, no flamboyance, just a quiet brilliance that was at once professional and inspiring. Gil Hodges was the Dodger parents told their kids to be like; my parents never had to tell me. To my young boy's eyes, he was the first grown-up I was aware of who exuded that force that is usually called character. It felt almost reassuring to realize that he would be at bat with Campanella on third base in a scoreless game.

Hodges took the first two pitches for called strikes. The next pitch by Byrne to Hodges was a virtual carbon copy of the pitch to Campanella. It was not quite as high, roughly around Hodges's Dodger letters, and a bit more toward the middle of the plate. Byrne remembers it as a changeup.

From my couch the result was exactly the same as Campanella's double. Byrne had made a mistake in his pitch, and Hodges made him pay for it. Like Campanella before him, Hodges swung hard at the inviting offering and hit a bullet well over the vain leap of Phil Rizzuto into left field in front of Elston Howard. There was not an instant of doubt about the course of the ball from Hodges's bat to the outfield grass; it was as solid a single as a premier slugger could hit. On that hit, my father could have scored from third as easily as Campanella did; the ball was hit so hard, however, that it is highly unlikely he could have scored from second. To underline the now-second-guessed decision by Stengel, Hoak then proceeded to tap an easy ground ball to Rizzuto for the third out.

The phone rang before my father could make eye contact with me. Once again, there were some quiet words that I couldn't hear, clearly with my mother. When he hung up, my father didn't repeat any of their conversation. He simply stared warmly at me and I simply stared back. It never occurred to me to blurt something out or to ask why we weren't speaking during the game. I don't remember feeling at all intimidated, merely happy to be looking to him for my cues. The silence increased my attention to the game. It also made it ten times as tense.

One run meant nothing. Worse, it was a prelude to even more dread of those fabled Yankee comebacks that made years of defeat all the more bitter. I had no earthly idea what to expect as the fourth inning concluded, but winning the World Series was definitely not in my young head.

For the first time that day, I began paying closer attention to Johnny Podres. He had survived the first three innings, but he did not seem overwhelming, and there had been two close calls already—Bill Skowron's shot to right field could just as easily have made the seats on the fly, and but for the fluke with Phil Rizzuto, Yogi Berra could have come to bat in the third inning with the bases loaded. When one looks back over the batter-by-batter summary of the game, it is apparent that the Yankees had not been particularly aggressive to that point. They were mostly waiting for Podres to throw strikes before they swung. The changeup was definitely in his repertoire, but he was throwing it less frequently than he had the previous Thursday in Brooklyn. It had been effective, but there was something tentative about the first third of the game.

Tommy Byrne had seemed more in command. The Dodger run had happened suddenly, two line drives wrapped around a slow ground ball. For the most part, however, the Dodgers weren't hitting him and there was a methodical efficiency about his pitching that was itself intimidating.

With the Dodgers on the scoreboard first, the Yankees' at-bat in the bottom of the fourth inning was especially important, and the most dangerous hitters were due up to hit.

Having missed his chance to bat with the bases loaded, Yogi Berra lead off the half inning. Swinging a bit late on another off-speed pitch, he sent a very high pop-up into shallow left-center field. It was one of those plays where the first thing you notice is that two outfielders are converging on the ball and it isn't immediately apparent whether they are going to get to it in time or collide. In others words, the play was instantly nerve-racking.

Berra's pop-up brought Junior Gilliam in from left field and Duke Snider in from center; it was just deep enough that Pee Wee Reese was in no position to make a play going backward from shortstop. It was gradually clear that getting to the ball would be no problem for the two Dodgers; the problem was going to be avoiding a collision. As the film shows, Gilliam and Snider charged toward the ball's landing spot in obvious disregard of each other. Neither was waving his arms or clearly yelling the hoary pop-up command—"I got it!"

At almost the last instant, Gilliam finally reacted properly, acknowledging the center fielder's dominant role in these situations. He darted quickly to his right, leaving Snider alone with the rapidly descending ball. Snider, however, did not react at all, and, shades of the prewar Daffy Dodgers, it fell to the ground in front of him. Berra was by now standing on second base; it is listed as a double in history, but it was as legitimate a hit as McDougald's "single" that struck Rizzuto the previous inning.

I have a vivid memory of the play. On any other occasion it would have produced a groan or an angry shout; in the odd circumstances of my living room that afternoon, I remember just pursing my lips. After the game, Snider said the bungled pop-up was entirely his fault, that he should never have stopped his charge to the ball. History can forgive as graceful and acrobatic an outfielder as ever played the game. The preceding day, Snider had stepped on a metal sprinkler in the outfield chasing a fly ball off the bat of Bill Skowron in the third inning, twisting his left knee. The injury was severe enough that manager Walter Alston used Don Zimmer to pinch-hit for him. There is a picture that survives of Snider after Game Six wearing a large bandage over the knee; he played the seventh game in pain and with limited mobility. But the injury, he later said, had nothing to do with the way he played Berra's fly ball.

The obviously ominous fact of Berra on second base with nobody out added still more tension to the atmosphere but appeared to have no effect whatsoever on Podres. Moving to his fastball in response to a shouted command from Campanella, who walked halfway to the mound and yelled at him to throw hard, he got a late swing and routine fly to Furillo in right field from Hank Bauer—short enough to give Berra no chance to tag up and try for third base against Furillo's famous arm.

Continuing to bear down under the pressure, Podres now faced Skowron. Again Campanella walked toward the mound, this time telling Podres to shake his head after the next sign as if he were rejecting it when, in fact, he was to throw the pitch for which Campanella had signaled. The Dodger catcher's purpose was to get Skowron thinking, trying to guess what Podres would throw to him. Podres told me Skowron was known as a "guess hitter," the kind who made up his mind before the pitcher threw what kind of pitch was coming his way. In the continuous search by pitchers for even the slightest edge over the hitters they faced, it was gospel that the more the hitter thought about it, the better position the pitcher was in. Whatever Skowron was guessing he would throw, Podres got him swinging late on another fastball, producing a ground ball to Zimmer at second. As with Furillo's ground ball in the top half of the inning, it was hit slowly, and because it was behind him, Berra had no trouble moving over to third base as the second out was recorded.

The tension remained thick as Bob Cerv stepped in to hit. Campanella called for yet another fastball. Cerv's swing was timely, but he hit under the pitch, popping it up high in the air behind Reese. The shortstop backpedaled a few steps and caught the ball for the third out. The Yankees had missed their third genuine opportunity to score in four times at bat and had failed to respond to the Dodgers' first run. A game that could not have been more tense by definition was now established as tense in fact, and there was now a favorable trend to it.

The main reason it didn't feel significant, apart from the omnipresent danger that the Yankees could strike like a sudden summer storm, was Tommy Byrne's masterful pitching. He was no longer the hard—and wild—pure thrower he had been in his youth. Now thirty-five, he moved the ball around the plate continuously, varied his speeds, and used the pitch that had probably length-ened his career (his slider) to keep the Dodgers off balance.

He also appeared to be enjoying himself at times. In the fourth inning, just before Campanella exploded with his double, Byrne had toyed with Duke Snider before striking him out. This was the one occasion when there is a consensus that he was talking to a hitter from the mound. Byrne yelled at Snider that a slider was on its way just before throwing one and falsely advertised a fastball (it turned out to be a curve).

Any hint, moreover, that the Dodger breakthrough in the fourth might be a sign the team was timing Byrne's pitches better and getting ready to hit him hard was quickly dispensed with by his performance in the fifth inning. Don Zimmer struck out swinging, Johnny Podres popped up in foul territory to Gil Mc-Dougald, and Jim Gilliam sent a weak ground ball to Billy Martin at second base, ending the first half of the game.

The torture that I was doing my best to endure was far from unique. Coming to grips with the possibility that the Dodgers might actually have a chance to win the game and the Series was now a fact of life in the diverse national circle of Dodger fans, but nowhere was the tension building the way it was building in their unique home across the East River. Brooklyn was beginning to stir, and other young people also were struggling to come to grips with what was unfolding over in the Bronx.

BROOKLYN, USA

Florence Rubenstein, like a million or so kids that day, had ar-rived home from her Brooklyn school (Montauk Junior High in Borough Park) during the second half of the game. She climbed the stairs to her apartment on Ocean Parkway and plopped down on the couch in the den where the television was of course on.

She asked her mother, who was ironing, whether there had been any more scoring. The reply did not surprise Florence. "It won't matter," her mother said, reflecting the most emotionally safe way of enduring a Brooklyn Dodgers World Series game—by preparing for defeat.

"The Yankees were always the winners," Florence recalled years later, "and they always had this infuriating arrogance about it. I had cried every year after I would get my hopes up for the Dodgers only to see them lose again. I would get in bed, put my head under the pillow, and just cry."

The cycle never stopped, including the annual rekindling of hope that came with the spring. Her father was the optimist, a genuine Wait'll Next Year-er; her mother refused to indulge.

"I was a little of both," Florence said. "Each time a World Series would start it would be like here we go again, and how unfair it all is. But I would hang in there. After all that time and the way we kept coming back, and tried so hard, we should win already."

Florence Rubenstein learned her baseball in Brooklyn sort of the way I did in Lower Manhattan—very, very young and from her father.

In Prospect Park's sylvan and expansive splendor, she and her brother spent hours with him growing up, learning to catch, to throw, and to swing a bat. He was from Canarsie—one of Brooklyn's scores of neighborhoods—hadn't got very far in school, but had played a lot of ball as a kid. Scouts had looked at him; baseball, along with advanced education, was among his might-have-beens.

As it was, he and his brother owned a liquor store over in Bedford-Stuyvesant, one of the neighborhoods where African-Americans were an increasingly large presence, to which they had been migrating from the South since the turn of the century (Lena Horne was born there in 1917). He and his family lived near the park.

Ocean Parkway is one of Brooklyn's boulevards of happy dreams, gorgeous testimony to the possibility of livable cities. It is superwide, tree lined, with both a bicycle path for young people and scores of park benches for the more sedentary. From north to south, it is for six miles or so a particularly pleasant route to Coney Island. Along the way, the old apartment buildings that frame it bring vividly to mind Berlin or Paris or Vienna.

That is exactly what two of the patron saints of the urban outdoors—Frederick Law Olmsted and Calvert Vaux—had in mind when they laid it out in the 1870s. For a kid in the 1950s, Ocean Parkway made possible an almost seamless indoor-outdoor life that encompassed an open neighborhood, public school, Hebrew school, the park, and Ebbets Field. Via subway or the Rubenstein family's green 1948 Chevy, the arts in Manhattan as well as the Coney Island cottage of Florence's grandfather (who was in the hat trade) beckoned.

In an essay of typical insight and warmth a few years ago, the writer Pete Hamill said that the visual key to Brooklyn was the striking presence of sunlight and of the sky, a dramatic and special openness that gave the famed borough, until 1898 a city in its own right, its distinct feel.

Woody Allen (née Allen Konigsberg in Flatbush) has written of the unique glow that the sun's light produces on the facades of Brooklyn's brownstones, even at midday.

Other writers speak of a distinctive Brooklyn personality—the descriptions regularly include decibel level, accent, chip-on-shoulder aggressiveness as well as defensiveness, fixation on the elemental turf of block and neighborhood, an absence of illusion, a presence of biting humor, and a passion for family.

One of my favorite Brooklyn sites on the Internet is lovingly and informatively maintained by a professor of Germanic languages (Yiddish especially) at Ohio State who was to the borough born—David Neal Miller. He summarizes the place where he was born and brought up, left but obviously took with him: "cradle of tough guys, Nobel Laureates, fourth largest city in the United States, proof of the power of marginality, and homeland of America's most creative diasporic culture."

It is easy to romanticize all this to excess, another fabled Brooklyn trait. It is also easy to forget that what is celebrated so eloquently can be found in cities all over America. You can even recognize elements of the famous accent in port cities as far apart as San Francisco, Baltimore, and New Orleans.

New Yorkers, myself included, famously forget there's a world out there—ironic, because the world out there is central to Brooklyn's nature and to its vast reputation. Brooklyn is uniquely connected to the rest of America, just as the rest of America is uniquely connected to Brooklyn.

The Dodgers have no national appeal without Brooklyn.

Brooklyn was the essential, perfect, diverse place for Jackie Robinson's courageous destruction of many of the bigoted myths about race. And for many people, and more than a few even today, part of Brooklyn's essence was the Dodgers.

An outsider, even one who was raised just across the river in Lower Manhattan, knows to approach Brooklyn carefully, even fearfully. As a boy, however, I approached Brooklyn gleefully, and not just to visit Ebbets Field and my Dodgers. I played hundreds of innings of baseball on the spacious fields of Prospect Park. I learned to love cemeteries with my father, prowling the delightfully diverse headstones of Green-Wood (from both Currier and Ives, all four Brooks Brothers, and Samuel F. B. Morse to Albert Anastasia, "Boss" Tweed, and Frederick Augustus Otto (FAO Schwarz). I was desperate to attend classes at the Brooklyn Academy of Music, reluctantly settling on a day program at Julliard. I rode the Cyclone at Coney Island in the front seat with my first serious girlfriend. I was actually at one of Alan Freed's rock-and-roll shows at the old Brooklyn Paramount at Flatbush and DeKalb— to my mother's horror and my father's bemusement.

And especially after Barbara Cahill moved to Brooklyn I ached to move, too; I said so at home, though I didn't give the real reason. Barbara Cahill lived near my neighborhood and often played in our pickup games; she had light hair, a brash disposition, and mesmerized me. On my ninth birthday (she was a year or two older), I saw her running toward me and, acting my age, I sprinted the other way. She caught me after a hundred yards or so and, pinning me in place by the shoulders, kissed me on the mouth. The sensation was bewildering and exciting for something I expected to hate. And then she was gone—to Brooklyn. I was miserable for weeks.

The place I always imagined living in is, first of all, gigantic. Its seventy to ninety square miles (depending on which agency is counting) dwarf Manhattan. Brooklyn is at least ten times the size of Washington, D.C., roughly the size of greater Boca Raton where many of its residents have retired, and of the entire island nation of Aruba.

With that kind of size there naturally come scores of quite different neighborhoods within a widely varied geography. You can see little bits from the Manhattan side of the East River (my childhood view), including the three imposing bridges—the Brooklyn, Manhattan, and Williamsburg. To the right is historically ritzy Brooklyn Heights, and moving left the eye catches the indentation where the Brooklyn Navy Yard once ruled, and then not-so-ritzy Williamsburg and Greenpoint. That is just the tip of an immense iceberg that includes, toward the center, African-American neighborhoods (Brownsville and Bedford-Stuyvesant), residential neighborhoods toward the east (East New York and Canarsie), famous addresses near the water to the southwest (Bay Ridge and Bensonhurst), and real beach towns to the extreme south (Brighton and Coney Island).

In the heart of Brooklyn lies Prospect Park, every bit Central Park's equal and for me its superior because of its more open feel and sports opportunities. To the east of the park is my favorite neighborhood, Crown Heights, where you can sample both kosher delicacies and soul food in the streets off Eastern Parkway, another boulevard of European dimensions and beauty. Like the Dodgers, Brooklyn didn't simply happen. It evolved over the three hundred years from its founding by Dutch settlers to the year (1946) the Dodgers suffered their first play-off indignity against the St. Louis Cardinals, in response to the elemental forces of geography, economics, and migration. By the time the British colonial era was firmly established at the end of the seventeenth century, what had become Brooklyn was the seat of one of the six counties in the populous area that would eventually be termed metropolitan (New York itself, Richmond, Queens, Westchester, and Suffolk).

It was also an obvious target for the British as the Revolution began, not to put the first of many chips on Brooklyn's shoulder but because the British were occupying the major colonial cities and the town was the preferred route for an assault on New York itself. It was also a target because George Washington's greatly outnumbered army was ensconced there. The Americans fought bravely, but as their situation became hopeless, Washington managed a mass escape across the river, preserving his army for another day (shades of Wait'll Next Year). When I first began reading about the Revolution in the books I took out of the public library, I remember my father dutifully taking me a bit farther downtown from our building; Washington's forces landed in the neighborhood (Kip's Bay) just below mine and marched up Murray Hill on their way out of town to safety; I recall my father joking that they could have stopped for food at the Automat on Third Avenue.

Brooklyn evolved differently from the bustling money center based on the long, narrow island across the river. Initially, its orientation was toward the east as the hub for another long island that became known as Long Island—a land of farms and residences more than an urban hub of commerce. Its history is not merely a story of population explosion and settlement but also of the other favored route for American community expansion— annexation. In the nineteenth century, Brooklyn gobbled up Bushwick, Gravesend, Flatbush, New Utrecht, Williamsburg, and New Lots. It formally changed from town to city in 1834, and by the year Abraham Lincoln was elected president only Philadelphia and that other place across the river contained more people.

America's industrialization—spurring the three mass movements of people off the farm, up from the South, and out of Europe—led to explosive urban growth. As often as not, the first stop for new arrivals who had nothing with them but dreams was a tenement on the Lower East Side; for many, their first decent place that had running water was in Brooklyn. With the construction of the bridges, above all the Williamsburg, the steady flow across the East River became a flood. There were factories and major businesses—the Pfizer pharmaceutical empire began there before the Civil War; the navy yard (where the *Monitor* was built) was established by then as well—but Brooklyn was more residential than commercial, and to oversimplify, that is why its existence as a separate city from the monster just to the west was probably doomed.

As America became urban, there were no more powerful engines of change than money and water—money to fund the immense infrastructure required for the housing and transportation of millions of people and reasonably safe water to sustain life. As the nineteenth century's end neared, it gradually became obvious that Brooklyn had reliable access to neither. In New York itself, Wall Street and the commercial banking giants that emerged in tandem meant access to a growing market in municipal bonds, the instruments that financed infrastructure, including the pipelines required to bring water down from the mountains to its north. By the end of the century, the major financial institution in Brooklyn was a thrift institution—the Williamsburg Savings Bank—that was built on the meager savings of working people hoping to accumulate enough to buy a house.

Across the river, primal forces were creating a unified, if not exactly united, New York City. The western part of the Bronx was annexed back in 1873, with the rest of that community incorporated twenty-two years later. The response in Queens was a split, with roughly a third of it joining New York in 1899 while the rest became Long Island's Nassau County. Brooklyn's turn, via a hard-fought referendum that pitted sentiment against reality (not for the first time), came the previous year. The pivotal issue was water. By then, the absence of access to an abundant, reliable supply had become obvious to both eye and nose. The newspapers of the time were filled with tales of a foul, dark liquid that mixed disease with hydrogen and oxygen. It was said to be so hideous that the traditional public health remedy—boiling—was not an option because it only spread the foul odor around.

The referendum vote was close for emotional reasons, but the annexation was inevitable in the remorseless context of finance and infrastructure. Everything that made Brooklyn a gigantic, largely residential community for working families also made independent existence all but impossible. The annexation is still treated with resentment in popular lore—as if it were one more victory by the Yankees—but Brooklyn was not so much gobbled up by a greedy neighbor as it was absorbed into a larger reality.

Since before the turn of the twentieth century Brooklyn has been gigantic in population. When it was absorbed into New York City, Brooklyn was even then the fourth largest city in the country. At its peak, a little before the year the Dodgers won the World Series, some 2.7 million people lived there. Even after the exodus to the Sunbelt and suburbia, its 2.4 million residents today would still make it the country's fourth largest city.

Brooklyn is also uniquely diverse, as in really diverse. For a hundred years it has been the ultimate home not to the oversimplified melting pot but to relatively recent arrivals to America and to the North. From Irish, Italian, and Eastern European Catholics, to Eastern European Jews, to black Americans crowding the trains leaving the segregated and largely agricultural South, Brooklyn was a destination city. It remains so.

Today nearly 40 percent of Brooklyn's residents are foreign born, compared to barely 4 percent for the country as a whole. That is a lot different from the Brooklyn that was home to the Dodgers, but the difference has much more to do with country of origin than with the importance of immigration itself.

Brooklyn remains a community with much less wealth and considerably more poverty than the rest of the country. Brooklyn's median household income (at thirty-two thousand dollars as the twentieth century ended) is also below New York City's. That is not a lot different from the Brooklyn that was home to the Dodgers. In modern times, Brooklyn has always been a residential community (overwhelmingly renters) for working families not much more than a few missed paychecks above catastrophe.

The change in the borough that was a city until 1898 has involved the pattern common to all major American cities after World War II—white people moving on to what were at first openly segregated suburbs along with jobs, their places taken by nonwhites seeking better lives in much more restricted circumstances.

The African-American percentage of Brooklyn's population was 36 percent in the 2000 census, more than double what it was after the war; and as much as 10 percent of the total is Latino, from Puerto Rico and Mexico to a slew of nations farther south. This trend was well under way in the mid-1950s.

Today's majority-minority Brooklyn contrasts with the Brooklyn of midcentury that was still mostly white and largely Catholic. But what made Brooklyn special, and still does today, was its Jewish community.

It was enormous after World War II, after the better part of a half century of constant immigration. By then, more than a third of Brooklyn's population was Jewish, and the term doesn't begin to do justice to the variety of stripes of the faith that in fact thrived there.

People came, basically, because others had before them. For people accustomed to bigotry and unspeakable violence, the reputation of safe haven meant everything. They did not just come to Brooklyn from Europe; they also came from Lower Manhattan. Having learned firsthand and with pain about hate, Jews made Brooklyn, for all its clannishness and parochialism, a borough with open arms and a visceral, street-level tolerance borne of necessity. Jews in the twentieth century in effect comprised Brooklyn's soul.

Jill Schuker was in school that day in 1955. In her fourth-grade classroom—literally across East 40th Street in East Flatbush from her family's row house—her teacher, Mrs. Bromberg, had placed a large radio on her desk in the afternoon. Jill and her classmates were eight years old, but they didn't move.

Jill Schuker's mother was the baseball nut in the family, which was not observant; organized religion, Jill said, took a dive in her family after a rabbi said that it cost you a year off your life if you didn't keep kosher.

But listen to the local social conscience through Jill: "In our house, Richard Nixon was the devil and Adlai Stevenson walked on water. My mother really loved baseball, the radio with the games was always on, but she loved the Dodgers as much as she did because of Jackie Robinson. To us, the Dodgers had been on the side of the angels and had been an example to the whole world. The Yankees were not just the rich team that always won; they were the rich team that was prejudiced. She was filled with pride that it had been the Dodgers that did it, right in our own town. To us, Branch Rickey was as big a hero as Gil Hodges."

In school, it was natural for Jill to reach out and be a friend to a little boy who was known back then as a "war refugee" and would be called a Holocaust survivor today; she stopped by regularly at the first-floor classroom that was used by the CRMD kids, the impersonal, bureaucratic term of the times for children who were crippled, retarded, or mentally defective; and though there was discomfort in her parents, Jill brought a friend from summer camp in the Catskills, a black girl, into their home for visits.

Carey Aminoff was on the trolley that afternoon in 1955, going for the religious instruction he received three days a week at the Brooklyn Jewish Center. He had just left public school for the day from Winthrop Junior High and could follow Game Seven as he went, excited as he was.

"In those days," he recalled, "you could just be outside or traveling or walking down the street and you never had any trouble keeping up with a game because the games were on everywhere."

Carey Aminoff's parents were determined, assimilating immigrants. His father was from Uzbekistan, his mother from northern Europe near the Baltic Sea, in an area where country names changed depending on who had won which war.

"They lived for my two brothers and me," he said. "Absolutely nothing but English was spoken in our apartment. Education was everything. The intellectual content of our life, and of Brooklyn, was quite high, as were the expectations. It really typified the Brooklyn of those days."

His father, who was in the gem trade, and his mother were not avid baseball fans, but young Aminoff absorbed Brooklyn's pastime through osmosis and his peers. He was a catcher and right fielder in school and a Dodger fan who frequented Ebbets Field with his friends, who sat in the left-field bleachers together.

He grew up in Crown Heights, in a building at Utica and Montgomery, which meant that to get to Ebbets Field all he had to do was walk down the latter until he literally bumped into the ballpark.

"The Dodgers were not just a source of fun and torture," he said. "They were also a source of the stability in Brooklyn, in part because of the continuity of so much of the team, in part also because they were an object of real influence, people that you could very easily look up to."

The central place of education and learning in Carey Aminoff's life was anything but unusual; it was commonplace, as it was throughout the urban world where first- and second-generation Americans lived. It was the way to get somewhere and make something of yourself. Education was also the way urban kids discovered there was a world out there, in effect guaranteeing their ultimate departure from a nurturing culture they loved fiercely; for girls, the impact was especially transforming.

Over on Ocean Parkway, Florence Rubenstein's mother, a real blonde, had been a stocking model as a young woman (a jolting hint of an independent spirit, coming as she did from an ultra-Orthodox family on the Lower East Side). She had also been a legal stenographer, but after her first child was born there had been no question that she would stop working.

In East Flatbush, same story. Jill Schuker's mother also had not been to college. She had been a model (of sweaters), too, and then worked in a medical office. Her father, with a degree from Columbia, worked at the Abbott Laboratories operation in Queens, and after she came along her mother plunged into the local Girl Scouts and PTA at her two daughters' school. Jill recalls one time when her mother packed the auditorium for an evening appearance by Gil Hodges (whose wife, Joan, was a regular at the beauty parlor up the street on Albany Avenue); it was the best-attended PTA event anyone could remember, with the possible exception of the time all the fathers had shown up for a performance by a hula dancer from Hawaii.

Education opportunities that had been restricted by the depression, by the war, and by a culture that shoved women into dead ends were suddenly exploding. Even in the mid-1950s there was no question that many girls were not only going to have the chance to go to college and at least think about careers; they were also being actively encouraged by parents. For everyone, education was not only the key to a better life; it was also a means to a different life. In Brooklyn, this culture was not unique; but its size and variety were.

Florence Rubenstein made it all the way through Brooklyn College, living at home, and then was off to graduate school in Pennsylvania. At the train station her father's words to her—more a moment of poignancy than rebuke—were, "You're not coming back, are you?" She got her master's degree in social work at the University of Pennsylvania, which led to a career as a child therapist in addition to raising a family with her husband, public-opinion genius Peter Hart.

Education did not have to mean training beyond high school back then. Today it is the key difference between a chance at a middle-class life and an economically marginal existence. After World War II, high school had the same open-the-door meaning.

Billy DeLury grew up near the enormous Brooklyn Navy Yard. His father drove a truck to support his wife and family, which included another son and daughter as well. The rules were that if you took school seriously, got used to working diligently, maybe benefited from a connection or two, you had a decent shot at a decent life.

I met DeLury fifty-three years after he got out of high school, fifty-three years after he started by doing odd jobs in the Dodger front office. He is a thin man, with a full head of wavy hair and a million stories to tell, the embodiment of an institutional memory the team has always cultivated in California. There is virtually no job in the organization he hasn't done. Eventually, he became the person in charge of the complex task of moving the team around the country during the season and was in the process of overseeing a successor's training. We spent an afternoon chatting under the grandstand at Wrigley Field in Chicago while his Dodgers were playing the Cubs.

Early in elementary school, his parents decided on parochial school for him. He graduated in 1950 from St. Leonard's Academy on Clinton Avenue near his home, a source of many a Brooklyn diploma that was run by the Franciscans.

He did well in school and worked on the side as well, but when he graduated, as he put it succinctly, "I didn't have even the slightest idea what I was suited for or what I wanted to do right away or with the rest of my life."

The one idea that had stuck in his mind was to go the seminary route to the priesthood, but when he consulted the priest who mentored him, the advice he got was that after years of rigorous Catholic school he should work for a while in the allegedly real world before making a commitment like that. In those days, there were numerous routes to a decent job, but one of the surest was through the church itself; the Propagation of the Faith Office in Brooklyn functioned in part as an employment agency, and it was there that DeLury first went for some referrals.

When he arrived, a fresh listing had just been received from the Dodgers, who were looking for an office boy. He arrived at the team office at 215 Montague Street to find a half-dozen other kids sitting around waiting to be interviewed. The only question he remembers being asked by the Branch Rickey man filling the job (Spencer Harris) was whether he was a Yankee fan. He was told the office would call him in a couple of days, but when a week went by without a call he was on the verge of exploring an equally promising opportunity.

Billy DeLury's uncle, John, was one of New York City's most important labor union leaders from midcentury on—the president of the ten-thousand-member sanitation workers. More than once he battled mayors from Robert Wagner to Abe Beame to keep ordinary working people from having to suffer the most whenever there was a budget crisis. He had gone to jail once or twice during strikes and was a person of enormous respect in town. He would have a job for his nephew.

The Dodgers, however, called him first. Billy DeLury reported for work on September 1, 1950, just as Walter O'Malley's front office coup was unfolding. By the time of the 1955 World Series, Billy DeLury had run errands, delivered stuff, picked up stuff, helped arrange things, and worked on programs, concessions, and tickets.

He had also met the love of his life, Eleanor, the old-fashioned way—in the neighborhood. He had been injured at the time, was resting up at home, hanging out on the stoop in front of his building when he noticed her. She lived directly across the street, but he had never noticed her before; she had gone to public school. He asked her sister to introduce them but ended up having to do the honor himself.

One of the Dodger officials who took a shine to Billy DeLury was Buzzy Bavasi, who kept after him to get engaged. Around the time DeLury proposed, Bavasi arranged a reservation at Mama Leone's in Manhattan and two tickets to a hit Broadway show, *No Time for Sergeants*, starring a young actor from the South named Andy Griffith.

During the World Series games at Ebbets Field, DeLury sat with the other front office workers in a section of the grandstand (number seven) between home plate and first base. At Yankee Stadium, the Dodger office workers were spread all over the ballpark with single tickets. During Game Seven, he just happened to be down the left-field line in front of the foul pole, staring straight at the Dodgers' left fielder, Sandy Amoros. Even with virtually his entire adult life ahead of him, Billy DeLury was living the American Dream.

On October 4, 1955, John Sexton must have thought he was living the American nightmare, but his story underlines the priority given to education even in the middle of the World Series. Sexton and his best friend and fellow Dodger nut, Bobby Douglas, had just turned thirteen and attended St. Francis de Sales Grammar School in Belle Harbor.

The nuns in the convent there had always been generous with their radio at World Series time, but there had been recent misbehavior at the school and the punishment forced the one hundred and two kids in their space-shortage-era class to sit through that school day with no access to the only thing on their minds. They endured the torture and then came bursting through the school doors about ninety minutes into Game Seven to learn that the Dodgers were ahead.

They then sprinted nearly thirty blocks to Sexton's home on Beach 136th street and scampered downstairs to his room in the basement where the radio was immediately turned on. From the windowsill, Sexton took down a small, metal crucifix; he and Douglas then knelt, each grasping a side of the crucifix, and prayed while they listened to the final innings.

Belle Harbor is a lovely spot on the water. The homes on it and near it are occupied by people of consequence in New York, if not always of great wealth. Sexton's grandfather had been the tax commissioner under the famous and infamous Mayor Jimmy Walker—a position of both opportunity and responsibility. His father was the leader of one of Brooklyn's most important political organizations, the Jefferson Democratic Club. The Sexton home, a legacy of his grandfather, was a two-family house on a forty-foot lot almost on the water, with ocean views from three sides. Ultimately, their view was blocked by the construction of a house occupied by Carmine DeSapio, the eternally controversial boss of Tammany Hall itself.

Belle Harbor, of course, is in Queens. I identify with Sexton's story because living in that neighborhood meant having to deal with a great many Yankee fans. Some of the older ones—Sexton calls them the guys in the black leather jackets—regularly beat him and his friend up to force them into blasphemous utterances, such as praising Phil Rizzuto over Pee Wee Reese. He remained rabidly steadfast, however. Now the president of New York University, Sexton had one unusual request when he was invited to help design his academic robe—he asked that one of its cuffs display the number 42, Jackie Robinson's number.

It was not necessary to be a native to be part of all this magical combination of tough struggle and delicious life. By the tens of thousands, people moved into and out of Brooklyn—doctors and nurses, businesspeople, and those who were either in uniform or drawn to the civilian jobs at the still-huge navy yard.

Gary Hymel came from New Orleans in 1954, an army lieutenant blessed with an assignment to one of Brooklyn's miniature historical jewels—Fort Hamilton, on the water at the East River narrows, with Bay Ridge its residential neighbor. We have known each other off and on since the late 1960s, long after he had moved on from his Brooklyn hitch to get into politics and government as one of Capitol Hill's most knowledgeable senior staff members—serving both the late House Majority Leader Hale Boggs from Louisiana and Speaker Tip O'Neill.

Hymel came out of the ROTC program as an undergraduate at Loyola of New Orleans. Instead of Korea or Europe in this intense Cold War period, he drew Brooklyn and the smattering of activities run out of Fort Hamilton, an outpost that dates to the 1820s, when construction was begun on a facility to help guard the harbor area between Brooklyn and Staten Island. It was originally simply called the Narrows but was then named after Alexander Hamilton. In 1841 its engineer was a promising captain, Robert E. Lee, and its commander as the Civil War began was a fellow who made a couple of contributions to baseball, Abner Doubleday.

Hymel settled in Bay Ridge with his wife, Alexandria. One of their children, Amy, was born in August of 1955, the year not only of the Dodgers but also of Hurricanes Connie and Diane—two particularly vicious Atlantic storms I remember well that hit just as the Dodgers were moving to clinch the pennant. The Hymels rented the back half of a row house on 65th Street from a Swedish woman, one of thousands of Scandinavians who flocked to the area in the early twentieth century. The Norwegian church that my mother had attended was literally next door to them.

As Hymel was a baseball fan already, Ladies Day at Ebbets Field became a staple of Hymel family entertainment on their tight budget. With him in uniform and a pregnant wife, the total cost of admission was one dime and the ushers were especially solicitous about seating. On the morning of Game Six, he had a day off (his assignments included MP duties and administering the band based at the fort) and went to Yankee Stadium in uniform on a lark.

World Series games almost never sold out at Yankee Stadium ahead of time, and he had no trouble getting into the bleachers for five dollars. Delighted at the spectacle, he had asked for a second day from his colonel and was back in the bleachers for Game Seven, with a scorecard he has held on to ever since.

He and his family are the tip of an enormous demographic iceberg. Brooklyn may have the deserved reputation as an insular, parochial place, almost a world unto itself, with its own accent and purported personality. However, it is also a place that was both a major destination for the millions of new Americans who arrived there before and after World War I and in turn a gateway to the country as a whole for those who left after school and those who spent time there because of work. From census and other data, the well-known-around-town boast by Brooklyn borough president Marty Markowitz that "Brooklyn is America's favorite hometown" does not appear to be hyperbolic.

The estimates only differ in degree. According to the urban writers Grace Glueck and Paul Gardner, "One out of every seven Americans was either born here, lived here once, had relatives here or got here by taking the wrong subway."

One of the country's preeminent urban historians, Yale's Kenneth T. Jackson, goes even further: "As many as a quarter of all Americans can trace their ancestry to people who once lived in its eighty-one square miles." In numbers, that works out to an eye-popping 40 to 70 million people.

On reflection, it is more comprehensible. After the Revolution, roughly 80 percent of the entire country lived within fifty miles of the Atlantic Ocean; those settlers, including the people then farming in Brooklyn, have done a little moving and breeding since then. And for more than one hundred years, Brooklyn was either a primary destination or the second stop for the tens of millions of people who flocked to America's shores, a phenomenon that continues to this day.

Gary Hymel is one of those people with a claim on the place; so am I.

Hollywood for years has recognized this special connection, alert as it always is to demographics and the mass market. There are arguments about when it all started for real, but there is no question that the popularization of Brooklyn, including the general idea of Brooklyn, was given a huge shove by World War II. Within months of Pearl Harbor, hardly a war picture could be shot that didn't have a scrappy kid from Brooklyn in the starring platoon.

The catalyst appears to have been *Wake Island*, made in 1942, about the Japanese assault on the tiny atoll early that year. It was vintage war propaganda but also a pretty good movie, winning several Academy Award nominations, including one for its star, William Bendix, the actor who first made the Brooklyn character famous and beloved.

Bendix was born near my neighborhood in a poor section of midtown Manhattan in the shadow of the old elevated train tracks along Third Avenue that were ripped down in 1956. He had been a batboy for the Babe Ruth–era Yankees as well as the Giants (he would eventually play Ruth in the movies in 1948), but it was as a marine in the South Pacific that he became famous.

The character that made the country and the rest of Hollywood take notice was a courageous private facing the impossible odds—Aloysius K. "Smacksie" Randall. To show it was no fluke, *Guadalcanal Diary* was released the following year, an account of America's first big victory in a land campaign in the Pacific and where my father served and got his first bad case of jungle fever. This time, Bendix had been promoted to corporal—Aloysius T. "Taxi" Potts, a fighter from Flatbush.

The country loved these guys and so they proliferated, even unto today. One of the soldiers whom Steven Spielberg enlisted to save Private Ryan was a Brooklyn kid, and the only baseball hats visible in the combat scenes from Jerry Bruckheimer's *Pearl Harbor* have the big *B* on the front. In Phil Alden Robinson's fantasy *Field of Dreams*, the old-timers who came out of Ray Kinsella's cornfield after he built his diamond included "Shoeless" Joe Jackson, his banned teammates from the Black Sox, Mel Ott of the old Giants, and, gratuitously, Gil Hodges; the reclusive novelist who hits the road with Kinsella, Terence Mann, had shunned baseball ever since the Dodgers left Brooklyn; his Dodger disillusionment helps establish his character.

The mass appeal of Brooklyn, however idolized and even schmaltzy, is also apparent in dramas, musicals, and comedy. The popular film version of Betty Smith's hugely successful novel of immigrant life, *A Tree Grows in Brooklyn*, came out right after the war and made Dorothy McGuire famous. Local boy Danny Kaye (born David Kaminsky in Brownsville, a runaway to show business at the age of thirteen) also had his first big hit that year (1946), as the tongue-tied milkman who becomes a prizefighter in *The Kid from Brooklyn*.

My favorite from this period—*It Happened in Brooklyn*—is a classic illustration of how Brooklyn and mass market were virtually synonymous. Released in 1947, it is a musical (Frank Sinatra, Jimmy Durante, Peter Lawford, and Kathryn Grayson) and was one of the year's major hits. The story involves the adventures of a Brooklyn kid overseas during the war who comes home to a tough restart in life, while he and his friends try to help a promising pianist get into the Brooklyn Academy of Music.

The songs include a Jule Styne and Sammy Cahn number, the score was by Johnny Green, and the piano playing was by a seventeen-year-old kid fresh out of Beverly Hills High School, Andre Previn. The school scenes were shot at New Utrecht High School in Bay Ridge.

As the television age dawned, the dependence on Brooklyn for characters and themes continued, in a sense celebrating both ends of America's ethnic journey. One of the first hits came off a radio program that dated from the war years—*The Life of Riley*, about a father, wife, and two kids who have migrated to California, where Dad works in an aircraft plant. Chester Riley was William Bendix.

Ironically, the original star of the television program bombed in the ratings and was forced to look for a new vehicle. His name was Jackie Gleason.

Gleason was a Bushwick boy, born in the same year (1916) that Margaret Sanger opened the country's first birth-control clinic on Amboy Street and Nathan Handworker began selling his famous hot dogs on Coney Island's Surf Avenue. In the 1950s, Gleason made a bus driver from Bensonhurst, Ralph Cramden, into one of the most recognized and beloved characters in the country. By the tens of millions, people tuned in each week to watch Ralph and Alice and Ed and Trixie do their best to cope with life at 328 Chauncey Street (the same address Gleason grew up at in Bushwick).

These characters could be foolish and buffoons, they were barely comfortable, they could be simple-minded and stubborn, but they were also hardworking, warm, and loving people. At that time, most of America did not carry briefcases and go to work in fancy surroundings. It was still a blue-collar country with a broadening middle class, still mostly urban, and not transfixed by luxuries. Brooklyn was the perfect setting, at least until about the time Johnny Podres was pitching in the seventh game of the World Series.

Within Brooklyn, there were many people who took offense at the television and movie portrayals, claiming to see insults where others saw humor, stereotyping where others saw compliments. The chip was never far removed from many a resident's shoulders. There was even a classic Rorshach test in the famous form of artist Willard Mullin's Bum. Some saw a slur; others saw a lovable, universally recognized character.

In 1941, a legend in the public relations trade, Sid Ascher, actually founded an organization called the Society for the Prevention of Disparaging Remarks Against Brooklyn. It eventually claimed anywhere from forty thousand to 1 million members (Ascher's preferred figure). Each year, it claimed a growing number of "investigations" of disparaging media references, the highest being three thousand in 1946.

Ascher was a Brooklyn boy and a PR genius. He developed the Miss Rheingold contest for the New York beer company, was one of the Boy Scouts' most active promoters, and wrote the famous speech in which Franklin D. Roosevelt solemnly defended the honor of "my dog, Fala," against Republican attack. His organization is often used as a metaphor for Brooklyn's ethnic defensive-aggressiveness, but the fact is his tongue was often clearly visible in his cheek in this hype-filled endeavor.

The proof that Brooklyn's storied attitude was as much myth and shtick as genuine is to be found in one of its most recognized exports—comedy. It ran the gamut from Mae West and Gleason to Phil Silvers and Zero Mostel, from Henny Youngman and Woody Allen to Joan Rivers and Buddy Hackett, from Phil Foster and Alan King to Sid Caesar and Joey Adams, and in more recent times from Chris Rock and Eddie Murphy to Andrew Dice Clay and Mary Tyler Moore. The Brooklyn theme is part self-mockery, part in-your-face, but always supremely confident and never ashamed.

Still another Brooklyn Kaminsky, Melvin, dealt with the borough's alleged reputation as the butt of jokes with some deft wit of his own. Working as Mel Brooks, he noted that the three place names most likely to evoke a laugh—Brooklyn, Burbank, and Podunk—each contained the letter *k*, and he argued that all such words are inherently funny. What makes the observation witty is that it is not clear if Brooks was being serious (he wasn't).

9

The Man from Fordham

For millions of Dodger households that day, the last out of the Dodger half of the fifth inning of the seventh game in 1955 did not simply mean that the game—barely an hour old—was half over. It also meant that Mel Allen's southern accent and booming baritone was about to be replaced by the flatter, already beloved, Bronx accent of Vin Scully. My parents detested Mel Allen—less because he was a notorious "homer" in his adulatory descriptions of Yankee games than because he was corny. I was used to his relentless hype and more amused than turned off by his folksy demeanor; most of my friends could recite his tobacco and beer spiels for White Owl cigars and Ballantine beer and ale ("Make the three-ring sign and ask the man for Ballantine").

Allen had two trademark expressions when he did games. By accident early in his career (he had started doing Yankee and Giant home games in 1939), he had described a long fly ball he wasn't sure was going to be caught or, as it happened, end up a home run: "Going, going . . . gone!" And after a particularly sterling play, usually by a Yankee, he always exclaimed, "How 'bout that!" He seemed pleasant enough.

But Vin Scully was way beyond pleasant. Astonishingly, on that historic day he was only twenty-seven years old, Junior Gilliam's age, broadcasting his second World Series, having emerged almost immediately from the shadow of as hard an act to follow as a person could imagine—Red Barber.

Despite their different origins and accents, and very different ages, each was renowned for essentially the same reasons: economical use of language, absence of noisy hype, almost casual tone, and a continuous flow of detailed information communicated in clear English.

Barber had been hired by Larry MacPhail in Cincinnati and went with him to Brooklyn. He achieved iconic status in the 1940s, a trailblazer in the difficult arts of wise understatement and wry wit that more sophisticated listeners in postwar America appreciated. By contrast, Vin Scully had barely had time to learn from the master as the very junior member of his broadcasting team when circumstances thrust him into the national limelight with virtually no warning.

"It was 1953," he told me when we talked in his booth at Wrigley Field in Chicago, where he had accompanied the Dodgers on a road trip fifty years later, still at the very top of his profession. "Gillette was offering him two hundred dollars a game for the Series, and Red wanted more, and Gillette made it clear that they were not offering a penny more. Red was just not going to do the broadcasts for that amount of money."

In the Dodgers' booth that year, the second man at the microphone was another broadcaster with a rich résumé, Connie Desmond. If Barber was a father figure to the young Vin Scully, Desmond (out of Toledo, Ohio) was the big brother. However, he also drank heavily, there had been an episode or two on the air, and NBC did not have confidence in him before a national audience for the World Series.

Ever the diplomat as well as the professional, Scully called his colleagues before formally agreeing to join Mel Allen in the booth. He sought the blessing of each and made it clear he was not in such a career hurry that he wanted to proceed without that blessing. Barber and Desmond each graciously told him to do the games; Dodger owner Walter O'Malley took Mel Allen aside before the Series and urged him to "take care of my boy." Scully went out and drew raves.

He was a recently married man, very close to his parents and sister, and living in New Jersey. On the morning of Game One in 1953, he had a big breakfast, drove to Yankee Stadium, promptly threw up his breakfast, and entered the booth.

Scully is from Yankee territory, the Bronx, but he grew up closer to the Polo Grounds and was a Giants fan. When he was a boy his mom wheeled him around the nearby campus of Fordham University, where it was always hoped he would go to college. As it turned out, he attended Fordham Prep as well.

A decent athlete in school, he developed his passion for broadcasting listening to games, especially college football games, on his family's large radio that perched atop a four-legged console. Lying on the floor underneath it, he was mesmerized by the sound of the fans. He first used his narrative gifts shouting summaries of what was transpiring to neighborhood kids playing in the alley five floors below his family's apartment.

The war interrupted his time at Fordham, but after navy service he returned, focused on being sports editor of the college paper and hanging out at a tiny FM radio station that had started up on campus.

In his senior year, he sent job application letters out by the dozen, but the only serious response came from the CBS affiliate in Washington, D.C., whose sports operation was presided over by one of the pioneers in the field, Arch McDonald, who did the Washington Senators' play-by-play and a daily sports show as well. It was in the evenings when McDonald was stuck at a game in Griffith Stadium that Scully got his opportunities to be on the air. The summer job led to an offer of a real one, but because it was not to begin until the spring of 1950, he was back in New York hoping for temporary work.

His big breaks came from Red Barber, who did CBS work during the college football season. Scully got two assignments, the 1949 Maryland–Boston University and Harvard–Yale games, which in turn led to his really big break. The junior man on the Brooklyn Dodgers' broadcasting crew was the legendary Ernie Harwell. He had not yet landed in the city that would make him famous, Detroit, but when he took a better offer from the New York Giants over that winter, the job opened up. Barber called Scully to arrange an interview with Branch Rickey, which produced the flimsiest of job offers—spring training with the Dodgers on a month-to-month deal, renewable at the Dodgers' option. Scully was barely out of college, but he was blessed with a sharp mind and a rich voice and determined to apply the lessons he had first learned lying under the family radio.

"I loved to hear the roar of the crowd," he told me, "and when I started broadcasting I loved to let the crowd roar without my interference."

This virtual silence at climactic moments when no words were really necessary has long since become a Scully trademark; that afternoon his trademark reticence would produce a famous concise sentence at the end of the game.

His sparse language and wry wit were always adorned either by a telling or merely delightful nugget of information. In our talk, Scully remembered Game Five of the '53 Series, a complete game 6–5 victory by the beloved Dodger pitcher Carl Erskine.

"It was Game Five, and the fifth anniversary for Carl and his wife, Betty," Scully recalled. "The Yankees scored all five of their runs in the fifth inning, and I noticed that the game ended at five-oh-five in the afternoon of October 5. I was determined to get all of those fives into one sentence and somehow I did."

For the record: "On Carl and Betty Erskine's fifth wedding anniversary, the Dodgers made it a game of fives, winning Game Five of the World Series on October 5 by a score of 6–5 in a game where the Yankees scored their five runs in the fifth inning before yielding to Brooklyn at five-oh-five in the afternoon of the fifth."

That, of course, was a head-scratching hint of still another Scully trademark. Whenever someone was at bat with two outs and the count on him ran to two balls and two strikes, the "deuces" were forever "wild."

Scully also made marvelous use out of the encyclopedic compilations of numbers kept by a genius the Dodgers had also hired, in 1947, to be their "statistician"—the amazing and pioneering Alan

Roth. Data is of course only numbers until it is reported and analyzed in understandable fashion. The combination of Roth's information and Branch Rickey's leadership produced some important player decisions as the Dodgers evolved into a powerhouse.

After Rickey departed for Pittsburgh, Roth brought his genius, as well as his trivia, to what would become a twenty-plus-year career in broadcasting. With Vin Scully, the combination of his data and the broadcaster's style and interpretation gave Dodger fans an insight into the game not previously available, even in print.

Scully and Mel Allen could not have been more different in their style and content, but it turned out that they shared an important career connection—with Arch McDonald, whose folksy Arkansan approach to sports fit with the then-sleepy southern town of Washington. Allen had come north from Alabama as Melvin Israel after doing the university's and Auburn's football games on a lark after getting both his bachelor's and a law degree. He literally walked into CBS in New York and got a job assisting the network's stars, Robert Trout in news and Ted Husing in sports. Allen could have gone in either direction, but two flukes— nearly an hour ad-libbing through an auto race and then being junior man for the 1938 World Series—sealed his fate.

The following year Allen was teamed with Arch McDonald for baseball, the first step in a plan to anchor the better-known McDonald in New York and send Allen to do the Senators in Washington. The idea was blocked when owner Clark Griffith exercised his local owner's prerogative to instead hire pitching immortal Walter Johnson for the job. That left McDonald in New York, which he hated and soon left to return to Washington, putting him in position to assist the young Vin Scully a decade later. Allen thus got the top job by this default; during the war years he was in turn assisted by none other than Connie Desmond.

I was of course not even remotely aware of any of this broadcasting history during the seventh game in 1955. In our apartment, Scully's voice was already a familiar and welcome guest. As he began doing the game, he didn't reduce the tension level one bit; it simply felt better to have a friendly voice guiding me through the excitement, just as it felt better to look across the room and see my father.

Scully was hardly tested by the Yankee half of the fifth inning. Elston Howard's fly ball to Junior Gilliam in left field was routine. Despite his well-earned reputation as a dangerous-hitting pitcher, Tommy Byrne struck out for the second time that day. Phil Rizzuto's ground ball to third was a bit more than routine; it was hit sharply, backing Don Hoak up, but he fielded the ball cleanly and his long throw to Gil Hodges was perfect. Through five innings, the Dodgers had a 1–0 lead, as tentative and tenuous a lead as there is. The feel of the game, as well as its details, more than justified the observation of *The New York Times*' Arthur Daley that "the Brooks never had a firm hold on it."

At that point, they had but two hits, both solid, off Byrne, who had walked two and struck out two. Podres had walked just one Yankee, while striking out three. The four Yankee hits included the bouncer by McDougald that Rizzuto slid into and the bloop by Berra that had dropped in the Gilliam-Snider confusion. Neither team had a clear advantage.

It was also of absolutely no consequence to me that the Dodgers at the end of the fifth inning were flirting with something achieved only once before in the seventy-plus years of their franchise's tough history—a lead in the deciding game of a World Series. In Game Seven in 1947, they had scored first at Yankee Stadium but had blown their lead in the third inning and fallen behind in the fourth. In their other seventh game, in 1952, they had tied the contest after five innings but fell behind in the sixth.

The true analogy at that point, unfortunately, was with Game Six in 1952, when the Dodgers could have won the Series in Brooklyn. The team took a one-run lead into the seventh inning only to lose it and the game under bizarre (even for the Dodgers) circumstances.

Vin Scully told me that the older players were acutely conscious of recent hideous, tragic Dodger history; it motivated them, but it also preyed on their minds. It did so for good reason; there had never been any recent history like it in sports. In the nine seasons after World War II ended, the Dodgers had lost the chance to win the National League pennant on the final day of the season three times and had come back from the World Series empty-handed four times. The other two years—the Boston Braves' pennant-winning season in 1948 (the Dodgers finished third behind St. Louis, eight games back) and the Giants' World Championship season in 1954 (the Dodgers finished five games back in second) seemed as much emotional respites as off-years.

I was steeped in this lore. My father had been as patient but persistent in my baseball education as he was with school and music. One thing—playing catch, learning to swing a bat—led to others, above all talking and reading. My parents doted on me, but what I remember most vividly is talking with them, not being a little kid around them. I had a cowboy outfit, complete with a cap pistol, and I had a shovel and pail for the sandbox, but I only have memories of playing in the parks of Tudor City with other little boys, not being indulged by my parents in our apartment; the only games we ever owned were checkers and chess, plus a deck of cards for Hearts. I have no memories of baby talk, only conversations in which I felt more part of the household than its junior member. Perhaps the fact that the roles in our household were scrambled by contemporary standards was part of it, but I grew up in an atmosphere where discussion and argument took precedence over obedience; I was encouraged to have no compunction about talking back as long as I understood that I then had to stand my ground against two people who used persuasion far more than power.

By the time I had started school, our family had a weekend ritual, interrupted only after I had started singing professionally and there was a Saturday matinee at the opera. Sundays were reserved for the laundry; my mother washed it in our bathtub, while my father and I squeezed out the water and hung clothes on a line strung across our postage stamp–sized balcony—two people could barely stand on it. But Saturdays were special. While my mother grocery-shopped, my father and I took the crosstown bus on 42nd Street to the massive temple of my young life, the New York Public Library, on Fifth Avenue.

My reading had quickly become voracious. I would get a book to take home on my library card, and more often than not as a treat my father would lead me to the periodical rooms to read old baseball stories in the newspapers and magazines. He—and my mother, too—would embellish the stories with their memories, shared around the card table while we ate or on my cherished trips with them to Ebbets Field. Years later, my mother told me that we babbled among ourselves so incessantly that people sometimes looked at us funny in the stands, on the street, or in the subway. I never noticed; I was in heaven, because on those occasions we were sharing good times, the focus for a change wasn't just on me, and they never treated me like a kid except when I did stupid things.

Even then, their disapproval was offbeat as well as corrective. For some reason, I recall developing the bad habit in a tiny living room of kicking off my slippers instead of taking them off in the morning. My father had gently reproached me for this without impact until one day I launched a slipper into a long, high arc; as if by black magic it descended right into the cup of Postum he was drinking. I have few memories of him yelling at me; this time, he looked at me with an exasperated disappointment that was ten times as reproving. Saying nothing, he produced his yellow pad, on which I was commanded to write a paragraph explaining why kicking off your slippers was wrong. I could not have been more than seven.

Sometimes the learning experience was in the opposite direction. One of my rare treats in those early years was a Sunday excursion to one of the grand ice-cream parlors of the day, Schrafft's, which had an outlet near Grand Central Station. A vanilla ice-cream soda was my usual, while my father favored milk shakes, the plasma of ulcer patients. Among my bad habits was a tendency to lean over the soda, sipping through my straw without holding the tall glass. One day, my father had just finished a lengthy declamation on the dangers of tipping the tall glass over this way when his elbow knocked his own glass into his lap. The waitress and I laughed until we cried—with him.

My only resentment, nurtured in private, was that I detested being shown off in any way to my parents' friends. I loved learning, but I hated performing because it made me feel more like a freak than a person. The one exception involved my father more than me. Whenever he was able to work and completed a free-lance piece, he would take me with him to a bar on Third Avenue a couple of blocks away from our building to celebrate and, I suspect, to show off. It was one of the writers' shrines of that era—Tim Costello's. Tim and his brother, Joe, attracted newspapermen, authors, playwrights, poets. The walls were decorated with drawings by James Thurber. I don't remember, but the family legend was that before I was five I had had whiskey spilled on me by Dylan Thomas and Brendan Behan.

My mother and father had hung out there before the war, when he was just beginning to establish himself. He knew both Costellos well, and there was always a ginger ale for me with a cocktail cherry in it after one of them hoisted me up on the long bar, where there was often another kid or two as well. My mother feigned disapproval, but all my memories of her in that famous joint include smiles and laughter (pride, I suspect) as she nursed her one manhattan; after my father got sick, even a shot of whiskey caused him intense pain, so we tended to share ginger ales. The noise was continuous as the writers shouted to one another about their "stuff" and these strange people they called editors. I don't recall any Yankee fans, but there was always plenty of Dodger talk, every word of which I soaked up like a sponge.

Through this somewhat unusual educational process, long before the 1955 season, I was an expert on everything from the evolution of the Dodgers from town teams after the Civil War, the maturation period under a onetime odd-jobs guy named Charles Ebbets and the construction of the cozy ballpark that bore his name, the disappointments of 1916 and 1920, the slow descent into the horrid but lovable Daffy Dodgers, and then the climb back to excellence followed by the amazing string of *Almosts* after the war.

This mixture of possibility, bad breaks, perseverance, disappointment, the nobility of effort, was hardly unique, but it certainly fit my family history. The Dodgers were made for us, as they were for so many millions of working families in those days.

After the fifth inning of the seventh game ended, I had no basis for believing what the scoreboard undeniably had recorded. Instead of the fact that the Dodgers were ahead 1–0 and Johnny Podres was pitching marvelously, the only thing that mattered to me was that the Yankees had come within an eyelash of scoring three of their first five times at bat. There was nothing beyond more of the same to look forward to—the atmosphere in my apartment was not rah-rah; it was quiet and intense, as established by my father's example. What was unspoken between us was both the fear and the expectation of disaster.

It could not have been otherwise. It was not superstition or a vague sense of foreboding that produced our mood. It was historical fact or, more comprehensively, a string of historical facts. We sat in silence because based on everything we knew in excruciating detail about the Brooklyn Dodgers, the game on the television set was anomalous to that point; it made no sense at all. Each at-bat by each player was simply an opportunity for something to go horribly wrong—again.

It is useless to say simply that the Dodgers lost real chances to win championships many times just before and for ten years after the war. The point is that each of those tales from 1941 through 1954 added bricks to the foundation of the team's unique lore and that the details of each (tragic, tragic-comic, maddening, infuriating, heartbreaking) are what gave the saga its meaning and its force. The Dodger fan's cry after every one of these *Almosts*—Wait'll Next Year—was not a cheery, uplifting chant; it was a fist waved with cockeyed optimism and defiance at adversity itself. The Dodgers themselves kept coming back; so did my parents and the millions of people who didn't have to study metaphors to know in their bones what the team represented. Any one of the stories of their setbacks would be astonishing by itself; strung together over such a short period, the stories provide a sense of what it took to keep trying and excelling.

There were twenty years of experience with the Dodgers in that living room that afternoon in 1955; each of those years taught us that a 1–0 lead was not only inconsequential but also most likely a cruel hoax.

10

The Sad, Crazy Saga

The Dodgers didn't become annual lovable losers in September and October via predestination. The famous reputation formed gradually, each year's late flop adding to the lore and legend of the previous one. To understand what Wait'll Next Year really means is to understand the individual Last Years that comprise this sad saga.

These were also my formative years. As I came to consciousness, I didn't then, and don't today, mark time by each of the Dodgers seasons, but the connection between them was obvious as I became a fully conscious fan during the worst of all their disasters—the historic pennant race of 1951. For my parents—at first pulsating with postwar optimism and pride in their war service, only to face the agony of my father's disability—the unique life of a Brooklyn Dodger fan was not overpoweringly obvious at first.

For the Dodgers, the postwar era also began in an atmosphere of optimism. A strong team was back from the fighting with legitimately high hopes and the added glow from Branch Rickey's signing of Jackie Robinson at the end of 1945. Their history had not been very successful, but the record of no championships was not the same as a curse.

The saga did not start with the first two World Series in 1916 and 1920. Those were simply disappointing ends to successful seasons, the first pennants in the team's modern history.

It hadn't started with 1941, either. That was also a disappointing end to a successful season, the first Brooklyn National League pennant in twenty-one years, proof that the Larry MacPhail–Leo Durocher era was synonymous with winning as well as prosperity. The Dodgers had performed before more than 1.2 million fans at Ebbets Field and drawn another million for their road games. Except for two weird plays—the line drive by Marius Russo off Freddie Fitzsimmons's leg and the ball that got past Mickey Owen—the Dodgers, not the Yankees, might have been in position to win the World Series.

It was the following year when the team's performance began to get frustrating, setting the stage for a repeat nonperformance four years later—each against the St. Louis Cardinals. Recalling the 1942 season, my mother once told me that there were two occasions that year when she simply felt sick, just the way she would so many times through so many later seasons. It wasn't the same as disappointment, she said; it was like getting kicked in the stomach.

My mother was one tough woman, famously spare with her emotions and anything but a baseball hero-worshipping premodern groupie. Until 1942, she had only two idols—Franklin Delano Roosevelt and my father. That year, however, she flipped for Pete Reiser, much to her astonishment. She said she was mesmerized by his baseball playing, at the graceful ease with which he fielded, ran, and hit. At Ebbets Field, she said, Reiser was the first ballplayer who drew her out of her shell and got her to yell during the games. In addition, like a lot of knowledgeable Dodger fans, she had developed a deep respect for all the moves Larry MacPhail had made to transform the team into a contender.

My father was already in basic training when the 1942 season opened, but my mother was in the stands at the Polo Grounds for the game against the Giants, courtesy of her boss. Baseball would be her hobby for the next forty months. She had a hard core of girlfriends at her law firm and then the U.S. Attorney's Office, all with husbands away in the war, who would go to ballgames together for the next fifteen years. During the war, she found it the perfect distraction from long days, and it reminded her of the good times with my father before Pearl Harbor. She described herself as lucky to have a job and even luckier to have one that usually demanded work on weekends and at night. She hated being alone with the unavoidable thoughts and worries about my father—where he was in the Pacific, whether he was safe. She never got used to it and she never got over it.

If anything, the Dodgers were a stronger team in 1942 (the flood of ballplayers who eventually left for the war was but a trickle that season) than they were the previous year when they squeezed in front of the Cardinals by two games in the standing. In fact, the Dodgers ended up winning four more games. The Cardinals, however, won the pennant, finishing the season white-hot and overcoming a Dodger lead that had stretched to eight games with barely a month to go.

Two events put an exclamation point on the collapse. In July, in just his second full season as a Dodger, Pete Reiser chased a long fly ball hit over his head in center field by Enos "Country" Slaughter of the Cardinals. Fast and fearless, Reiser caught up to the ball just before he crashed, headfirst, into the wall near the exit gate. The ball fell out of Reiser's glove as he crumpled in a heap on the grass, unconscious, and Slaughter sped around the bases for a home run that figured prominently in the Cardinal victory that day. At St. John's Hospital, the diagnosis was severe concussion, and the recommendation of every doctor who looked at him was that he not play for the rest of the season. Larry MacPhail and Leo Durocher paid no heed, however, and Reiser was back playing before he had stopped having vision and equilibrium problems. He had been hitting close to .400 before he was hurt but finished the season barely hitting .300. His enormous promise remained, but he had been seriously damaged by Dodger decision making as well as by Ebbets Field's outfield wall.

And then, just days before the season ended, Larry MacPhail was canned by the team's board of directors. He had repaired the team and repaired Ebbets Field, he had greatly reduced debt, and he had stitched together the beginnings of a lucrative broadcasting network. The profits, however, were puny in the board's stern view;

the directors wanted fat, annual distributions, and MacPhail was viewed as not only mercurial but spendthrift. Once again, the directors consulted Ford Frick in the league office, and once again he consulted his friend Branch Rickey, the Cardinals' famous architect. This time, Rickey recommended himself. He and MacPhail were both baseball geniuses—pioneers in the development of farm team systems for young prospects and in making deals for more established players—but Rickey was both famously straitlaced and deeply religious as well as a legendary tightwad with salaries.

MacPhail was ushered out. The cover story for his departure was a supply service job, at a lieutenant colonel's rank, in the army he had served in World War I. Meanwhile, a new ownership group had been assembled that would rule the team for the next eight years. The change was managed by an important figure in Brooklyn's modern business and political history—George V. McLaughlin of the Brooklyn Trust Company, which was both the mortgage holder on Ebbets Field and the team's operating lender.

McLaughlin's bank was represented on the Dodgers by a Brooklyn lawyer—a graduate of Fordham Law, with engineering credits as well from the University of Pennsylvania—who had thrived during the depression representing failing companies in bankruptcy proceedings. In addition to handling mortgage foreclosures for the bank, he gradually assumed responsibility for the Dodgers' legal needs. His name was Walter O'Malley.

In the lore of John Sexton's family, this was no automatic elevation. His father had been both an attorney and a powerful figure in Broklyn's Democratic Party organization. He also had been close to Branch Rickey and the family legend is that Rickey had offered him the position of general counsel in the Dodger management. Sexton declined, and it is far from clear Rickey could have prevailed over the bank's power and O'Malley's ambition. However, there are never enough what-its in Dodger history, and this is another

Rickey owned twenty-five percent of the team, as O'Malley eventually did. A third quarter share was held by another stalwart of the business establishment—John Smith of the Pfizer Company, the drug giant that eventually sold penicillin and had been based in Brooklyn for nearly one hundred years. The final share was owned by the last link to the Charlie Ebbets era, the heirs of one of his partners, Steve McKeever.

During the war, Rickey continued to build the nucleus of a Dodger future around young prospects whom he stockpiled in an elaborate farm team system that came to include more then five hundred players, financed in part by the strategic selling of the contracts of older Dodgers judged to be past their prime; Rickey became deservedly famous for his sales and his purchases, motivated strongly by the fact that his contract guaranteed him 20 percent of the profits on these transactions.

Rickey also launched his secret project to desegregate the sport; his cover story was that he was looking for black players with which to stock a new Negro League venture. The atmosphere around the Dodgers was very positive during the war years and as the global conflict drew to a close. There were reasons galore to expect that the Dodgers were about to become one of the sport's premier teams and no hints at all of the nine nightmarish seasons ahead.

A COIN TOSS

In 1946, the first full season after the war, the Dodgers and Cardinals were back at it again, battling all year long and down to the final games of the season. Pee Wee Reese was back, along with a MacPhail-era rookie, Carl Furillo, in center field; a scrappy second baseman in the Leo Durocher mold, Eddie Stanky, had replaced the thirty-seven-year-old Billy Herman at second; Reiser was still contributing solidly in the outfield, as was the Dodgers' most popular player, right fielder Fred "Dixie" Walker (known famously in Brooklynese as the People's Cherce).

The 1946 season was also my debut in Brooklyn. My father was getting regular magazine assignments through his agent and war buddies—*Harper's, Reader's Digest,* and trade publications. He was making good, not great, money, but it was enough so that for the first time in her life, my mother didn't have to work. She kept house and spent every day when the weather was nice wheeling me around the parks in Tudor City, getting to know the other Baby Boom mothers. Just months old, I witnessed several games from the outfield bleachers at Ebbets Field, passed between my father and mother, and for one glorious inning was held by none other than Hilda Chester. My parents had gotten to know possibly the most famous baseball fan ever during her heyday in the 1930s. A formidable woman with a foghorn for a voice and a delightfully coarse, occasionally vulgar wit, she had haunted Ebbets Field since the 1920s. Her life is truly the stuff of legend, much of it unverifiable. There is general consensus that she had worked bagging peanuts for sale at ballparks and that after a heart attack her doctor had told her to stop her trademark yells and harangues from her customary bleacher seat. She responded by developing two new trademarks—a cast-iron frying pan that she banged with a ladle, and then a cowbell (the gift of some Dodger players) she rang while leading processions of her groupies through the stands. My father, a master at conversing with odd people as though they were senators, who engaged her before and after the war, told me that behind her raucous behavior was a tough, often sad, life, but that she was warm and decent under a very gruff exterior. Her favorite Dodger by a mile was manager Leo Durocher. She did not show up in Brooklyn much after he left for the Giants, but I remember seeing her famous sign in front of her seat (Hilda Is Here) on occasion as a boy, and her presence during the 1955 World Series is a matter of record.

In the final week of the season, however, there was a harbinger of the disaster to come—another injury to poor Pete Reiser. Playing despite a bad leg and leading off first base, he tried to slide back to beat a pickoff attempt, caught his spikes in the dirt, and broke his ankle.

On the last day of the season, the Dodgers were shut out at home by journeyman Mort Cooper of the fourth-place Boston Braves, leaving the players in their dressing room and thousands of fans in the ballpark to wait for the result of the game between the Cardinals and Chicago Cubs that would determine whether the Dodgers were finished for the season or would be in a play-off. There is a picture of the throng, largely clustered on the outfield grass in front of the famous scoreboard in front of the right-field fence, between the signs then advertising Botany neck-ties and Gem shaving blades. Somewhere in the crowd is me, at the ripe age of nine months, with my parents.

As it turned out, the Cubs crunched the Cardinals at home, cre-ating the first tie in league history and requiring a best-of-three-game play-off to determine the pennant winner. For reasons that old-timers still argue about, the Dodgers won a coin toss to deter-mine where the first game would be played and elected to start on the road in St. Louis, requiring an immediate, long train trip. The game featured the Dodger future (twenty-year-old Ralph Branca) against the Cardinal present (twenty-game winner Howie Pollet).

Branca was not effective, yielding three runs in less than three innings. Howie Pollet pitched a complete game for the win.

The second play-off game in league history was played in Ebbets Field, matching two pitchers coming off strong seasons—Dodger left-hander Joe Hatten and Murry Dickson of the Cardi-nals. Hatten was even less effective than Branca had been, giving up five runs in less than three innings, including a run-scoring triple by Dickson.

A powerful team being slowly assembled under Branch Rickey had been beaten by a St. Louis Cardinals team that Rickey had al-ready helped build. Around Brooklyn, the talk was mostly about the decision to open the play-off on the road; it was assumed the Dodgers would be contenders the following year—which they were.

LAVAGETTO, GIONFRIDDO, AND DEFEAT

The year 1947 belonged to Jackie Robinson, a season of struggle but of triumph as well. Hitting, fielding, running, he was the spark of a team that began to slowly pull away from the Cardinals.

Toward the end of the season the team had a night for him at
Ebbets Field, a fitting tribute to a man who was the runaway
choice as Rookie of the Year while he was making much larger history as well. In the end the Dodgers won the pennant going away,
finishing five games ahead of St. Louis. At this point in their development, Robinson was the one addition to Reese and Furillo
among the Dodgers who would be on the field eight years later,
playing first base at the time.

Until 1947, the famous term *Subway Series* primarily meant the
Yankees and the Giants, who had played memorable World Series
against each other in the 1920s and '30s. The only exception had
been in 1941. This was the year the great rivalry was joined in
earnest between the Yankees and the Dodgers—between the team
of the borough where working families lived and a team based in
the blue-collar Bronx but suffused with the glow of Manhattan
and more than a generation of unparalleled success.

Even before the season, bad blood had begun to flow. By this
time, Larry MacPhail had resurfaced as one of three Yankee partners, forging an alliance with two men Dodger fans loved to hate:
The first was Dan Topping, a trust fund child with movie star
looks and gobs of money from the Anaconda copper fortune.
Among his lesser distinctions, he was one of silent movie star Ar-
line Judge's eight husbands. Topping had dabbled in professional
football as well, including a team in Brooklyn. The second man
was Del Webb, the boss of a real estate development empire that
filled up the postwar West with tract houses sold with restrictive
racial covenants forbidding sales to people of color. Webb also
had been involved in the construction both of the internment
camps where Japanese-Americans were confined during the war
and of the Frontier casino in a spot of Nevada desert called Las
Vegas, the postwar brainchild of mobster Bugsy Siegel.

After the deal acquiring the Yankees from the estate of beer
baron Jacob Ruppert (the modern team's as well as Yankee Stadium's builder), MacPhail resumed his madcap life that combined baseball wheeling and dealing with large-scale misbehavior
and binge drinking. Like more than a few sports figures of the

time, he also hung with people who were called colorful or gamblers in the popular press, euphemisms for gangsters. In 1947, however, it was not MacPhail who got in trouble for his escapades; it was Leo Durocher of the Dodgers.

Among their shared acquaintances were two legendary gambling figures who belonged in a Damon Runyon story—Memphis Engleberg and Connie Immerman, the latter the operator of a casino in Havana and an "associate" (to use another euphemism) of mobster Charles "Lucky" Luciano. According to legend, the two had been part of the group that crime figure Arnold Rothstein used to fix the 1919 World Series. Back then, baseball and gamblers were no strangers, and separating them was high on the agenda of the commissioner hired by the team owners in 1945: A. B. "Happy" Chandler (a former governor of Kentucky and the man who sanctioned the signing of Jackie Robinson).

Durocher was a mere manager; MacPhail, however, was part of an ownership group. What is more, Durocher had lived a publicly notorious life for years, including a messy divorce involving assault charges in 1934 and an even more famous affair that turned into marriage with the actress Laraine Day. In the morality politics of the day, moreover, Durocher was a favorite whipping boy for the stern disciplinarians of the Catholic Church, who regularly inveighed against him for corrupting the young and in Brooklyn threatened to discourage parish kids from attending games.

In the end, MacPhail's behavior was officially ignored and Durocher—by then a team and borough fixture for nearly a decade—was suspended for the entire historic season. For the first two games, the fill-in manager was Clyde Sukeforth, the scout Branch Rickey had sent to look Jackie Robinson over and bring to Brooklyn; for the rest of the season, and for the following three years, Rickey hired a contemporary and friend, Burt Shotton, who had managed the Phillies twenty years before. A quiet, dignified man who dressed impeccably off the field, he was the anti-Durocher.

After the manager melodrama and the debut of Jackie Robinson, the pennant-winning season was almost anticlimactic, with one tragic exception again involving Pete Reiser. Once again, the speedy star was playing a shallow center field against the Pittsburgh Pirates on June 4, when a long-forgotten outfielder named Cully Rikard hit a shot over his head to the deepest part of the ballpark. Once again with Reiser racing back with no thought of the rapidly approaching unpadded wall and forgetting that the fences had been moved in by more than ten yards, it was a virtual repeat of the disaster five years ago, except that this time he could have died. He hit the wall with his head at full speed, collapsing with the ball still in the webbing of his glove. He was virtually paralyzed for more than a week, eventually needed surgery to remove a blood clot from his head, suffered repeated episodes of double vision and grogginess, and never played the outfield consistently again. He could still hit (his average in 1947 was .309), but the full-time career of a man many baseball people considered the best natural all-around athlete in the game's history, with the possible exception of Shoeless Joe Jackson, was at an end.

There was nothing forbiddingly awesome about the Yankees in 1947. They won three more games than the Dodgers, but in a weaker league. They were anchored by Joe DiMaggio, but with a large collection of new players and a new manager (Bucky Harris had replaced a team legend, Joe McCarthy), there was no obvious favorite that fall.

In the first game, it was the Dodgers who broke on top for a run off the Yankees' Frank Joseph "Spec" Shea. In Yankees–Dodgers lore, pitching is central, and one of the dominant themes of the torture Brooklyn endured was the seemingly endless emergence of journeymen who had career moments against them in the World Series. Spec Shea, whom the newspapers also called the Naugatuck (as in Connecticut) Nugget, won fourteen of his fifty-six career victories that year. He also pitched two excellent games in that Series, winning both of them.

Through four innings, however, young Ralph Branca was magnificent, retiring all twelve of the batters he faced, five on strikeouts. In the fifth inning, he fell apart. The disaster began with a ground ball that DiMaggio hit toward left field, which Pee Wee Reese chased down too deep in the shortstop hole to have a chance of throwing him out. Unnerved, Branca walked a batter, hit another, gave up a two-run double, walked another hitter, and was in the process of walking a third when Shotton yanked him. Before the inning was over, the Yankees had batted around and scored five runs.

The Dodgers' pitching also collapsed in the second game, but after their hitters awoke to break open the third game at Ebbets Field, the stage was set for one of the weirdest games in World Series history. For eight innings plus two outs, still another journeyman pitcher—Floyd ("Bill") Bevens, 7–13 for the season—had held the Dodgers hitless. He had given up a run on two walks, a sacrifice, and a ground ball out, but no one had ever come that close to a no-hitter in the Series and the Yankees had scored two runs. The ninth inning was for the ages.

The Dodger catcher, Bruce Edwards, very nearly tied the game with a long fly ball that Joe DiMaggio caught in deepest center field. Carl Furillo then walked, and for speed Shotton sent in a small kid outfielder from Pennsylvania named Al Gionfriddo to run for him. After the Dodgers' third baseman, John "Spider" Jorgensen, fouled out, Shotton sent Pete Reiser up to bat for pitcher Hugh Casey. In a display of daring that would be almost unthinkable today, Gionfriddo took off for second with the count two balls and no strikes on Reiser. He dived at the base, just beating the throw, whereupon the Yankees intentionally threw the fourth ball to Reiser. This was a highly unusual move, putting the winning run on base, but Harris's thinking was that because Reiser had a bad ankle that month his famous speed was not in play. Harris's thinking backfired, however, when Shotton sent in utility infielder Eddie Miksis to run for Reiser.

The stage was thus set for Harry "Cookie" Lav of the MacPhail era in the late 1930s who lost his war. He might not have made the Dodgers after th

An.

except there was a special rule that permitted teams to keep three additional players on the roster if they were war veterans.

Lavagetto swung at Bevens's first pitch, a fastball that rode in on him, and missed it. The second fastball was over the plate; Lavagetto went with it and drove a hard line drive straight at the huge wall in right-center field.

There was never any doubt about the only hit the Dodgers got that day. When the ball bounced off the wall, hit Yankee right fielder Tommy Henrich in the chest, and rolled away from him, there was also no doubt that Gionfriddo and Miksis were going to score easily. One moment, the Dodgers were two strikes away from being no-hit and going down 3–1 in the Series; the next moment, they had won the game and tied the Series. My father always told me that the celebratory eruption that ensued was the most positive emotional moment surrounding the team that he experienced until that afternoon eight years later.

The Dodgers' hitters remained quiescent the following day when Spec Shea pitched a marvelous complete game victory—a tense 2–1 win—to send the Series back to the Bronx. This time, the Dodgers' bats woke up, taking an 8–5 lead into the sixth inning, when a second famous Series moment from that year occurred. For defensive purposes, Gionfriddo had been sent into the game to play left field in place of Miksis. Two men were on, there were two outs, Joe Hatten was pitching, and the most dangerous Yankee of them all was next. As Joe DiMaggio came up to bat, representing the tying run, Gionfriddo was moved even closer to the third-base line in the Dodger expectation that he would try to pull the ball. Instead, he hit it on a low, hard line toward the Yankee bullpen in left-center field.

Not unlike another Dodger left fielder eight years later, Gionfriddo took off at the crack of DiMaggio's bat and ran, and ran and ran and ran. Miraculously, he got near it, just in front of the 415-foot sign, reached out in midstride with the glove on his right hand, snared the ball, twisted in the air so he bumped the fence with his rear end and came down on his feet. As with Sandy ˙ros's play in 1955, the run was more spectacular than the catch. In the papers, Gionfriddo compared it to an end in football running under a long forward pass. On his way back to the Dodger dugout, he noticed a scene famously captured on film—the normally controlled DiMaggio kicking the dirt around second base in disgust.

This set the stage for the first time in Dodger history that the team would play a game in which they could win the World Series. All the pitchers were tired from the grind of the previous six games, with the Yankees choosing to start Spec Shea again on two days' rest and the Dodgers going with journeyman Hal Gregg, who had pitched seven strong innings in the Game Four miracle against Bill Bevens. In Dodger lore, there is an amazing succession of small turning points that are as maddening as they were pivotal. In their first Game Seven, it was base running.

In the first inning, both Eddie Stanky and Pee Wee Reese were thrown out by Yankee catcher Aaron Robinson while trying to steal second base. These were not foolish attempts: Robinson's relatively weak throwing arm was well-known; this just happened to be his day. Then, in the second inning, Carl Furillo was thrown out trying to score on a ground ball to Phil Rizzuto at short. The Dodgers had five hits and a walk in those two innings but only two runs.

The Yankees, meanwhile, pecked away at the Dodgers' pitchers, getting one run in the second inning, two in the fourth, one in the sixth, and one in the seventh. After the fourth inning, the Dodgers got exactly one hit the rest of the way—a two-out single in the ninth. The man who shut them down—as he had for four innings in Game One before taking the loss in Game Six—was one of the pioneers in the then-infant art of relief pitching, a tall specialist in the forkball (so-called because it is held between the first two fingers) named Joe Page. He had three marvelous seasons with the Yankees beginning that year and two productive World Series, both against the Dodgers. This time the disappointment was keen; the team had every opportunity to win, but losing late was becoming familiar. Three little-known ballplayers in that World Series performed feats that are still talked about today, but

Bill Bevens, Cookie Lavagetto, and Al Gionfriddo would never play another inning of major-league baseball.

The 1947 World Series was not like 1941. It is was more than a disappointment after a successful season that made history and gave the Dodgers a national following with the arrival of one courageous player. This time, the first chorus of Woulda, Coulda, Shouldas, Mightas could be heard. They didn't just almost win; they probably should have.

CHAOS AT HOME AND ON THE FIELD

It was during 1948 that my parents' lives changed. Their happy, essentially carefree postwar life gradually unraveled as my father's health slowly but inexorably deteriorated.

My mother described my father upon his return from the war as thin as a rail, pale, and weak. He had been through malaria and dengue fever as well as countless other bouts with germs Western medicine had not yet named. He was never down for long and rarely in medical facilities that offered much more than a little rest and symptomatic relief, but the cumulative effect got him assigned back to New York after the invasions of Saipan and Tinian.

With no memories of anything but a bubbly, strong man before the war, my mother was alarmed at his appearance and general condition at first, but thousands of men came home from the Pacific in poor health and thousands more had been seriously wounded. At first, he seemed to recover, but within six months what he thought was a chronic stomachache turned out to be a bleeding ulcer. Unable to imagine that his health was deteriorating, he braved his way through a quick recovery, only to get knocked on his back a few months later.

The syndrome slowly became chronic. At first, my father had to pass on the occasional writing assignment; eventually, he was passing on most of them. He did not have access to fancy medical care to begin with, but what really drove him to distraction was his difficulty in finding someone who could tell him what was wrong beyond the fact that the linings of his organs were weak, his digestive system didn't work right, and he was in constant pain, sometimes agony. Eventually, he managed to get a firm diagnosis for one complaint and it was terrifying: a tumor on his right kidney that demanded surgery. Back then in the days before lasers and other modern marvels, surgery to remove a kidney was a huge deal; the scar went halfway around him.

What had begun as a frustrating irritant rather quickly became a family crisis. Fat savings accounts were for rich people; in those days most everybody was just a few missed paydays from disaster. There was never any doubt or discussion about what to do; my mother simply went back to work. Her old law firm was healthy and expanding, and she had been a valued secretary and office manager; she was welcomed back enthusiastically, but she returned with a heavy heart and budding doubts that her dreams of a secure life and another kid were just around the corner.

For me, it meant nursery school, at a place run by a church up First Avenue from us. It would be called day care today, but it was most of my day for the next three years—so that my father could work when he was feeling well and rest when he wasn't. He bore his burden stoically, but his continual illness was accompanied by a constant battle for the official attention of the heavily burdened Veterans Administration. Years later, he told me we would have had a much less difficult time if he had returned from the Pacific all shot up instead of infected.

Anything courtesy of the Dodgers to distract him would have been embraced; it would have been the perfect time for the Dodgers to win. But alas, this was when they became the Dodgers of fable and lore.

Following their second and thrilling World Series, the Dodgers and the Yankees spent 1948 rebuilding teams that had been veteran-heavy. They also spent the year in turmoil. After a display of drunken brawling astonishing even for him, Larry MacPhail's two partners, Topping and Webb, decided to get rid of him, bought him out for more than $2 million, and installed the highly respected George Weiss as their general manager. Headed toward a third-place finish just behind the Boston Red Sox and the eventual World Champion Cleveland Indians, the Yankees also decided that Bucky Harris was not their field manager of the future. They replaced him after the season with the man who would be running the team for more than a dozen years, including that day in 1955—Casey Stengel, the stylish, mischievous Brooklyn outfielder on the 1916 pennant winner who had managed mostly unsuccessfully after his playing days with the Dodgers and Braves before rekindling his reputation at the Pacific Coast League's Oakland team.

The Dodgers' experience was much more traumatic. After leading the abortive petition drive against Jackie Robinson's promotion to the team, Dixie Walker had asked to be traded, and the Dodgers obliged him in one of the better steals of Branch Rickey's fabled career. Shortly after the World Series, Walker was shipped to the Pittsburgh Pirates along with pitchers Hal Gregg and Vic Lombardi. In return, the Dodgers got a solid left-handed pitcher whose best years were still ahead of him, a tall Arkansan named Elwin Charles "Preacher" Roe; a third baseman, Billy Cox, who was a decent hitter but, more important, may have been the best-fielding third baseman of his day; and for good measure a utility infielder (Gene Mauch) who eventually became a famous manager.

But 1948 was also the year Leo Durocher tried to come back from his suspension only to run into the implacable ill will of Walter O'Malley, then beginning to flex his muscles on the Dodgers' board. Unable to save Durocher's job as the team lurched toward last place in late June, Branch Rickey put him in touch with the owner of the Giants, Horace Stoneham, who was also looking to make a managerial change. Just as the Giants were beginning their own rebuilding process, Durocher skipped across town in midseason, replaced once again by Burt Shotton. The Dodgers made a run at the pennant, but an August injury to Ralph Branca probably doomed their chances and they skidded to third place, just a game in front of Pittsburgh, a game behind the Cardinals, and eight games behind the pennant-winning Braves.

In 1949, the modern Dodgers burst on the scene. The year before, Durocher had moved Gil Hodges from backup catcher to first base. After Eddie Stanky was traded to the Braves, Jackie Robinson was installed at second base. (Stanky was another signer of Dixie Walker's infamous petition.) From Compton near Los Angeles, a young Duke Snider was installed in center field as Furillo moved to right; and Roy Campanella had replaced Bruce Edwards as the catcher. Except for a hole in left field, it was almost instantly a powerful, fast, and superb defensive team. This was Jackie Robinson's Most Valuable Player season; he led the league with a .342 batting average, drove in 124 runs, got more than two hundred hits, and stole thirty-seven bases.

This was also the year that Don Newcombe arrived in the major leagues with a flourish, pitching a shutout in his debut in late May and winning seventeen games in his Rookie of the Year season; Preacher Roe, with a delightful assortment of pitches that included the occasional spitball, added another fifteen victories, to go with Ralph Branca's thirteen.

The Yankees were just as impressive, but both teams had to survive famous scares at the end of the season to slip into their third Subway Series by one-game margins. The Yankees, needing two victories against the Red Sox, got them; and the Dodgers had to beat the rapidly improving third-place Phillies to avoid another play-off with the Cardinals.

The World Series is typically described as a Dodger collapse, in part because that is precisely what it was as they lost in five games. Its place in Dodger mythology, however, is more interesting than that because the first three games were Series classics, nail-biters that could have gone either way, featuring fabulous pitching and enough what-ifs and might-have-beens to keep increasingly neurotic, truly knowledgeable Dodger fans talking for years.

The wild finish of the regular season disturbed the Dodger pitching rotation, with Preacher Roe needing an extra day of rest. In his place, Don Newcombe became only the second rookie to open a World Series (the first, Paul Derringer, had started the first game for Branch Rickey's Cardinals in 1931). Newcombe was opposed by Allie Reynolds, whom Larry MacPhail had obtained from Cleveland after the 1946 season for veteran second baseman Joe Gordon. Part Native American from Oklahoma, Reynolds was already one of the league's best pitchers, could relieve as well as start, and had won Game Two against the Dodgers in 1947.

For eight and a half innings, the two men pitched one of the best World Series games ever. Newcombe yielded four hits, Reynolds just two; Newcombe struck out eleven, Reynolds nine. If anything, the Dodgers had been slightly more threatening, getting three runners into scoring position at second base to the Yankees' two. It all came down to the bottom of the ninth inning at Yankee Stadium, with Tommy Henrich, the Yankee right fielder who had struck out on the ball Mickey Owen let past him eight years before, leading off.

Newcombe fell behind Henrich, who took the first two pitches for balls. Behind the plate, Campanella signaled for a curveball, and said later that Newcombe obliged with his best pitch of the day. Henrich was ready for it and hit it hard into the right-field seats to end the game. This was as close as Newcombe, famously overworked during the regular season grinds that brought the Dodgers three of their pennants in his day, ever came to winning a World Series game (in all, he lost four).

Game Two was just as exciting, another 1–0 pitching duel that matched Preacher Roe against another solid Yankee, Vic Raschi. This time, fortune was with Preacher Roe, who scattered six hits and walked nobody in a masterful performance. Raschi was almost as good over eight innings of six-hit pitching before giving way to a pinch-hitter and then Joe Page in the ninth. The difference in the game was a two-out single in the second inning by Gil Hodges that scored Jackie Robinson, who had doubled.

In Brooklyn, incredibly, the third game was tied 1–1 after eight innings. Ralph Branca battled first Tommy Byrne and then Joe Page for the Yankees and had two outs in the ninth inning around a walk to Yogi Berra when he once again collapsed. Three singles and a walk later, the Yankees had scored three runs, but with Page tiring after more than five innings in relief, the Dodgers rallied in their half of the inning. With one out, the answer to one of the better Dodger trivia questions hit a home run into the left-field bleachers. His name was Luis Olmo. He was Puerto Rican, had played regularly only during the war, and had only appeared in thirty-eight games that season. Two months later, he was gone to the Braves for the last two seasons of his career.

With two outs, it was Roy Campanella's turn to put one in the bleachers to bring the Dodgers within one tantalizing run, but Bruce Edwards (batting for relief pitcher Jack Banta) took a called third strike to end the maddening game. It was only then that the team truly fell apart, losing the next two games 6–4 and 10–6, with late rallies in both games shut down first by Allie Reynolds and then by Joe Page. It was the beginning of a historic winning streak for the Yankees and the beginning of a long nightmare for the Dodgers.

TRYING TO SCORE

Looking back on his epic career, Duke Snider observed that exactly two innings kept the Dodgers from doing what the Yankees amazingly did beginning in 1949—win five pennants in a row. With two more chances against them in the World Series and fielding what Dodger after Dodger from Buzzy Bavasi to Johnny Podres say were their strongest teams, it is possible that the Yankees might not have done what they also did that had no precedent—win five World Series in a row. As it was those two innings were the exclamation points on a mind-boggling string of late-September and October catastrophes that set the stage for 1955.

Those two innings Snider was referring to are among my first baseball memories as a child. In the fall of 1950, I was in my final year of nursery school at the church up First Avenue from our apartment building. I was home with my father every afternoon.

When he was working, he arranged his life so that he wrote late at night and saw people in the morning. The afternoons were for me, and they were idyllic. I was given lunch at the church, after which my father would be waiting downstairs. We only took the bus down to 42nd Street when the weather was bad; the rest of the time, hot or cold, we walked. On afternoons when the Dodgers were playing, the radio was always on; the family lore was that I could recite the Dodgers' lineup that year, stumbling only over the name of the more-or-less regular left fielder, Gene Hermanski (the first few times, I'm told, it came out "Waterski"). This was the heyday of the Red Barber era, and if I close my eyes I can still hear that soft voice with the strange but pleasantly odd accent of his native Mississippi. Because Barber was free of the hype germ, my memory is more of a third person in the room, conversing. My father and I would sit at the card table in front of the Murphy bed where my father set up his typewriter; he took his notes on long, legal-size yellow pads that my mother brought home from work; it was on those pads on those afternoons that he taught me the odd art of keeping score.

My actual baseball education commenced in the parks of Tudor City, true fields of dreams. All we had to do was turn right out of our building and head up a flight of stairs that matched the layout on the other side of 42nd Street. On each side were two parks, a lower playground for older kids with a sandbox and an upper park that had gravel paths and benches along with swings for toddlers. At all the entrances, the city had a sign that said No Ball Playing, but it was never obeyed during my childhood; in fact, cops walking beats in the neighborhoods often joined in the pickup games that punctuated life between April and November.

Baseball for me began in the sandbox. For what seemed like hours, my father and I played catch; he taught me to slide in the dirt; and with a kid's bat in my little hands he tossed soft underhand pitches to me that I gradually learned to hit. For a ball we used a New York icon, a pink rubber ball that the Spalding people made for the city's concrete handball courts and for stickball in the streets; it was known then and will always be known through the slightly nasal New York accent as a Spaldeen. This was the middle of the Baby Boom, so the parks were always filled in the afternoon with kids and their mothers. Naturally, the sight of a man playing ball with his son lured the curious and the jealous to us. In short order, my father was supervising the baseball education of a dozen children at a time, arranging and then supervising makeshift games. Through a child's eyes, he was the man who operated the Tudor City baseball clinic, not a writer who got sick regularly and couldn't work full-time.

I remember the last day of the 1950 season, a Sunday, sitting in our apartment and hearing my mother and father shout, "Shit," at the same time. I was so impressed that for weeks I, too, shouted it in moments of excitement until it was explained to me that either I would stop doing that or there would be no baseball in the park for an entire weekend. I was so pleased with my obedience that in a long-distance chat with my grandmother back in Indiana (a big and rare event in our household) I told her in response to the standard question about what I was doing, "I've stopped saying 'shit,' Grandma."

My parents were reacting to one of the plays that looms huge in the Dodger saga, the failed attempt by Cal Abrams to score from second base on a single by Duke Snider in the bottom of the ninth inning against the Philadelphia Phillies. It left the game tied, but only until the Phillies won it convincingly in the following inning.

The Dodgers' predicament was slightly worse at the end of that season. The year before, they had to win their final game to get into the World Series; in 1950, they had to win their final three games to force a play-off with these same Phillies, an exciting team of mostly young players remembered as the Whiz Kids: a relentlessly consistent, winning pitcher named Robin Roberts; a durable second starter in Curt Simmons; one of baseball's first star relief pitchers, Jim Konstanty; a very fast center fielder, Richie Ashburn; and a collection of dangerous sluggers in outfielder Del Ennis, catcher Andy Seminick, and third baseman Willie "Puddin' Head" Jones. They had dominated the league all year, and the Dodgers had to climb back from as many as ten games behind on Labor Day to even have a chance to tie them. They won the first two games at Ebbets Field, setting quite a stage for the final one.

The game offered the ideal matchup—Robin Roberts against Don Newcombe, who had won another nineteen games that year, as had Roberts. After eight and a half innings, the score was 1–1. In the Dodger half of the ninth, the first batter was one of the many outfielders who tried to catch on with Snider and Furillo in the outfield—Cal Abrams—but who rarely got a chance to show his skills despite excellent minor-league credentials; for Brooklyn, with a million and a half Jews anxious to cheer someone besides first-base coach Jake Pitler, he would have been perfect. He had played more than usual that year because he had been called up from the farm team in St. Paul, Minnesota, after an injury to Furillo.

With Roberts pitching a bit too carefully, Abrams worked him for a walk. The next batter, Pee Wee Reese, got a sign to bunt him over to second base but was unable to get one fair through two strikes. As can happen in baseball, his adversity was followed by a single that left two men on and nobody out.

That brought up Duke Snider, far from the greatest bunter in history but fresh from a learning experience earlier that year that caused him to pause—when there was no signal for a sacrifice— and walk over to the Dodger dugout to be certain. In the spring, Snider had failed in the same situation, popping his bunt up. After the play, he threw things in the dugout and yelled about the silliness of having a power hitter bunt. Manager Burt Shotton heard him, fined him fifty dollars on the spot, and gave him a lecture about team play after the game.

As Snider recalled, Shotton told him to swing away that Sunday. He did just that, hitting a clean single up the middle. Richie Ashburn, charging the ball from center field, had a relatively weak arm, but his throw this time went quickly through to catcher Stan Lopata as Abrams rounded third, was waved toward home by coach Milt Stock. He was tagged out by a mile.

The Dodgers were far from dead, Reese and Snider having

advanced to third and second base respectively on the throw, Jackie Robinson having been walked intentionally to load the bases, and Carl Furillo coming up to hit. He failed, however, popping up to the right side of the infield. When Gil Hodges flied deep to left for the third out, the game was still tied, but the fans and the Dodgers had lost their spirit.

In the Phillies' tenth, Newcombe gave up two singles to Roberts and first baseman Eddie Waitkus, but got a crucial out when he fielded a sacrifice attempt by Ashburn and threw to Billy Cox at third, a split second before the sliding Roberts arrived. The next hitter was left fielder and left-handed hitter Dick Sisler, who already had three hits that day. Sisler's father was one of the game's most famous hitters, George Sisler, who after a Hall of Fame career with the St. Louis Browns had stayed in the game as a hitting instructor. One of his most satisfying projects had been a young rookie with the Dodgers, Duke Snider.

Newcombe was ahead of Dick Sisler in the count, one ball and two strikes, when he swung late on a fastball and sliced a line drive into the left-field bleachers. When the Dodgers went down meekly to end the game, the first vigorous second-guessing of the long postwar Dodger nightmare began—focusing almost entirely on the Abrams play instead of Newcombe's pitching in the final inning.

A few years later, during one of our Saturday morning outings to the public library, my father and I for some reason began talking about that day. Ever alert to the chance to instruct me on some point, he went off to the magazine room while I busied myself with a school project. When he returned, he announced that I was about to learn why the things you hear about immediately following a major event are often not the whole truth or even the truth at all.

In the newspapers at the time, most fingers pointed at Milt Stock, the third-base coach. Within days he had been cruelly fired by the Dodgers, and he never worked in baseball again. It seemed like callous treatment of a man who had been in the game since 1913, played more than a decade as an everyday infielder, and finished up with the Dodgers in the mid-1920s. One reason for the intensity of the reaction to his having waved Abrams home was what happened after he was out. Had Stock held Abrams at third, the long fly ball Gil Hodges hit would have been the second out and Abrams would have scored the winning run on the play with ease.

Other fingers pointed at Abrams, who according to several players had seemed to hesitate before running on Snider's single and had also taken a very wide turn as he rounded third base.

And still other fingers pointed at Burt Shotton, who perhaps might have been expected to put in one of his faster players to run for Abrams. He, too, was gone after the season, though for other reasons.

What was missed, my father said as he put two magazine articles in front of me to read, was what actually happened on the play. Several of the Phillies said much later that before Roberts's pitch, a sign had flashed from Stan Lopata calling for an attempt to pick Abrams off second base. Even before Roberts threw the ball, Ashburn was running in as a precaution in case the throw to second base was wild. Roberts, however, did not see Lopata's signal and threw to home plate. As a result, the charging Ashburn had the ball in his hand even as Abrams was rounding third. It is fair to argue Stock should have seen all this and held Abrams at third; it is equally fair to argue that with nobody out it was a decent gamble that he could score anyway if Ashburn made a typical throw. The argument has gone on for fifty years, but my father's point was that it was not resolvable. In terms any Dodger fan could understand, it was a fluke.

My father's other point was that the second-guessing missed the larger point that Newcombe had then proceeded to give up a single to the opposing pitcher and a home run to a man who hit only fifty-five in an eight-year career. Losing a pennant in the last inning of the season on a three run home run was a bitter pill to swallow. Surely nothing like that could ever happen again to such a talented team.

But it did.

In addition to the arguments over the famous ninth inning, the off-season was also dominated by arguments over the boardroom maneuvers by Walter O'Malley that had sent Branch Rickey—the team's architect and the man with the plan to fracture the so-called color line—packing. Famously ambitious and single-minded, O'Malley was determined to take over the team, he had the controlling power (the catalytic event was the death that year of his partner, John Smith, following which O'Malley convinced his widow to allow him to run her business affairs), and he used it. His leverage came from the fact that over his opposition Rickey could not get another contract to run the Dodgers as president.

In order to get another job in baseball (the Pirates quickly beckoned), Rickey had to sell his interest in the Dodgers under league rules, and, believing he had him over a barrel, O'Malley tried to make him sell for no more than the few hundred thousand dollars he had paid years before. But when Rickey found a potential buyer—real estate magnate William Zeckendorf—O'Malley had to match his $1 million offer and was then forced to pay him an additional fifty thousand dollars as the disappointed suitor. That last requirement drove O'Malley to distraction, and his continuing feud with Rickey would eventually cost the Dodgers four years later when Rickey backed out at the last minute from a deal that would have brought the widely praised young outfielder to Brooklyn from Puerto Rico—Roberto Clemente.

DISASTER

There is no one who followed baseball at midcentury who cannot recall where he was when a twenty-seven-year-old outfielder from Scotland named Bobby Thomson hit the home run for the New York Giants that became forever known as the Shot Heard 'round the World, the three-run blast off Ralph Branca that ended the Dodgers' next season; there is not a Dodger fan who doesn't still wince at the endless replays of that stab-in-the-heart moment when Giant broadcaster Russ Hodges began shrieking, "The Giants win the pennant," over and over again.

I was with Abe Slutsky in his station wagon.

That fall I had started school in Miss Allen's kindergarten class at the Browning School for Boys on 62nd Street, between Park and Madison Avenues. To this day, I have not the slightest idea how my father got the school to help us so I could go. I had been at least dimly aware of the stakes for both my parents, which must be why I remember sitting in Miss Allen's room taking the entrance test a few months before and hearing my father tell me at nursery school that I had been accepted. What they did to wangle a scholarship out of a place that, as near as I could tell in grammar school, didn't give them then remains a mystery.

Browning, which had opened in 1888, was in a small building with four classrooms on each floor and room for a cafeteria, a woodshop on the ground floor, and a gymnasium in the basement. It is little different today, except the school has acquired the building next door. Browning was rigorous and demanding on the fundamentals but culturally nurturing as well. We were drilled and drilled on grammar and arithmetic but encouraged in music and art; sports were in the afternoon. A jacket and tie were required even for Miss Allen's class, which met (all nine of us) around small tables in her room.

I had not been conscious of much outside my own neighborhood to that point, except for Ebbets Field. This was a different world. All of my classmates either lived in huge apartments on Park or Fifth Avenue or in town houses on Upper East Side streets. By some miracle I was conscious of the difference but not obsessed with it. I was acutely aware that my parents were struggling and that my father was often sick and that my classmates lived in places that were palatial by my confined perspective, but for some reason I was not preoccupied by the difference. They were almost all Yankee fans and therefore much more severely disadvantaged.

In part, my attitude was conditioned by the fact that my parents had prepared me superbly for school. I was already reading voraciously by then, every argument or misbehavior episode at home ended with my having to write my way out of trouble, and my parents and I talked all the time. I had been taken through the fundamentals of music lovingly by my father and could already read and play simple pieces. I had my unique neighborhood, and I had the Dodgers. I thought I was fortunate. The only emotion I bottled up was my frustration that for all their loving attention to me, my parents were not happier. In school, I was not cocky, but I felt confident from the beginning, and except for sloppy penmanship and a chronic inability to draw, my preparation and habits helped me excel.

Abe Slutsky worked in my neighborhood at one of the buildings in the amazing complex known as Tudor City. On the side, for not many extra bucks, he drove kids in the area to and from private and parochial school in Manhattan. He was an older man from Brooklyn, pleasant and warm to me once he discovered I was a Dodger nut, and fun to be around. New York was not a car town, so the idea of having a ride in a station wagon twice a day was more than a novelty at first. I remember that Mr. Slutsky's had red leather seats.

In the late summer and fall of 1951, the Dodgers were going through the same torture that the Phillies had endured the previous year, losing a huge lead in the pennant race and trying to hang on for dear life down the stretch. The torture was especially severe because the team gaining on them was the Giants. If the Dodgers–Yankees rivalry seemed grand, battling the Giants was more like a neighborhood grudge match. Before I was born, it was the Giants who had initially dominated baseball life in New York when legends like John McGraw and Christy Mathewson were around, and it was the Giants–Yankees rivalry in the 1920s and early '30s that captured the city's attention while the Dodgers wallowed in entertaining mediocrity. That all changed just before and after the war.

I was of course too young to have any memory of Leo Durocher as the Dodgers' high-profile manager in the Branch Rickey period. By the time I came to baseball awareness in 1951, he was managing the Giants and therefore a figure who to a Dodger kid conjured up both fear and loathing. They had two other figures that inspired the same feelings: a hard-nosed shortstop, Alvin Dark, a mean-looking man who had been involved in some of the early harassment of Jackie Robinson while on the Boston Braves; and the meanest-looking man I remember as a child, a pitcher with a perpetual five o'clock shadow named Sal Maglie, who was known as the Barber for the pitches he threw close enough to a hitter's face to give him a shave. I was also aware, however, that like the Dodgers the Giants had not only been desegregated early; they were also integrated. That year, their regulars included a legitimate slugger, Monte Irvin, a solid third baseman, Hank Thompson, and a rookie from Alabama who could hit with as much power as Mickey Mantle, play center field acrobatically, and run like the wind—Willie Mays. The contrast with the rigidly still-segregated Yankees was obvious.

In our apartment, the Dodgers were always on the radio—a black Zenith box—when they were playing, but when they were playing the Giants we really paid rapt attention. It was an exciting rivalry, central to baseball's most glorified decade when three marvelous teams fought in the same city, and for the most part it was an enjoyable one because the Dodgers usually won. Just not that year.

As I began to actually follow the Dodgers, there were four things about them in 1951 that were different. In June, my father got a chance to explain to me what a trade was because the whole city was buzzing about the one the Dodgers made to get what it was hoped would be (at last) a solid left fielder. He came from the Chicago Cubs and his name was Andy Pafko. To get him, along with a new backup catcher (Al "Rube" Walker) and two other players, the Dodgers sent four players west: their older backup catcher, Bruce Edwards, pitcher Joe Hatten, the swift infielder Eddie Miksis (whom the second-guessers thought Burt Shotton should have put in to run for Cal Abrams the year before), and Gene Hermanski. The trade, however, happened during a year when Pafko was struggling, and while he had an excellent 1952 he was gone in another trade to the Braves by 1953.

There were also two more pitchers whose major contributions

to the team began that year. After getting burned in the World Se
ries by the likes of Joe Page and Allie Reynolds, the Dodgers fi
nally found a pitcher who could start or relieve—Clem Labine. A
right-hander from Rhode Island, he could throw an assortment of
breaking and sinking balls to go with a fastball, and he excelled in
his first full season. His best opportunities came in midseason af
ter an injury to one of the stars of the first part of the year, Clyde
King. The favorite in my family, however, was Carl Erskine, because like Gil Hodges he was from my father's Indiana—the small
industrial city of Anderson in the north-central part of the state).
Erskine was relatively small, under six feet tall and never weighing more than 170 pounds. He threw hard, however, with a
smooth delivery, very high kick, and almost overhand throwing
motion. A popular and religious family man in Bay Ridge, he was
the famous "Oisk" in Brooklyn. But perhaps because he threw so
hard for his size, he had shoulder problems for much of his career. He had first come up in 1948 but was down and up from the
Montreal farm team more than once over the next three seasons
and was often used in relief. In 1951, his hard work and talent
paid off with sixteen victories to go with Preacher Roe's twenty-
two (his best year ever) and Don Newcombe's twenty.

It was also the first year as manager for Charles Dressen—a
coach under Leo Durocher when Larry MacPhail was in Brooklyn who had followed MacPhail across town to coach for the Yankees. In addition to teaching Johnny Podres to throw the
changeup, Charlie Dressen loved to talk baseball, to be quoted in
the papers, and to gamble. He was the precise opposite of Burt
Shotton's understated dignity in demeanor and quickly became a
Brooklyn favorite again.

With banner seasons from the stable lineup of well-established
hitters (1951 was Roy Campanella's first Most Valuable Player
year), the Dodgers exploded from the start of the season. By August they were more than thirteen games ahead of the Giants, at
which point just about everything started to go wrong. At first it
was injuries to the pitching staff—to Clyde King especially and
then to Ralph Branca, who strained his pitching arm and, after

winning more than ten games by the summer, finished up with only thirteen. To make matters worse, Pee Wee Reese and Duke Snider each endured horrific hitting slumps after July.

The Giants chipped away at the huge Dodger lead and then chipped away some more. In September, the Giants went on a tear (they were 38–7 over the last forty-five games) while the Dodgers were losing as much as they were winning, and actually tied them at the end. On the last day of the season, the Giants won first over the Braves, and only heroic relief pitching by New-combe and Clarence "Bud" Podbeilan and a home run by Jackie Robinson in the fourteenth inning got the team past the Phillies.

After 1946, the last-day heroics in 1949, and the crushing disappointment in 1950, the Dodgers were headed into still another play-off. There was a coin toss again, won by Brooklyn, which elected to open at home this time, meaning games two and three (if necessary) would be in the Polo Grounds.

With pitchers on both sides tired from the crazed stretch drive and with the pitching rotations out of whack, the teams' best pitchers did not start the series. Leo Durocher opened with Jim Hearn, a decent pitcher over seven seasons with the Giants who won the most games of his career that season (seventeen); Dressen countered with Ralph Branca. It was a good, low-scoring, exciting game. Not for the first time, the Dodgers scored first—a home run by Andy Pafko in the second inning.

The person who beat Branca that crucial day was none other than Bobby Thomson, who would play a role of some importance later in the series. It happened in the fourth inning. After breezing through the first third of the game, Branca started the fourth by hitting Monte Irvin. With two out, Thomson hit a fastball he later said was right down the middle of the plate, belt high, into the left-field bleachers. In the eighth, Monte Irvin hit another Branca mistake into the seats, and while the Dodgers largely slept at bat (five hits and four double plays), Jim Hearn had enough support to win. The second game was a 10–0 Dodger blowout: four home runs (another by Pafko and one by the other player in the Cubs trade, Rube Walker, who was playing for the injured Roy

Campanella, who pulled a thigh muscle in the final game against the Phillies and aggravated it during the first play-off game at Ebbets Field). Clem Labine, asked to start for the depleted staff, responded with a six-hitter.

The final game of the fateful series begin with the perfect ingredients for a pitching duel (Newcombe versus Maglie) and that was precisely what happened. Through seven innings, the score was 1–1. The Dodgers (the script rarely seemed to change) scored first in the first inning—two walks by Maglie and a single by Jackie Robinson. The Giants tied the game in their half of the seventh inning on a hit (hardly anyone remembers this fact) by Bobby Thomson.

It was in the top of the eighth inning that the Dodgers appeared to break the game open as Maglie tired—he allowed three runs on a wild pitch and singles by Pafko and Billy Cox. Newcombe retired the Giants routinely in their half of the inning but had begun complaining in the dugout that after more than 270 innings of work that year he was running out of gas.

The inning that epitomized the postwar Dodger experience began just as I walked out of school and got into Abe Slutsky's car, his final pickup before the drive downtown. It started with what they call a bleeder in baseball, a ground ball by Alvin Dark that just made it through the hole between first and second base. With Gil Hodges holding Dark on first, the Giants' right fielder, Don Mueller, took advantage of the inviting gap on the right side by hitting a sharp single between Snider and Furillo in right-center field. By the time Furillo got to the ball, Dark was headed safely to third. A brief respite followed when Monte Irvin hit a pop fly that Hodges caught in foul territory, and then the roof fell in.

By now, I think Mr. Slutsky was across town and had turned onto Second Avenue. There were four other kids in the car besides me. Before the next Giant batter came up, I have a fairly clear memory of Mr. Slutsky pulling over to the right side of the street and stopping to listen.

The next Giant batter was a slender first baseman—a good but not powerful hitter who had been playing with the Giants since he came up in 1945 at the age of nineteen. His name was Carroll Lockman, and he was called Whitey because of his light hair. A left-handed batter, Whitey Lockman sliced a line drive into left-center field that was far enough away from both Pafko and Snider that Dark could walk home and Lockman could easily reach second base with a double. On the play, Don Mueller also had an easy time making it to third base, but he slid very hard coming into the bag and broke his ankle—forcing a pause in the game while he was being removed from the field and a pinch-runner was being inserted. For the historical record, his name was Clint Hartung, he was huge (nearly six feet, six inches), he was fast, and after four years as a mediocre pitcher he was in the first of two years as a reserve outfielder; he was from the small town of Hondo in Texas and in those days of nicknames he was called the Hondo Hurricane.

While Clint Hartung was jogging to third base, Charlie Dressen was walking to the pitcher's mound. On the phone to his bullpen he had been told by coach Clyde Sukeforth that Ralph Branca had thrown decently while warming up, so Dressen took the ball from Don Newcombe and signaled for the man who wore the number 13 on his Brooklyn uniform. Bobby Thomson was due up, with Willie Mays on deck. With men on second and third and only one out, the historical consensus is that walking Thomson intentionally was not an option because that meant putting the potential winning run on base, but the situation also dictated that he not be given easy pitches to hit with first base open, even if that meant he ended up being walked anyway.

Also by historical consensus, Branca's first pitch was a huge mistake—a fat fastball right down the middle of the plate, not unlike the pitch Thomson hit into the bleachers two days before. Fortunately, Thomson took it for a strike. The second pitch, all the participants agreed at the time, was supposed to be off the plate, inside. Instead it was also out over the plate.

The participants also agree that the line drive off Bobby Thomson's bat was hit very hard as it went over Billy Cox's head toward the left-field wall just three hundred feet away, but that it lost speed and height as it traveled farther. For a second or two, it was not clear whether it would make the stands, hit high off the wall, or fall into the glove of Andy Pafko, who stood with his back pressed against the barrier. It made the stands, just barely, falling in with its last gasps of kinetic energy.

I will always remember Mr. Slutsky pounding his steering wheel with an open hand over and over again before turning off the radio and driving on; I can see the scene clearly but have no memory of saying anything, which is why I'm convinced that *shock* is the right word for my young reaction. I also have no memory of arriving home after the tragic end of the first baseball season I followed. What I do remember is sitting at the card table in front of the Murphy bed, writing on one of my father's legal pads.

It was a letter to Ralph Branca. Apparently after solemn embraces that afternoon we had eaten supper in near silence (very, very unusual for my loquacious family). When conversation finally began it had been about "poor" Ralph Branca and how terrible he must feel about what had happened. Ever alert for a chance to use an event for its probative as well as sentimental value, the idea of writing a letter was my father's. I have no memory of what I wrote, but my mother mailed it the next day on her way to work. I never got an answer, but on a half-dozen other occasions in my childhood I wrote similar letters—always to Dodger players who were having a tough time. There was no dearth of subject matter.

The reaction by my family to Ralph Branca's ordeal was not common. According to Duke Snider—whose parents had come east in anticipation of seeing their famous son play in the World Series and whom he gallantly took out to dinner in Brooklyn after the game—there were already effigies of a stuffed figure with the number 13 and a Dodger hat hanging from light poles as he drove home to Bay Ridge. After the disappointments that began in 1941 and continued through 1949, the reaction had been almost entirely pained sadness and frustration. It was after Cal Abrams was thrown out at home the year before that second-guessing became part of the ritual. After the Bobby Thomson home run it became epidemic. Through the years, three questions remain for eternal argument in addition to the obvious one that Branca threw two fat fastballs in a row over the plate to a power hitter who had homered off him earlier and had two hits already that day:

First Charlie Dressen erred in not acceding to Campanella's intense desire to play. He could have either helped Newcombe through the final inning or issued a definitive opinion that he was too tired to continue. Campanella also would never have let Branca's first fat pitch pass without an angry comment to the pitcher.

Secondly, Dressen erred in ordering that Erskine and Branca be the pitchers to warm up in the bullpen during the inning. There were three other pitchers who had performed regularly during the season and were available—Preacher Roe, starter-reliever Erv Palica, and Bud Podbeilan. Roe was relatively rested and Podbeilan had a decent record against the Giants. According to Snider, Roe had tried to get loose before the ninth inning but couldn't. Also according to Snider, Clem Labine was not warming up because of his complete game shutout the previous day and because the Dodgers had not yet learned that Labine had a rare "rubber" arm and in his youth could routinely pitch with no rest; interestingly, however, Labine was up and throwing after Branca had walked in to pitch. Bud Podpeilan is the more credible, and unresolvable, might-have-been.

And finally, Dressen erred in not making a public stink about cheating by the Giants at the Polo Grounds, specifically the stealing of signs by binoculars from a spot inside the center-field scoreboard and the flashing of them by walkie-talkie to the bench. *The Wall Street Journal* published a long account of the affair in 2001, but it was not unknown at the time and was the subject of frequent discussions between Dodger coaches and Dressen. Sign stealing is to an extent part of the game, but a ruckus about the Giants' elaborate system would have disrupted it and disrupted them.

Interestingly, none of these issues involved the bullpen coach, Clyde Sukeforth. When Dressen called him instants before making his decision, Sukeforth was an accurate reporter of the facts. Erskine, who was always observed closely because of his arm woes, had bounced at least one of his curveballs into the bullpen dirt, while Branca was throwing normally. Naturally, even more flagrantly than the previous year's case of Milt Stock, it was Sukeforth who got blamed in public by Dressen. The Dodgers offered Sukeforth a minor-league job during the off-season and after the team got criticism for such cruelty even offered him his old job, but sensing the withdrawal of support, Sukeforth moved on to Pittsburgh and back with the man (Branch Rickey) he had helped make history.

Ralph Branca hurt his back the following spring and never recovered his pre–Bobby Thomson form or spirit. One of the best young pitchers ever was inconsequential in 1952, gone to the Detroit Tigers in 1953 for cash, and gone from the major leagues after two farewell games with the Dodgers in 1956.

TWO MORE

The Cold War military got Don Newcombe for 1952 and 1953 at the comparatively advanced age of twenty-six. Despite the loss of an All-Star workhorse and the obvious aging of Preacher Roe, the team on balance improved. In each season they won the National League pennant going away, and in each season they had a better record in a tougher league than the Yankees. The Dodgers also lost the World Series twice more in succession to their nemesis, both times under exasperating circumstances.

This was the period when my devotion to the team flowered. My parents took me to at least a dozen games each season—on the weekends and usually on Ladies Day, when my mother got in at a deep discount. She loved these family outings. Being a pure

Scandinavian, my mother was famously reserved—except at Ebbets Field, where she yelled and laughed and groaned and beamed. She never joined one of Hilda Chester's famous parades through the bleachers behind the famous woman with the clanging cowbells and borderline vulgarity, but my mother was a genuine, loud baseball fan. My mother always brought a paper bag with her on the subway to the games; in it were three sandwiches, three pieces of fruit, and three paper cups that she filled with water from the drinking fountains at the ballpark. During the games, she would get me an ice-cream sandwich from which she and my father always demanded one bite each.

Our time in the bleachers was one of the infrequent occasions when I didn't see my mother as someone who dressed with meticulous care every morning to go downtown and be a secretary on Wall Street and then came home to make us supper in impossibly cramped circumstances. She taught by example that there was a place for neatness and order that complemented the chaos of my father's life and his effusive romanticism around me. In the bleachers, when she was laughing and yelling, I got a glimpse of the immigrant's daughter who fished and did farm chores, played with Indian kids, and walked to school through deep drifts in the bitter winter wearing snowshoes.

For those days in 1950s America, the reality in my household was radical; it didn't take me long to realize that my mother was the principal breadwinner and that she was the mortar in the family's foundation. Because that was our norm, it never struck me as odd. When my father was sick—his problems came in waves a few weeks apart when the ulcers would bleed or his digestion would just stop working and he was either groaning in the bathroom (I hated the sound) or stuck in bed, exhausted, for days—I can never recall feeling scared. My mother by this time gave me things to do in the apartment. I could wipe furniture and surfaces; I could even stand on a chair over the sink in the kitchenette and wash dishes; my little space in the second room was never cluttered because the apartment had no room for a kid's clutter. Sometimes, when my father would be asleep during the day on weekends when she had chores to do and I couldn't go down to the park by myself, she would take me on long walks. She talked to me the way my father did; in effect, we conversed. These were the occasions when I heard about Norway and Minnesota and learned rudimentary Norwegian, while we were folding clothes or putting dishes away. On the East Side and at school, I felt and acted like a kid—but never at home.

On our floor—an atmosphere where most of the doors were usually open and many of the dozen residents were in one another's apartments a lot of the time—I was the only child and therefore a continual object of attention. My father had introduced me to the basics of reading music and playing the piano primitively, but it was in the tiny studio of a young, budding Canadian pianist from Vancouver that I first heard music that seemed to soar. His only possession of consequence was a concert grand that took up least a third of his space. Normally he played and practiced with a felt damper over the strings to mute the sound, but on the occasions when he took it off I would sit spellbound in the middle of the symphonic noise.

Down the hall was another Canadian, from Quebec—a young diplomat at the UN who shared an apartment with his artist sister. They spoke French and took it upon themselves to slowly introduce me to their language. The war widow in 2509 who often shopped with my mother and sometimes looked after me also worked at the UN, and it was through her that I escaped one childhood ritual, dressing up in costumes to go trick-or-treating on Halloween. Instead, beginning the year Don Newcombe went into the armed services, I would go around the building in the early evening, with my mother tactfully behind me, collecting money for the United Nations Children's Fund, for which she worked, known better as UNICEF. The money was usually accompanied by candy (a forbidden commodity in my apartment), which provided the incentive to keep going. I can't remember how much I collected, but I turned out to have had one of the largest hauls in the city that first outing. To my mother's shock, this produced an invitation to the giant Secretariat building on First Avenue, where there was a little ceremony in which a bunch of other kids and I got certificates from the secretary-general. For my mother, this moment was from heaven, because the secretary-general was a Norwegian, Trygve Lie. For the occasion, I practiced a few phrases over and over under her guidance so I could respond in Norwegian. I have no memory of the occasion beyond the sight of her talking in Norwegian to one of her heroes, who she had explained to me had helped lead his government into exile after the Germans invaded in 1940.

The twenty-fifth floor was also home to a dark-haired woman who was beautiful and spoke with an unusual accent that turned out to be Russian. She could cook stuff I had never heard of, strong-smelling stews and vegetables, and sweets I can still taste. Vera Brynner had a brother who the previous year had made it big on Broadway in a new Rodgers and Hammerstein musical, *The King and I*, which, thanks to Vera, was the first Broadway show I remember attending. The film version, four years later, along with *The Ten Commandments* and *Anastasia*, would be Yul Brynner's breakthroughs to superstardom.

He visited his sister occasionally, including a few of the occasional evenings the people on our floor spent together when everyone contributed a supper dish. He was the first completely bald person I had ever met, a bit of a forbidding figure as I recall. On one occasion, my father decided that I was to perform on the piano for the famous man, the one aspect of his paternal behavior that I hated. I was marched down the hall to our place, where I was encouraged to play a simple melody I had learned by a well-known Russian émigré composer of this period, Alexander Gretchaninoff. Normally, I felt uncomfortable performing on command, but on this occasion before this mysterious man I recall being terrified. Somehow I got through the piece, at which point my mood was erased by the thrill of riding back down the hall on Yul Brynner's shoulders.

One consequence of this casual-seeming but in fact relentless instruction was that school at first was easy for me—too easy. I was reading and writing by the time I started, my conversational French was decent, and I found Miss Hurt's first-grade class a breeze. Apparently, the school worried that I was becoming restless and a little bored in this atmosphere, and the first minicrisis I remember in my own life was the discussion about whether I should be put into Miss Lamont's second-grade room in the middle of the year. I remember liking it immediately because the work was harder and therefore more satisfying, but what I remember best was my introduction to the first teacher who deeply affected my life.

Margaret MacMillan was the music teacher, and second grade meant an hour a day in her classroom, for basic instruction in reading music and singing—back when the arts were considered part of elementary education. Mrs. MacMillan was widowed, a bit younger than my parents—a striking woman who was completely comfortable with music and awkward in everything else. From my parents she knew I was already playing the piano, but on her own she decided that I had a boy soprano's voice that was worth trying to train, and she gradually cajoled me into stopping by her music room for lessons. My initial time with her was spent being taught how to breathe, to project, and (the great challenge for me) to jump octaves and sing arpeggios in key. I enjoyed it so much that my father began encouraging her to take me on in piano work as well.

Mrs. MacMillan was a professional, which meant long hours getting basic techniques and exercises under my belt. The real thrill, however, came because Mrs. MacMillan introduced me to expression. Her relentless instruction was that music expressed emotion, that it was a method of communicating, that it could be happy and sad, exciting and tragic, and that the reason to work on mechanics was to unlock emotion. Previously, I had learned via simple classics—mostly early Bach and Mozart. Mrs. MacMillan threw Chopin at me. She was demanding and warm at the same time, and it was with her that I first realized there was a way to get at the confusing mix of feelings I had as a youngster without having to worry about finding the right words for them. Audiences never meant much to me because it was not approval I was looking for; for me, music was above all personal.

Mrs. MacMillan had one other serious pupil from the school. He was eight or nine years older than I, much more advanced on the piano—a sensitive, warm, and friendly teenager who sometimes worked with me. His name was Arthur MacArthur, and he was the son of the most famous military man of the era—much more of a public presence than Dwight D. Eisenhower, who was on his way that fall of 1952 to being elected president. Douglas MacArthur, his wife, Jean, and their son had settled in New York in the apartment tower of the Waldorf Astoria Hotel on Park Avenue after MacArthur was dismissed by President Truman following his Korean War insubordination. My parents couldn't stand MacArthur's politics, but because of World War II my father revered his leadership in the Pacific.

At school assemblies, Arthur MacArthur and I often performed on the piano (once, we played a simple four-hand sonata together), with both our sets of parents in the audience. I never forgot after we were finished how cold, aloof, and remote General MacArthur seemed, in dramatic contrast to his warm, encouraging, and friendly wife. I was too young to know very much about family economics or the nature of fame, but I was more than old enough to sense his son's discomfort and to feel fortunate in my family's embrace. Years later, I smiled upon learning that Arthur had eventually changed his name and lived his own life, actively involved in the arts, down in Greenwich Village.

Mrs. MacMillan's voice instruction had more public consequences. In the congregation at the church we attended was a part-time talent scout for choral groups in the city. As my voice developed she suggested to my parents that I try out for some of them that paid their singers a few bucks a performance. Most of the work was in churches, and it was out of this activity that I was invited to audition for the opera. I did not have a stage mother or father, but their attitude was never discouraging. It was clear to me that they were always nudging me into a music world far beyond just taking lessons but it was always equally clear that they would never have done so over my adolescent resistance or discomfort. The real point was that I was the one pushing myself, for the same reason I couldn't wait to be able to stop playing primitive games with my bat and glove in the sandbox and start getting into the pickup games with older boys in the park itself. I have often compared growing up in these circumstances in postwar New York to hanging around a candy store with an unlimited allowance. There were all these choices and opportunities and just a limited number of hours every day.

My mother never had trouble getting me up in the morning. I was always eager to get going, and that spring I had a new ritual to start each day from April until October—poring over the box scores of major-league baseball games I was learning to decipher.

I had Brooklyn Dodger memories before the season of 1952—images of the 1950 and 1951 heartbreaks—but this was the first season I remember as a season, when I was aware of actually following the team, knowing about the players, listening constantly to the soft voice of Red Barber on the radio, looking at least at the pictures in the papers, and being in what my six-year-old brain considered the enormous, cavernous green beauty of (actually) tiny Ebbets Field.

It was a good year to begin. The Dodgers were an astonishing, stable powerhouse of hitters, all of them well-established figures in the game. They even had a solid, productive left fielder for a full season in Andy Pafko. What was different was the pitching, an interesting collection of younger players and a now-settled star (Carl Erskine), who more than made up for the victories lost by Newcombe's departure and Preacher Roe's decline and arm woes. The Dodgers won the same number of games they had in the regular season the year before, losing three fewer. What was different in the National League was that neither the Giants nor the Cardinals were as strong.

This was the second season of Carl Erskine's stardom. He anchored the starting rotation, winning fourteen games and providing my first happy baseball thrill that was attached to a Dodger story. It was the first of his two no-hitters in the majors (the second came in 1956), in the middle of June, just before the Dodgers began to pull away from the rest of the league (they had to survive a near collapse in September but won the pennant by five and a half games over the Giants).

I can still remember the way the excitement built over the radio. It was an odd game (against the Chicago Cubs) because it was a rainy day and in the third inning the rain was coming down so hard that the umpires actually stopped play and sent the players to their dressing rooms. This produced another bit of Dodger lore. After most games, some of the players played bridge in the clubhouse, a game I didn't learn until I married into a bridge family years later, but which my mother played every day at work during her lunch break.

On this particular afternoon, the rain delay led immediately to a bridge game, with Erskine. According to Duke Snider, the pitcher had just finished making a four-hearts bid when an umpire reappeared to order the players back on the field. Erskine completed his masterpiece—the final score was 3–0 and only one runner reached base, on a walk—and the story of the bridge game made the papers. Shortly thereafter, the Dodgers got a call from Charles Goren, the reigning bridge authority, who had a syndicated column and wanted to reconstruct Erskine's hand. My mother saved the clipping for years, as amazed at Erskine's ability to make his bid as she was by his no-hitter. What she did not know, however, until Erskine revealed it years later was that in fact he had no memory at all of his bridge hand that day. Goren had simply made it all up for his column.

This was also the season when a succession of younger pitchers appeared as first Ralph Branca and then Preacher Roe went by the wayside. One of them was one of the few somewhat odd characters on the team. Billy Loes was a local guy, a native of Long Island City, brought up just over the Brooklyn border in Astoria. He won thirteen games that year, the first of a half-dozen consecutive years when he won more than ten.

He was fun to watch, but he marched to his own drummer. He was famously superstitious, always pitching in the same filthy uniform jersey. He also appeared to lack the competitive fire that characterized the decidedly blue-collar image that baseball in general and the Dodgers in particular projected in those days. Buzzie Bavisi confirmed one story to me that seemed too off-the-wall to believe. The following year, Loes had a clause in his contract guaranteeing a bonus if he won fourteen games. When he had done so by August, he demanded his money immediately and appeared to slack off on the mound, claiming that if he won twenty games the management would expect it of him every year. He was, however, one of the 1950s Dodgers' better pitchers.

The unexpected star that year and in fact the league Rookie of the Year was a twenty-eight-year-old African-American from New Jersey named Joe Black. He was almost as imposing a figure as Don Newcombe and could throw just as hard, and for that one magical season before his arm wore out he was magnificent. If there had not been segregation and he had arrived earlier instead of spending the first years of his career in the Negro Leagues, there is no telling what he might have accomplished. Charlie Dressen used him (some would say used him up) almost exclusively in relief in 1952; he appeared in more than a third of the team's games, starting just two of them, and pitched more than 140 innings. In the end, he won more games than any other pitcher on the team (fifteen), but the total understates his importance.

The Dodgers won one more game in 1952 than did the Yankees, who squeaked past the Cleveland Indians into the World Series. As had been the case in previous years, the Dodgers' late-season frustrations were famous, but there was no clear reason to consider them underdogs (especially since this was the first year the Yankees were without Joe DiMaggio) with the possible exception of their pitching. As it turned out, that very slight edge was pivotal in another, agonizing, seven-game Series.

This is the first year I can remember sitting in my school's gymnasium-auditorium, with the 21-inch television set perched on the edge of the stage. Amid a throng of noisy Yankee fans, there were just three of us sitting off to the side rooting quietly for the Dodgers: John Steinback's son, a second-grade classmate whose father was running the Bulova Watch Company at the time, and Mr. Kenrey, the fifth-grade teacher.

For the weekend games, we walked across the neighborhood to the apartment of a fellow writer whose son was a playmate of mine, because they had a television set (a Philco), which was our occasional visual entertainment in those pre-Scarlet days.

At Ebbets Field, the Dodgers won the first game. In a bit of in-spired managing, Dressen started Joe Black, who pitched all nine innings of a 4–2 victory over Allie Reynolds, the very first in a World Series game for an African-American. All of the Dodger runs came on home runs by Reese, Robinson, and Snider. Snider's two-run blast was the first of four home runs he hit in the Series, something that only Babe Ruth and Lou Gehrig had done to that point; when Snider did it again in 1955, he stood alone.

Game Two, however, was a dispiriting 7–1 thrashing of Carl Er-skine, who uncharacteristically walked six Yankees and lasted just three batters into a five-run sixth inning. There was more to it than a simple thrashing. Before the game, on a cloudy day, Ersk-ine had stood on a stool in the dressing room to look out a win-dow at the threatening sky. As he climbed down, his knee (tender from a high school injury) banged against a radiator. The pain was so intense, according to Snider, that Erskine actually fainted on the floor and had to be revived with smelling salts. Conscious, with a bandage over a cut on his chin from the fall, he went out to pitch in the World Series. The legions of second-guessers, my par-ents included, were certain that Dressen left Erskine in the game too long.

The third game, in the Bronx and won 5–3 by Preacher Roe, appeared to atone for Mickey Owen's infamous passed ball eleven years before. Going into the ninth inning with a lead of just 3–2, Pee Wee Reese and Jackie Robinson each singled and then executed a very rare double steal of second and third. With Roy Campanella at bat, a pitch from reliever Tom Gorman got past the normally flawless Yogi Berra, and both Reese and Robinson raced home. The daring base running and Berra's passed ball proved decisive because Johnny Mize pinch-hit a home run for the Yankees in the bottom of the ninth.

After Reynolds pitched a complete game shutout against Joe Black in the fourth game and Carl Erskine courageously went eleven innings to win Game Five (the contest with Vin Scully's famous fives), the Dodgers actually headed home needing but one victory to win the Series. They came maddeningly close.

In Game Six, behind Billy Loes, the Dodgers took a 1–0 lead, off the first of two Duke Snider home runs into the seventh inning. But Yogi Berra tied the game, with a lead-off home run, and after the Yankee left fielder, Gene Woodling, singled, everything fell apart.

Standing on the pitching rubber and about to go into his stretch with Woodling on first, Billy Loes then inexplicably let the ball fall from his right hand onto the ground. That is called a balk under the rules, and Woodling was awarded second base.

The batter was the Yankees' reliable pitcher Vic Raschi, on his way to winning his second game of the Series but never known for his hitting. He sent a bouncing ball straight at Loes, who seemed to freeze as it hit his leg, and by the time it was retrieved, Woodling had scored what proved the winning run. In the papers, Loes claimed to have been blinded by sunlight on the play, a comment that drew derision at the time, but over the years several Dodgers have backed him up, explaining that there was a space between the upper and lower decks of Ebbets Field through which the sun hit the pitcher's mound in late afternoon. In simple English, the Dodgers lost their chance to win the Series that day because a pitcher lost a ground ball in the sun.

Game Seven, the second time the Subway Series between these teams had gone the distance, was, if anything, more dispiriting. The seesaw game was tied, 2–2, after five innings, at which point the Yankees scored twice, first off starter Joe Black and then off reliever Preacher Roe, to go ahead 4–2 with the Dodgers coming up in their half of the seventh inning.

The tension built as Carl Furillo led off with a walk and with one out moved to second on a single to right field by Billy Cox. When Reese walked, the bases were loaded with but one out. At this point, the Yankees' pitching staff was exhausted, but Casey Stengel went to the mound to pull Vic Raschi from the game for one of those pitchers the Yankees always seemed to produce just for such moments.

Robert LeRoy "Sarge" Kuzava, out of someplace in Michigan, had been in the league for six years at this point. He was on his fourth team and would be on three more before ending up his career with a total of forty-nine victories. To this point, after appearing in just twenty-eight games for the Yankees during the regular season, he had not been used in the World Series at all. On this one day, however, he was ideal for two innings and two batters.

Most accounts of this Dodger disaster focus on the third out of the inning, but according to Duke Snider the second out (which he made) was just as important. It was a classic pitcher–batter duel; with the bases loaded, the count went full and Snider fouled off more than one pitch after that.

In the end, though, Kuzava threw him a fastball low and outside, which Snider more reached for than swung at, popping up to Gil McDougald at third. Two outs; Jackie Robinson coming up.

This time, Kuzava threw a fastball inside, and Robinson popped this one up, too. The ball was hit above a kind of no-man's-land between the pitcher's mound and first base. With Billy Martin playing deep at second, the ball was hit over an area where it wasn't clear who should come over to catch it. In fact, both Kuzava and the Yankee first baseman, Joe Collins, appeared frozen.

Eventually, the ever-hustling Martin began to run—and run and run and run. He caught the ball near the mound no more than six inches off the ground, saving at least two runs and the game. Kuzava's next two innings were almost anticlimactic.

To make the experience even more dispiriting, this was the World Series when Gil Hodges famously didn't hit—not once in twenty-one times at bat. Worse: except for Duke Snider, the entire heart of the Dodgers' batting order didn't hit. For the Series, Hodges, Robinson, Furillo, Campanella, and Pafko came up 116 times and got just fourteen hits.

The evening after the last game had ended, I sat down under my father's supervision and wrote the second fan letter of my life—to Gil Hodges. My very dim memory of my first attempt at contact with the person who was already my idol is that it included a feeble attempt to make Hodges feel less exposed; I noted that I also made out nearly every time I batted.

If anything, 1953 was even more crushing because the expectations for the Dodgers had been even higher. Branch Rickey went to his grave (in 1965) insisting that his 1949 Dodgers were the best team of the postwar period; most of the Dodgers who stayed with Brooklyn insisted that it was the '53 team.

No matter. It was a season during which the only suspense was whether the Yankees would beat the Dodgers yet again to win their fifth consecutive championship—an unimaginable accomplishment. The Dodgers won, for them, a record 105 games during the regular season, finishing 12 games ahead of the former Boston (now Milwaukee) Braves.

Still without Don Newcombe, the team was led from the mound by Carl Erskine, who won twenty games that year. While Joe Black's famous rookie season was followed by his sudden decline, the blooming of Clem Labine as a starter-reliever occurred that year. With more than decent years by Billy Loes and Preacher Roe (his final Dodger season, at the age of thirty-eight), the arrival of young rookie Johnny Podres, and the acquisition of Russ Meyer (he had been on the 1950 Phillies), the team had a stable core of consistent pitchers.

In the field, this was the year of Junior Gilliam—the Dodgers' fourth African-American Rookie of the Year out of the previous seven, following Robinson, Newcombe, and Black. The second throw-in player in the deal for Leroy Farrell at the end of Rickey's tenure, Gilliam was twenty-five in his rookie season; had baseball been fully integrated all along, this gifted athlete almost certainly would have been in the major leagues long before 1953. He was fast, he hit line drives (he led the league that year in triples, with seventeen), and he was a graceful infielder.

Gilliam's arrival meant a break for some of the Brooklyn veterans. An older Pee Wee Reese now could bat second behind him. With Gilliam at second, Jackie Robinson—by now in his thirties—could move to a position where he did not have to be so mobile; Dressen's choice was left field, after Andy Pafko was traded that winter, and sometimes third base. That was of course Billy Cox's position; he was still productive and enormously popular, but he was aging.

This was also the year when Duke Snider exploded into a superstar, as if the four home runs during the '52 Series had been a harbinger; in 1953, he hit forty-two (only Eddie Mathews of the Braves hit more).

But as fate would have it, the Yankees were also excellent, again with a slightly more experienced pitching staff. The team (led by Mickey Mantle and Yogi Berra and benefiting from the first big year by their brilliant left-handed pitcher Whitey Ford) won the pennant by ten games over the Indians. Still, the Dodgers won six more games that year than they did; they were not underdogs.

Through the years, the 1953 World Series has been mostly described as an almost routine Yankee triumph because they won it in six games. I remember it as a series of close, seesaw games, at least two of which the Dodgers almost won. They were within one break of sending the Series to another seventh game; they just didn't get the break. It was a Series whose star was Billy Martin, who tied a record with twelve base hits and batted an astonishing .500; and it was a Series of relatively poor performances by nearly all the pitchers on both teams in four of the games. Mostly, it was an immense frustration after such an excellent season.

Carl Erskine, the Dodgers' star that year, was the person on whom Charlie Dressen depended. Erskine was unable to come through in the first game at Yankee Stadium, giving up four runs in just one inning of work. What is usually forgotten is that the Dodgers had battled back to tie the game, 5–5, in their half of the seventh inning. It was the subsequent collapse of the bullpen that produced an 8–5 defeat.

It was worse the next day. Preacher Roe (no one knew he was making his last World Series appearance as a Dodger) pitched an excellent game into the late innings, and thanks to a Billy Cox double the Dodgers were ahead 2–1 going into the bottom half of the seventh inning. Roe tired; however, Dressen didn't pull him from the game, and home runs by Martin and Mickey Mantle cost the Dodgers a second game.

It was a risk taken by Dressen—starting Erskine after just a day off—that produced the Dodger highlight of the year. For nine innings, his high kick and overhand fastballs and curves kept the Yankees off balance. He yielded just two runs and was striking out batters with a frequency that gradually created a frenzy in Ebbets Field. When he fanned pinch-hitter Johnny Mize in the ninth inning, Erskine had set a new Series record of fourteen strikeouts. As it turned out he needed to be that good, because Yankee starter Vic Raschi had only given up three runs.

The next day, the Dodgers tied the Series in exceptionally uplifting fashion. Not only did they jump on Whitey Ford for three runs in the first inning; they also kept on scoring, piling up four more as the game progressed. Billy Loes, en route to the only World Series victory of his career, had yielded just two runs through eight innings.

In the ninth, however, he and the Dodgers flirted with disaster. Two singles—by Woodling and Martin—and a walk to Gil Mc-Dougald loaded the bases with nobody out, meaning the tying run would be at the plate from then on. For once, Dressen made a timely and correct pitching change; in came Clem Labine.

In baseball's ultimate tense situation, Labine began by striking out Phil Rizzuto. The next hitter, pinch-hitting again, was Johnny Mize, but his soft fly ball to Duke Snider in center field was much too shallow to even tempt Woodling to try to score on the play.

Mickey Mantle was next. Batting left-handed, the Yankee star sliced a line drive into left field for a single. Woodling scored easily, and Billy Martin came roaring around third, headed toward home plate as well. The left fielder, in the game that inning for his defensive ability (shades of things to come two years later), was a utility player named Don Thompson who had an excellent glove and arm but couldn't hit. Thompson fielded Mantle's hit cleanly and unleashed a strike to Roy Campanella. Billy Martin attempted to knock the ball out of the catcher's mitt, but the much smaller runner merely bounced off the stocky Campanella.

I had been spending the weekend with a schoolmate whose family had a weekend home in Westchester County. We were watching the television in the lounge of a country club—not one of my usual hangouts—and I was again a tiny Dodger island in a sea of Yankee fans. I remember giving a little yelp at the third out, but I remember more the glares that my noise produced in the room.

The Dodger collapse that then ensued was primarily a collapse in the final game at Ebbets Field. This was the game Johnny Podres started and got yanked from after he loaded the bases in the third inning, following the critical and rare error by Gil Hodges. Not only did Podres's replacement, Russ Meyer, then yield the famous grand slam to Mantle, but the rest of the relievers failed to do their jobs as well. It was a crushing 11–7 defeat.

Game Six, however, was exciting. The Yankees got to Carl Erskine early—three runs by the fourth inning—but then their hitting cooled off and the Dodgers began a comeback. They got one of the runs back on a classic bit of Jackie Robinson daring. With one out he doubled off Whitey Ford and then promptly stole third, coming home on a ground ball out by Campanella.

The ninth inning was at least thrilling. Allie Reynolds, pitching his final World Series inning after six years of brilliance and seven victories, walked Duke Snider with one out. The Dodgers were just two outs away from the end of their season when Carl Furillo lined an outside pitch into the right-field seats for the home run that tied the game. It was a remarkable feat by a determined baseball player who had been injured the final month of the season (Leo Durocher had stepped on Furillo's hand during a fight).

In the gymnasium with my little knot of Dodger fans, there was a sense that the team had momentum going into the bottom of the ninth—if for no other reason than the fact that Clem Labine had been pitching effectively since the seventh.

This time, disaster began with a walk to Hank Bauer. After Yogi Berra hit a line drive right at Carl Furillo in right field, Mickey Mantle hit a strange high bouncing ball (called a Baltimore chop in baseball) that landed between Labine and Billy Cox at third. By the time Cox had picked the ball up, Mantle was on first and Bauer was on second.

That brought Billy Martin to the plate. His record-tying twelfth hit of the Series was a "bleeder"—a ground ball that just barely got through the middle of the Dodger infield into center field. Hank Bauer scored the winning run less than ten minutes after Carl Furillo's home run—after a walk and two scratch singles.

The next day, after reading in the papers that Clem Labine had cried after the game (I almost did myself), I wrote him the third fan letter of my life.

I had actually experienced only the last few years of this long saga. From the library, from my parents and their Dodger fan friends, I had absorbed all of the rest. It was a rich, varied, interesting, exciting tableau of near misses and flops—from Babe Ruth's pitching to Billy Wambsganss's triple play, from Mickey Owen's passed ball to Don Newcombe's home-run pitch to Tommy Henrich, from Cal Abrams running around third base to Bobby Thomson's shot, from Billy Loes's balk to Billy Martin's seeing-eye ground ball.

Duke Snider was correct. Only two agonizing innings separated the Dodgers from five consecutive National League pennants, but a variety of twists of fate had left them just short of victories when it counted for a dozen years of frustration.

That is why the seventh game of the 1955 World Series to any fan of the Brooklyn Dodgers anywhere was far more than just another thrilling game. With a 1–0 lead after five well-pitched innings, there was no context, no basis of any kind, for a belief that this was the game when it would finally happen. Off this kind of detailed, demoralizing experience, that was one more reason to dread the sixth inning.

11

1955

There was another. The 1955 World Series was different from the other clashes between the Dodgers and the Yankees—in both how it looked ahead of time and how it actually unfolded. The professional gamblers knew what they were doing; the Dodgers were underdogs before the Series began, they were underdogs before each of the previous games in Yankee Stadium, and they were decided underdogs before Game Seven.

Going back to 1941, the two teams had seemed more evenly matched, both from their rosters of players and off their performances during the regular season. Part of what had made the five previous defeats so frustrating was the fact that the Dodgers had legitimate chances in each of them.

The 1955 season was different and so was the World Series until the seventh game. Following the loss two years before, Clem Labine may have shed tears, but Walter O'Malley did not. The pattern of second-guessing and scapegoating born from the last-day frustration against the Phillies continued, with the Dodger boss's ire focusing on Charlie Dressen.

After the season, Dressen had the temerity to ask for a two-year contract, apparently because his long-ago Dodger boss and pal, Leo Durocher, had extracted one from Giants owner Horace Stoneham. To O'Malley this was heresy, and after pretending to negotiate with the popular manager, he let him go. The Walter Alston era that would last two decades was about to begin.

To press and fans alike, and both were famously vocal, O'Malley had replaced a legitimate baseball mind and familiar public personality with a faceless organization man with no discernible personality or ability. That was certainly the instant verdict in my household, though with each year that passed this was a position that became increasingly untenable off the evidence. O'Malley was already an unpopular figure in his own right because of the circumstances of his move against Branch Rickey, but it was as if many of the negative opinions about him were simply transferred onto Alston.

Many of the Dodgers knew better than their fans. Alston had been a consistently successful molder and handler of young talent for the top farm team in Montreal, and Newcombe and Campanella had experienced his remarkable leadership in Nashua, New Hampshire, during their first Dodger organization seasons back in 1946.

The idea that Alston was simply an owner's stooge was also silly. As a large first baseman out of Miami University in his native Ohio he had been signed by Branch Rickey's brother for Branch Rickey's St. Louis Cardinals. He'd had exactly one at-bat with the Cardinals in 1936—a lone appearance in the major leagues in which he'd struck out against Cubs pitcher and eventual National League umpire Lon Warneke. After that, Rickey had given Alston a player-manager job in Trenton and then assigned him to Nashua. Alston's general manager there and in Montreal had been Buzzie Bavasi, who recommended him for the Dodgers job and summoned him to Brooklyn, flying in under the alias of Matt Burns to deceive the press.

Alston also appeared to have a personality—a wry, almost mischievous grin should have been the clue. Years later, I picked up a copy of the first of his two revealing books about his career, which showed the self-deprecating barnyard wit of an Ohio farm boy. The volume was inscribed by him to some guy named Kurt and reads: "I am sorry I left the pitcher in until we lost every fucking game. Retardingly, Walter 'Fart' Alston."

He had a hopeless job in 1954. Don Newcombe finally returned from the service but was ineffective in twenty-eight games. Roy Campanella suffered from hand injuries and had a severely disappointing part-time season.

This was also the year that Preacher Roe's skills declined sharply and Billy Cox lost his regular job at third base to a platoon arrangement with Jackie Robinson and rookie Don Hoak (after the season Cox and Roe were traded to the lowly Baltimore Orioles for three nobodies and some cash). Within baseball, two amazing pros were yielding to age, but in New York, Alston was defiling two icons of a glorious past. In the inevitable testing of a new manager's authority by established veterans—a ritual of baseball life—there was no way for the newcomer to avoid being painted as the heavy.

Despite all this, the Dodgers finished the season thirty games above .500, due in large part to magnificent seasons by Hodges and Snider. The problem was that the Giants were five games better than that. Worse, they rubbed it in by sweeping the Cleveland Indians in the World Series—the one where Willie Mays made an impossible catch over his shoulder in the deepest part of the Polo Grounds off a titanic blast by Vic Wertz.

The 1955 season had begun amid nothing but questions. There was no way to know whether Newcombe's arm would carry the team he hadn't carried since 1951, no way to know how much an aging Jackie Robinson had left, no way to know if Campanella's hands would recover, no way to know whether age was eroding Pee Wee Reese's skills, no way to know if any of the growing list of young pitchers would join Carl Erskine to comprise a consistent staff.

That only made the winning streaks and the earliest-ever clinching of a pennant sweeter. Amid the inevitable dissension that platooning can create, Alston juggled four players in and out of his regular lineup—Robinson, Hoak, Zimmer, and Amoros.

Robinson (his batting average plummeted to .256 on barely three hundred times at bat) and Hoak mostly shared third base. Zimmer played second mostly when Junior Gilliam was in left field.

For the first part of the season, Amoros was the pleasant surprise in his second full season with the team, batting well above .300 and fielding expertly. Edmundo Isasi Amoros had been a schoolboy star in pre-Castro Cuba, then a star on a provincial and then the national team. He had seen some action in the Negro Leagues and played at home during the winter, along with scores of players and coaches from the major and minor leagues. He was signed in 1952 by Fresco Thompson's chief scout at the time, Al Campanis.

I took notice of Sandy Amoros almost immediately, because according to the information on his baseball card he was almost exactly the same size as my father—about five feet, seven inches tall, weighing around 170 pounds. Both of them had large, in Amoros's case strong, legs, which helped him to accelerate quickly when he ran. I also took notice of his unusual batting stance. Just before the opposing pitcher started his windup, Amoros (who batted left-handed) would begin wiggling his bat. In the neighborhood parks, I quickly started wiggling my own bat—without Amoros's results.

In addition to his emergence, the other noteworthy change in the Dodgers besides the addition of their highly publicized but rarely used "bonus baby," Sandy Koufax, was the early summer arrival of two young pitchers from Montreal and St. Paul (their other Triple-A farm team)—Roger Craig and Don Bessent. They promptly won both ends of a doubleheader against Cincinnati. They proceeded to combine for a 13–4 record the rest of the way, shoring up a pitching staff that gradually became hobbled with arm injuries and illness—including Erskine, Podres, Loes, and Spooner.

Amoros also began to wear down after he hurt his back seriously enough to have to play in a corset; his average dived into the mid-.200s. And, as if on cue after their early pennant clinching in September, the entire team seemed to slump.

Here is how the *New York Post*—a favorite back then in my family for its liberal politics and bright sportswriting—put it on the eve of the World Series: "They talk about cold clubs going into the World Series. This Brooklyn team is probably the coldest on record. Duke Snider (he had forty-two for the year) and Roy Campanella (he hit thirty-two) haven't hit a homer since Labor Day, and Campanella hasn't hit one since late in August. Today's starter, Don Newcombe, won only two of his victories through August and September. Carl Erskine hasn't thrown a good curve since June and Johnny Podres has been knocked out of the box twelve straight times."

To further darken the atmosphere, the Dodgers had been taunted in public as perennial losers of big, late games. One insult was predictable and came from Joe DiMaggio on vacation abroad. But two were from closer to home—from guest Series newspaper columnist, now-minor-league manager Charlie Dressen, and from a bitter Billy Cox, who had played his final season with the Orioles—unlike Preacher Roe, who simply retired.

The Yankees, however, were not without major injury problems of their own. Mickey Mantle had pulled a thigh muscle late in the season running the bases against the Boston Red Sox. The injury left him barely able to walk, let alone run, as the Series approached. Hank Bauer was also hobbled by a bad leg.

Among the pitchers, the Yankees had won the pennant in large part behind excellent relief pitching from a home-grown talent, Tom Morgan, who appeared in forty games, and from one of those older stalwarts from other teams that the Yankees had a knack for acquiring: Jim Konstanty of the Whiz Kids Phillies, who had appeared in forty-five. Konstanty, however, was not on the World Series roster. The staff had pitched consistently well throughout the year and was not bothered by the late-season aches and pains that affected the Dodgers. This was the slight advantage that the Yankees had enjoyed previously; in 1955 it seemed more obvious ahead of time, which is why they were more clearly favored.

But by the time Game Seven began, the World Series had turned into a seesaw affair—three wins for the Yankees at the Stadium, three for the Dodgers in Ebbets Field. In reality, it was more complicated than that, games within games, not a lot of hitting but a great deal of slugging; excellent pitching and ineffective pitching. The Dodgers scored first in each of the games except the sixth, the only one of them that wasn't close at least until the middle innings.

By now, I was studying the sports pages instead of merely looking at them. From the box scores, pictures, and headlines I had started reading the articles closely—attracted by the material that went into the intricacies of games, repelled by the way the stories almost casually made players great heroes or dastardly goats from one day to the next.

I was in the fifth grade, Mr. Kenney's class—strict and fun. A younger man (he could throw a curveball), he organized his room into teams for the constant drilling in the fundamentals of grammar, spelling, punctuation, usage, and numbers on which the school based its elementary education. It was in his class also that I made my first stabs at expository writing, but this was in his American history lessons, and only after still more drilling in names, dates, places, and events.

It was in the arts that I had a chance to let go with feelings. On the piano, I preferred to take music apart and put it back together, a phrase or melody at a time; I tended to be technically proficient but flat in my playing. Mrs. MacMillan spent most of her time getting me to come out of my shell, to feel angry or excited or sad as appropriate.

It was on the stage where I found it more natural to lose myself in performance. This was the year when my parents' acquaintance at church suggested that they sign me up for the boys chorus auditions at the Metropolitan Opera. In those days, the opera was housed in an aging but magnificent structure at 39th Street and Broadway, an easy walk from the 42nd Street crosstown bus.

The auditions were held in a large rehearsal room shared by ballet dancers as well as chorus members. On the day in question there were perhaps two hundred people in addition to my parents and me there—probably half of them other parents, as well as a handful of quite stern-looking people from the opera and a pianist sitting at a beat-up Steinway upright very much like our own.

My parents never pushed me to do anything; they encouraged me. This was something I very much wanted to do. There was opera music all around me growing up, and I loved the way it took everything, from emotions to technical demands, to excess. I can't recall anything special about that morning or our bus trip across town, no elaborate preparations or sense of tension, just the audition itself. When my name was called, I went to the front of the big room, where each young singer had to belt out something slow ("America the Beautiful") and something fast (the title number from *Oklahoma*). I had never had lengthy instruction in voice, getting by on my fortunately natural sense of pitch, and I had always seemed to know that the trick to singing is to have absolutely no inhibitions of any kind, especially for choral work; you cannot hold anything back. I had not gotten much further than "my honey, Lem and I" in "Oklahoma" when the piano music suddenly stopped and a very large man—the chorus boss, Kurt Adler, who eventually conducted during a distinguished career and turned out to be a kind teacher as well—gruffly thanked me.

I had auditioned before, but while I was used to the abrupt ending of my supreme efforts, I never quite knew how to feel when I was halted in midphrase. This was not one of those tryouts where they took your telephone number and said they would get back to you. After everyone had sung, the opera officials retired for what seemed like ten years before returning and reading a list of the names of boys who were asked to remain.

When I heard my name, I remember glancing at my mother, who was in tears. I held one of her hands and my father held the other while the opera people passed out work permit forms my parents had to sign because of my age. They were then asked to leave, and within minutes, I and my new colleagues found ourselves standing on the stage where Enrico Caruso had worked, staring at a conductor's podium where Gustav Mahler had stood. The guy who was standing there was Dimitri Mitropolous, an austere tall man with not a hair on his head; he had conducted the New York Philharmonic, and now he was at the Met presiding over a walk-through of that year's production of *Tosca*. Maria Callas was standing on the stage next to one of the tenor stars of the day, Mario del Monaco, and I wasn't ten feet away. There was no rehearsing that day; the staff had simply wanted to give us a taste of what we had in store. I would have been more impressed, but I had no idea—yet—who these majestic people who carried themselves so regally were.

I flew up Broadway to the crosstown bus. It was a different era in New York. Now that I was in the fifth grade, I was entitled to one of the bus passes the city issued through the schools, and at the ripe age of nine I could go by myself; the rules were no subways alone and never out after five. At the apartment I was clutched and quizzed on every detail of my first day and then walked up to Schrafft's for the special treat of supper out.

My own good fortune was in contrast to my father's declining health that year. After the war, he had at least managed to sell a half-dozen freelance articles in a decent year. In 1955, though, he was off his feet a lot and had to be hospitalized twice for internal bleeding. By then, I knew too much about bleeding ulcers for a nine-year-old, but now I started to hear about how gallbladders, colons, and livers worked—or, in his case, didn't. Our apartment was so small that it made no sense to conceal any of this from me; it was all around me all the time. Instead of hiding it, my parents talked to me about it, trying to explain what was going on. It gave me a feeling of being involved, even if I didn't completely understand what they were talking about. By then I was as used to the routine as continually frustrated by it. With the pile of medical bills always high, it was my pay envelope that gave me a sense of meaningful participation in the family, however puny the proceeds actually were from perhaps ten performances and as many rehearsals a month.

After malaria, the first disease my father had been attacked by, with more ferocity than any Japanese soldier went after him with, was dengue fever. It is a virus carried by a mosquito that produces a rather brutal flu, but which can also produce dangerous complications that involve internal damage as well. He also had several bouts with bacterial and viral enemies that at that time had no name in western medicine. None of the ailments knocked him out for more than a couple of weeks, but after the war his susceptibility to internal bleeding was the dominant medical fact of his life. Throughout my childhood his treatment was symptomatic, his surgeries essentially emergency; but neither the Veterans Administration nor any doctor who would see him could figure out how to "cure" him. To my parents, I think the endless pile of bills was especially onerous because it appeared to have no lasting purpose.

My life was now a delightful mess of varied activity, with that always present cloud of confusion and sadness, which only made the Dodgers more special to me—as both refuge and cause. I can still remember the dread, though, with which the approaching World Series filled me. Don Newcombe and Carl Erskine were both tired and hurting from the long season; I could think about baseball now, not merely root, and I could not think of a way for them to win this time.

I could, however, think of so many ways for them to lose. Their three defeats in Yankee Stadium that historic year were straight from the Dodgers–Yankees textbook of frustration—a seesaw affair that inexorably slipped away and two overwhelmingly dominant pitching performances to support just enough runs in one case and a first-inning explosion in the other.

With hindsight and fifty years of contemplation, it was the Dodgers' three victories at Ebbets Field that were a bit unusual—initially a refusal to quit, at the plate and on the mound, and then a two-game combination of timely slugging and clutch pitching.

The fact that it was the Dodgers who scored first off Whitey Ford in Game One meant absolutely nothing; I had seen all that before. It surprised me, however, that Ford did not appear his usual masterful self that day. In the second inning, Carl Furillo had no sooner stepped up to bat than he hit a line drive to the opposite field that made the right field seats in no time. With one out, Jackie Robinson then hit another wicked line drive, this one into the gap in left-center field, which for him was an easy triple. When Don Zimmer followed with a single, the Dodgers actually led 2–0.

It was a lead Newcombe could not hold. With one out in the same inning, first baseman Joe Collins walked and Elston Howard then pounced on a not-very-fast ball, sending it into the left-field seats to tie the game.

The torture continued the next inning, when Duke Snider led off with a tremendous home run that made it into the upper deck in right field. That happy blast was then wasted when Newcombe blew an easy out and walked Whitey Ford, who came around to score after two groundouts and a single by Hank Bauer.

Inevitably, or so it seemed to me, the Yankees went ahead in the third on a Joe Collins home run and chased Newcombe from the game when Collins hit another one in the sixth inning (his second Series hit and second Series home run in the first game turned out to be the only hits he would get). For decades, Newcombe has been unfairly maligned as a poor performer in World Series games. Because of his military service, this was in fact only the third Series game he had pitched since his more-than-decent outings in 1949; he would pitch but one more the following year. More than any other pitcher of the postwar period, Newcombe was the reason the Dodgers were in the World Series in the first place.

After the Collins home run, Newcombe yielded a triple to Billy Martin on a line drive that went over Junior Gilliam's head in left field, and then turned the ball over to rookie Don Bessent. With Eddie Robinson pinch-hitting for Phil Rizzuto, Martin then took off in an attempt to steal home. The pictures taken from the right side near the Yankee dugout appear to show the sliding Martin sneaking the toe of his shoe across the plate before Campanella fell on him; from the left, they appear to show Campanella successfully blocking the plate. The view that counted was that of umpire Bill Summers, who called Martin out. As the two players jumped to their feet, the ever-aggressive Martin nearly elbowed Campanella in the head and then glared at him, but the Dodger catcher ignored the challenge and left the field.

The Dodgers got excellent relief pitching from Bessent and then Clem Labine but could not take advantage of subsequent opportunities to tie the game. It became a one-run affair in the eighth inning under dramatic circumstances. Carl Furillo, having singled and moved to third on an error by Gil McDougald on a ball hit by Robinson, scored on a sacrifice fly to Mickey Mantle's replacement, Irv Noren, by Don Zimmer (his second run batted in of the game).

With Jackie Robinson on third base and Frank Kellert (a throw-in in the Billy Cox–Preacher Roe deal with Baltimore) pinch-hitting for Bessent, Robinson executed his famous and controversial steal of home. Robinson said he attempted the steal (at the age of thirty-six) in an effort to ignite his teammates in what was now a close game.

The ignition almost happened in their last at-bat, with Bob Grim on to pitch the ninth inning for the Yankees. With one out, Duke Snider lined a fastball into right field for a single. Roy Campanella was next. Another fastball came from Grim, and this one Campanella almost punched toward right field, a fly ball that appeared to be drifting closer and closer to the seats. For an instant it looked like the go-ahead home run might have been hit, at least until the ball dropped into Hank Bauer's glove just in front of the stands—a frustrating end to another frustrating game.

Game Two was equally frustrating—another lost opportunity for Billy Loes to win an important game, and a chance for Tommy Byrne to show that he was back in control. After three well-pitched innings by both men, it was once again the Dodgers who broke in front—on a double by Reese and a single by Snider.

Loes then proceeded to have a nightmare of an inning, as all nine Yankees came to bat, with four of them scoring on a walk, a hit batsman, and five singles. The Yankees then proceeded to do nothing for the rest of the game against Bessent, Labine, and especially Spooner, who gave up just one hit and struck out five in three innings of work that suggested to Walter Alston (fatefully) that he might be good for one starting assignment in the Series despite his long season of arm troubles.

The four runs, however, were all Tommy Byrne needed. He was a bit wild (five walks during the game), but the Dodgers grounded out and popped up when it counted. After a run in the fifth inning, their bats also fell silent.

Byrne's complete game victory was the first by a left-hander in the entire season against the Dodgers; in fact, no left-hander had done it since an exceptional performance by Joe Nuxhall of Cincinnati the year before. Their actual record against lefties was 5–6, but as that statistic shows, the Dodgers rarely faced them, so intimidating was their right-handed power, especially in hitter-friendly Ebbets Field.

As the Series moved across the East River, there was far more talk about the fact that no team in fifty-two years of postseason play had come back to win after losing the first two games than there was bravado about going back to Brooklyn.

Before the Series began, all the papers had stories saying that Carl Erskine would start the third game. He had not had a spectacular season, and the wear and tear of throwing hard with such a relatively small body had been unusually severe. It was a surprise, however, when Alston suddenly went on a hunch and announced that instead of Erskine, he would pitch Johnny Podres—on his twenty-third birthday. The one good thing about the surprise was that it gave Podres little time to get scared. Before the game, the Ebbets Field announcer, Tex Rickard, announced to the crowd it was his birthday, and Gladys Gooding (the Larry MacPhail innovation who had become a New York sports institution) banged out "Happy Birthday" on the organ.

Alston also did something else that was unusual for this

normally taciturn, direct man. He called a meeting of the team before the game, simply to tell them that he thought they were just as good as the Yankees and that he had faith in their ability. According to Jackie Robinson, whose occasional clashes with the manager had been much-publicized, it was an unusual gesture both noted and appreciated.

Podres aside, there was much more pregame attention paid to his opponent that last day of September.

Bob Turley, who had turned twenty-five just eleven days earlier, had come to the Yankees over the previous winter in a big trade with Baltimore, along with another young pitcher who would become famous the following year—Don Larsen. To get them, the Yankees unloaded six players—including an aging Gene Woodling and two promising catchers, Gus Triandos and Hal Smith (who would burn the Yankees severely with a home run as a Pirate in the 1960 World Series).

Turley, a very large man, had been one of the mainstays of the pitching staff in 1955, winning seventeen games and leading the league in innings pitched. He threw very hard (his nickname on the sports pages was Bullet Bob), and he was an innovator. Instead of waving his arms down and up before throwing, he became a pioneer of what was called the no-windup delivery—starting with his hands at his waist and simply rocking back and then forward as he threw.

In the first of two games that Brooklyn could not afford to lose, it was Turley who faltered first. Podres had no trouble getting the Yankees in order to open the game, but in the Dodger half of the inning, after a one-out walk to Reese and a Snider strikeout, Roy Campanella jumped on a very fat pitch (after the game he said it was a fastball that wasn't fast) and hit a line drive home run into the bleachers in left-center field.

There was too much history to allow for anything resembling confidence this early, and the point was promptly demonstrated in the Yankee half of the second inning, when Mickey Mantle jumped on a Podres fastball and sent it more than four hundred feet into the center-field bleachers. (Despite his horrible leg injury, Mantle gamely played this contest and the next one as well.)

Perhaps unnerved, Podres repeated his mistake to Bill Skowron, who hit a sharp double down the left-field line. That brought Alston to the dugout telephone and Don Bessent up in the Dodger bullpen to throw. Podres kept Skowron on second base for two outs—a ground ball to Jackie Robinson at third base by Elston Howard and a Billy Martin strikeout—but with Phil Rizzuto due up, Alston took the slow walk to the mound.

The manager did not want to walk Rizzuto intentionally, even though Turley was up next, in hopes that the pitcher would be the first, nearly automatic out of the next inning. Alston told Podres not to make any more fat pitches.

The pitch to Rizzuto was low and inside, but the Yankee veteran nonetheless hit it cleanly into left field for a single. Skowron never hesitated as he rounded third base, but the left fielder—Sandy Amoros in his World Series debut—fielded the ball cleanly and let loose a perfect throw that Campanella caught well up the line from home plate as he braced for the coming collision.

It was less a collision between two big men than it was a perfectly placed collision between Skowron's left elbow and Campanella's mitt. The ball went flying toward the Dodger dugout as Skowron scored and the alert Rizzuto kept running around second base and into third.

The Dodgers then got a break. Instead of rolling around on the ground (backing up home plate, Podres couldn't see where it had gone), the ball landed in a special Series section next to the dugout that was constructed for the bulky television cameras of that primitive time. That made the play automatically over, and instead of scoring easily, Rizzuto had to go back to third base. With Turley coming up, the score was still tied.

Podres's pitch to his counterpart was hit on the ground right back at him, but it bounced high and Podres had to reach for it. Had it gotten past him, Alston would have taken Podres out of the game and the history of 1955 might have been very different.

The inning persuaded Campanella to start calling for more changeups from his young charge. As Pee Wee Reese explained the strategy after the game, "Speed alone won't beat the Yankees; you have to give them that soft stuff and mix it up."

The Dodgers did not permit the game to remain tied for long. In their half of the inning, Turley stumbled and then fell from Casey Stengel's grace, the Yankee manager deciding that he didn't have his best stuff that cloudy day. By now, Mickey Mantle's leg was hurting so badly that he moved to less demanding right field, sending Howard to left and Bob Cerv over to center field.

The Dodger eruption occurred with one out, and the catalyst, as he would be all day, was Jackie Robinson, who singled up the middle. His unnerving dance off first base upset Turley enough so that he hit Amoros in the leg. To make matters and Turley's composure worse, Johnny Podres (of all people) laid a bunt down toward third base that kept spinning toward the foul line as Turley lunged after it. Everyone was safe and the bases were loaded.

As ever, Robinson began his famous dance off third base, upsetting the young Yankee pitcher. Obviously bothered, Turley walked Junior Gilliam on five pitches, Robinson trotted home, and Turley left the game for Tom Morgan. Before the Yankee reliever could settle down and get out of the inning, he walked Reese to force in a second run.

That was all the Dodgers would need, but they kept pressing, getting two more runs in the fourth inning on a walk, two singles, and a sacrifice fly. Another two-run outburst occurred in the seventh, sparked once again by Jackie Robinson. With Tom Sturdivant now in the game (the fourth Yankee pitcher), he hit a line drive down the third-base line for an obvious double and then took advantage of a rookie mistake by Elston Howard to execute a classic Jackie Robinson maneuver. Often, when running the bases, he would take a deceptively wide turn, lure an outfielder into throwing behind him, and then take off for the next base.

That was exactly what happened to Howard, who had just made an excellent leaping catch that robbed Gil Hodges of at least extra bases, if not a home run. When Howard had chased the ball Robinson hit down, he noticed the Dodger star had gone several steps beyond second base, and quickly fired the ball there, hoping to throw him out before he could return to the bag. Instead, there was a cloud of dust at third base. Robinson then went into his patented dance and came home on a solid single to right field by Sandy Amoros.

As he put it with characteristically sharp wit after the game, "I must admit I had a pretty good day for an old, gray fat man."

Johnny Podres allowed but one Yankee run after the nearly disastrous second inning. In his living room all those years later, he told me that he normally threw his changeup four or five times in a game, as a way of setting up the curves and fastballs he used to get hitters out; on this occasion, he said, Campanella called for it more than twenty times.

The second time Mickey Mantle came to bat, after his prodigious home run, Podres threw him a low changeup, which Mantle grounded to Robinson at third. The third time, there were runners on first and second with no one out in the sixth inning when Mantle grounded the changeup right at Reese to begin a double play. The last time, in the eighth, there was another ground ball to Robinson. The final score was 8–3.

Bob Cerv, normally a decent hitter, struck out three times. As Billy Martin, who had nothing to show for four at-bats, put it later, "I tried everything, including running up on him, but I couldn't do a thing with it."

For a change, it had been a pleasant afternoon in my school gym with my two friends and Mr. Kenney. I had absorbed and been taught the entire history of the team's struggles, but I had not learned that up to that point, after forty-five World Series games going all the way back to 1916, they had never won one by more than four runs.

Having seen his young, competitive pitcher at the top of his game, Alston told Podres in the dressing room afterward that if there was a seventh game, he would start it. The trick was getting to a seventh game.

The prospect of trying to tie the World Series in Brooklyn via the Game Four pitching matchup of Carl Erskine and Don Larsen was superficially comforting but factually disturbing. Erskine's wins had dipped to eleven that year, and the wear and tear on his relatively slight frame had been considerable. He had labored down the stretch, and he was hurting. He was also famously gutsy; he would give the start all he had, but the uncertainty surrounding his impending outing was considerable on the eve of another game the Dodgers simply had to win.

By contrast, Don Larsen was a relatively unknown commodity. The less-publicized part of the Bob Turley deal, Larsen had pitched decently for the Yankees, winning nine and losing just two in his third full season, with a low earned-run average (3.06) after nearly 130 innings of work. He was also a very big man (Erskine's head barely cleared Larsen's shoulders in the pregame posing) but he pitched with more guile than power.

This time, it was the Yankees who scored first. We were watching at the apartment of my father's writer-friend in the neighborhood—children on the floor in front of the set, adults arrayed on a few folding chairs behind them. Television was not yet in nearly every American home. There was nothing unusual in an apartment or on a city block during a major event about an open door with friends and neighbors wandering in and out. My parents and I didn't move once.

The mobile antenna on top of the set had just been adjusted for the best reception when Gil McDougald jumped on a pitch and put it into the left-center field bleachers. It appeared from the beginning that Erskine was anything but overpowering that day; the third out of the dispiriting inning was a wicked line drive by Yogi Berra right at Duke Snider.

There was more trouble in the second inning. This time, Erskine walked Joe Collins. Elston Howard sacrificed him to second, and a ground ball out to second by Billy Martin moved Collins to third. He scored on a single by Rizzuto—one of those agonizing ground balls that seemed to take forever to bounce just past the best efforts of Pee Wee Reese to get to it.

The Dodgers got one of the runs back in their half of the third inning on a delightful play that I remember. Sandy Amoros (playing left field again with a right-handed pitcher on the mound) walked. With one out, Alston decided to play run-and-hit, and with Amoros moving on Larsen's pitch, Junior Gilliam sent a sharply hit ball into the left-field corner. Amoros never slowed down, rounding second, rounding third, and sliding home well ahead of the throw to Berra. It was fun to watch Amoros run; he was built low to the ground and seemed to pick up speed as he ran.

The Yankees, however, quickly scored another, frustrating run. A single by Berra and a walk to Collins brought Alston to the mound and Don Bessent into the game to pitch. Erskine did not have any real power behind his pitches that day. Because of his record and reputation, the fabled Oisk never drew boos from the fans; it was, simply, sad. After the game, Erskine said in the papers that he was in no condition to pitch anymore that year.

At first, it appeared the Dodgers might keep the Yankees from scoring more runs. Howard bunted a Bessent pitch too sharply, enabling the pitcher to throw Berra out at third. However, Joe Collins noticed that the Dodgers were not paying enough attention to him as he led off second base and alertly stole third. Billy Martin then sliced a ball weakly into right field that Furillo could not reach before it dropped in for a run-scoring single that gave the Yankees back their two-run lead.

It didn't last long. Roy Campanella was the leadoff batter in the fourth inning, and he hit a line drive that reached the left-field seats in a split second, it was hit so hard. Furillo then hit a ground ball that bounced over Larsen's head and he was safe at first base before Rizzuto could pick it up. That set the stage for a very long home run by my hero, Gil Hodges, that soared above the large scoreboard in right-center field and for the first time gave the Dodgers the lead.

The Dodgers very nearly lost it in the fifth inning. A walk and two singles loaded the bases with two out and sent Alston out to the mound once again, to replace Bessent with Labine. Disaster was averted when Joe Collins hit a routine ground ball to second baseman Junior Gilliam's reliable glove.

It was at about this point in the game that one of my favorite foul balls ever was hit. I can't remember which Yankee hit it, but it was a very high pop-up that drifted near the Yankee dugout. As the television camera followed Roy Campanella's pursuit of it, it became clear the ball was going to land next to the Yankee dugout in box seats filled with big shots. It not only did; it came down right on owner Del Webb's head. My mother had a high-pitched giggle when she really let loose, and she really let loose at Webb's discomfort. She had the most infectious laugh, radiating delight.

The Dodgers' power erupted again in their half of the fifth inning. Gilliam led off by walking and then stealing second. Larsen then fell behind Reese, throwing two balls far out of the strike zone; that was enough for Casey Stengel, who replaced him with Johnny Kucks, a promising Yankee rookie that year. He got Reese to hit a ground ball, but it was wide of first and though Collins fielded it, Reese was safe, while Gilliam scampered to third.

Duke Snider then hit his third home run of the Series to put the Dodgers ahead, 7–3. It was the kind of hit for which Snider was famous—a beautiful arching fly ball that went far above the forty-foot wall with the screen on top of it in right field and on into Bedford Avenue beyond. In contrast to Willie Mays (an explosive ballplayer who specialized in spectacular plays in the field, at the plate, or running the bases) and Mickey Mantle (who exuded glamour as well as power), Duke Snider above all displayed grace as the complement to his skill. In the papers he could come off sometimes as brooding, even insecure, but the person on the field made the improbable seem almost easy.

He had come from very little in California. Snider was raised in a working-family section of Los Angeles called Boyle Heights, a kind of mini-Brooklyn. It is near downtown and he would have walked as a boy through the nearby hilly neighborhood that would eventually contain Dodger Stadium. Both he and his dad served in the Pacific during the war at the same time. Each niche along his career path was earned the hard way and life was tough for his parents. His father handled dangerous, white-hot equipment at a Goodyear rubber plant. His mom packed pieces of cardboard into his sneakers so they would last longer.

Snider's development as an athlete (his role model was center fielder Jigger Statz of the minor-league Los Angeles Angels) began with his dad, who first called him Duke and forced his reluctant naturally right-handed kid to bat lefty so he would be a step closer to first base. At high school in Compton, where he played three sports, his reputation was enhanced by the glowing articles penned for the Long Beach paper by one of his classmates, a young man whose public relations talents eventually served another sport, professional football, with huge consequences for the country's culture—Pete Rozelle. Eventually, Snider was one of the other rookies on the Dodgers in 1947, the year of Jackie Robinson.

Years later, in his justly praised autobiography, Snider offered a compelling summary of what was going on in the country while he was hitting yet another titanic home run in the clutch of a key game in a special World Series:

"The Yankees were admired but the Dodgers were loved. The Yankees were the ultimate professionals—they even wore pinstripes. We were the colorful, scrappy underdogs. Somebody said rooting for the Yankees is like rooting for General Motors, but the whole world had a great time rooting for the Dodgers. We sounded like an assortment of characters straight out of Damon Runyon and in many ways we were . . . The sports world has never again seen the likes of Brooklyn and its Dodgers in the 1940s and '50s."

Snider's blast gave Clem Labine a soft cushion of a lead, but he let the Yankees back into contention with a rough sixth inning—singles by Howard and pinch-hitter Eddie Robinson, and a long double that Billy Martin hit over Snider's head produced two more runs.

The Dodgers got one of them back in their half of the inning on singles by Campanella, Furillo, and Hodges, and this proved to be all Labine needed to finish the game as the winning pitcher, the first World Series victory in an already important career, and especially sweet after the two games in which he was charged with losses in 1953. The Series was now tied.

The fifth game was played on Sunday, October 2. My father normally got the *Post* and *Times* on Sundays (he usually put on a long raincoat over his pajamas for the trudge to the stand on the corner of 42nd and Second), but on this day he picked up the *Daily Mirror* as well because it usually contained far more pictures and we were hungry for pictures in the wake of the previous day's slugfest.

It seemed incredible to me that I was going to the game, but it was not completely clear whom I was going to see pitch. The general consensus was that the most rested Dodger pitcher was Roger Craig, who had won several important games in the latter part of the season as a rookie after so many of the other pitchers began to wear down. For the Yankees, the speculation seemed to center on Bob Grim, who had only pitched the final inning of Game One (a crucial outing in a one-run game), but until I saw them both warming up at Ebbets Field the issue was in doubt.

Our neighbor came over for a late breakfast that morning. When she arrived I was already dressed, wearing one of the two sports jackets I had for school; given my mother's fastidiousness, I considered myself lucky not to have a tie on as well. For the game, she made us sandwiches and stuffed them into a shopping bag along with apples, cookies, and two paper cups for water.

As a clue to how excited I was, I can remember being on the subway with my wonderful benefactor for the trip across the East River to Brooklyn, and I can remember even more clearly walking into the bleachers and seeing the red, white, and blue bunting on all the railings. This may have been the first World Series broadcast in the fledgling technology of color, but I was unaware of that and, at any rate, had never seen the images on a color television. This was the first moment I experienced the pageantry of the World Series, and it was majestic.

We took our seats about twenty rows up in the bleachers be-hind left-center field. By then I was used to the view, which I liked because you could see the entire field.

Down near the field, there was a brief, very Brooklyn, epilogue to the foul ball incident the previous day. In the Yankee box, Del Webb was presented with a business card by a local undertaker, Michael Smith, emblazoned with his title, Mike the Merry Morti-cian. On the way into the ballpark, I had also spotted Hilda Chester holding court. With so many famous and important peo-ple at the World Series, she was bellowing the news that she not only had dressed up a bit but also was wearing a special perfume—Chanel Minus Five.

I was much too excited to want to keep score that day, and I don't believe we had a program (not that I needed one), because my mother would have saved it. We waited for the game to begin.

Roger Craig was twenty-five that season, a very tall, very skinny man who spoke with the accent of a Durham, North Carolinian. The previous season he had been pitching in the Piedmont League and was barely three months removed from the minor leagues in Montreal. He was not particularly fast but specialized in pitching low (he would later get credit for helping develop the split-fingered fastball); in ninety innings of work, he had com-piled an excellent 2.78 earned-run average.

Grim, more of a stocky man, was also twenty-five and more of a power pitcher. In his rookie season the year before, the native New Yorker had won twenty games, a most unusual feat. His arm troubles earlier that season, however, had created the opening for Tommy Byrne to have his remarkable comeback year.

The first thing I was conscious of as the game began was how much more vocal the crowd was. Ebbets Field was not a quiet place under normal circumstances, but in a World Series game people were reacting to every pitch. The tension in the air was palpable.

After an uneventful first inning, it was the Yankees who threat-ened first as the second inning began. Craig walked Joe Collins (playing right field that day so Stengel could have an extra left-handed hitter in the lineup against a right-handed pitcher) and then first baseman Eddie Robinson. To make the threat greater, Billy Martin hit a little squib in front of home plate; by the time Craig picked it up and threw him out, both runners had advanced to second and third with only one out.

The threat quickly ended, though, when Rizzuto hit a pop-up to Gil Hodges and Grim grounded to Jackie Robinson.

In the Dodgers' half of the second, with one out, Hodges got their first hit—a sharply hit single in front of us in left field. That brought Sandy Amoros to the plate. In the distance, I could see him in the stance I loved to mimic on the sandlots—a slight crouch, bat in tight and wiggling as Grim made his pitch.

The ball was clearly going to be a home run the instant Amoros hit it; I had spent enough time in the bleachers to know that a ball that gets past the infield that high and that quickly is guaranteed to clear the high fence in right field. As it happened, there was a roar in Ebbets Field unlike any I had ever heard; you could almost feel the noise vibrations, which followed Amoros all around the bases.

The noise was even louder the next time the Dodgers came up. The leadoff hitter was Snider, who swung as if he been waiting specially for the fat fastball Grim threw him. The ball went almost exactly where Amoros had hit his—to straightaway right field, way over the screen, and on into Bedford Avenue, where kids often waited with their gloves on in hopes of catching a home run ball. I was concentrating on the spectacle so fiercely that I don't remember much about being with our neighbor from 2509 in the bleachers. I do, however, remember her words as Snider circled the bases. "Isn't it wonderful," she said, an exclamation a bit demure for bleacher fans like me.

Craig was pitching well, but he was not overpowering; the Yankees were getting their chances, one of which produced a run in the fourth inning. Yogi Berra pulled a line drive off the scoreboard in right-center field, which would have been at least a double anywhere else, but with Furillo playing the carom and unleashing a typically hard throw back to the infield, Berra immediately stopped at first. With one out, Craig walked Robinson, whereupon the first Yankee run of the day scored on a single by Billy Martin.

Back came the Dodgers the following inning. With one out this time, Snider did it again—a towering blast that was hit more toward center field and easily cleared the scoreboard. This time the roar followed him all the way into the dugout. It was not just his second home run of the game; it was his fourth in five games of the Series, the second time he had accomplished this feat in a World Series, something no one had ever done; only Babe Ruth and Lou Gehrig had hit four home runs in a single Series to that point.

The Yankees were not finished. Bob Cerv made it 4–2 in the top of the seventh, hitting a Craig fastball into the deck above us in the bleachers. When the next batter, Elston Howard, walked, Walter Alston removed his rookie, who had given him six solid innings, in favor (once again) of Clem Labine, whom the Dodgers were beginning to realize indeed had a "rubber arm."

He was not, however, initially effective. When Yogi Berra poked a ball over the screen in right field to open the eighth inning, it had become a tense 4–3 ball game.

The so-called insurance run that the Dodgers then proceeded to manufacture was a thing of baseball beauty. With Bob Turley now pitching, Carl Furillo began the inning by hitting a sharp ground ball that bounced off Martin's glove at second for a single.

The proof that Alston was content to play for one run came when the next batter, the mighty Gil Hodges, followed orders and laid down a perfect sacrifice bunt in Turley's direction to move Furillo into scoring position at second. He scored when a Jackie Robinson ground ball just made it past a lunging Phil Rizzuto into left field for a single.

I distinctly remember the tension as the ninth inning began, but it dissipated almost immediately as the Yankees went meekly in order. Normally, baseball etiquette calls for handshakes after any game short of the Series finale, but I can still see Labine doing a little jump near the mound after the third out (a Howard ground ball to Gilliam). To that moment, Labine had been every bit as important a pitcher as Podres, getting a win and a save in the final two Brooklyn games. The Dodgers still faced the jinx of trying to become the first team to win it all after losing the first two games, but they had just become the first team to win three straight after being in that hole.

The real obstacle to that final historically elusive victory, as always, was pitching. Neither Newcombe nor Erskine was available anymore, which meant that for Game Six Alston had a choice among Loes, Spooner, and Meyer for the unenviable task of opposing Whitey Ford. Alston's choice of Karl Spooner is still second-guessed, but the fact is that he pitched very well in relief during Game Two and had been reported to be throwing well by Dixie Howell as he warmed up for a call that never came during the second of the games in Brooklyn.

The first inning of Game Six is a famous disaster in Dodger lore. What is sometimes forgotten is how tantalizingly close the plays were that produced it.

It was certainly Spooner's fault that he began the bottom of the first inning by walking Rizzuto. But while he was striking Billy Martin out, Junior Gilliam was late covering second when the Yankee shortstop took off on a steal attempt; he caught the quick throw by Campanella in front of the bag (that could have been the second out). Spooner then made the mistake of walking Gil McDougald.

The next three hits that ended his afternoon each came on two-strike pitches. The first, a run-producing single by Berra, was especially painful; it appeared to have eyes, bouncing over Spooner's outstretched glove and just under Gilliam's on its way into center field (it was almost a double-play ball). The second was another run-producing single by Hank Bauer (playing despite his bad leg for the first time since Game Two).

The third hit was an excruciating three-run home run on an outside pitch by Bill Skowron. It was a line drive that just made the seats in short-right field. On came Russ Meyer, and Spooner tragically never pitched in the major leagues again. Meyer was nearly flawless for five-plus innings, as was Ed Roebuck over the last two, giving the second-guessers a field day. For the Yankees, Ford's magnificent four-hitter, his first complete game in the World Series, meant the entire rest of the Yankee staff would be fresh for the seventh game.

For the Dodgers and their fans, Game Six meant a return to their traditional deflated state. That was the other reason a 1–0 lead after five innings meant only that the torture was now beyond severe. None of us imagined that it was about to get much, much greater.

12

The Longest Inning

In the official summary of the seventh game of the 1955 World Series, the time of the game is listed at two hours, forty-four minutes. It felt as if it took more like two years, but of those one hundred sixty-four minutes, at least forty of them were consumed by one of the oddest, most exciting, and most enervating baseball innings ever.

When it had ended, the score hadn't changed much, but it could no longer be ignored. There was no longer any question that the Dodgers really were ahead. I remember feeling mostly exhausted by it but more than a little aware that however historically weird it looked, good things had actually been happening, however difficult it was to accept that.

In all, eleven men came to bat in the famous sixth, seven for the Dodgers. There were only two base hits, each of them on the cheap side. The hardest hit ball was an out. There was one very serious error that made possible the only run scored during the long inning. There were two critical substitutions that will keep discussions of the managers' strategy alive forever. There was one defensive play so spectacular that it is among the handful of old World Series highlights still being replayed for disbelieving audiences. And throughout it all, there was this twenty-three-year-old pitcher who maintained his composure and his concentration through a series of ultimate distractions to continue his domination of the game.

Naturally, it all started with Pee Wee Reese, the Dodgers' captain, who to that point had the questionable distinction of being the only person in baseball history to have played through five World Series and been on the same, losing side each and every time through each and every inning—each and every time to the same team.

Tommy Byrne, still pitching smoothly and just as effectively as Johnny Podres had been, threw Reese a challenging pitch, down low in the strike zone. He hit it on the ground. It bounced past the mound and then kept on bouncing past second base and into center field, past the converging lunges of Phil Rizzuto and Billy Martin.

It was only the third hit that Byrne had given up to that point, the other two having produced the lone Dodger run in the fourth inning. It was also the only occasion in the entire game when the Dodgers got their leadoff man on base. Duke Snider—with forty-two home runs that season plus his record-setting four more in the Series—was up next.

From the Dodger dugout Walter Alston flashed the sign to his third-base coach, Billy Herman: sacrifice. Herman in turn flashed it to Snider, who touched his cap in acknowledgment. The years-earlier incident with Burt Shotton was still fresh in Snider's mind; the instruction to bunt also made perfect sense and had been used two days before in Brooklyn on a power hitter, when a bunt by Gil Hodges set up the Dodgers' insurance run in the pivotal fifth game. As Snider saw it very clearly, Alston was looking for one more run and was not interested in gambling on a big inning. If the Dodgers could get that run, it would take the option of one-run baseball away from the Yankees; instead of using the sacrifice to help get one run in, they would need to swing away with men on base, risking double plays.

The Dodger strategy was logical, but it remained an open question whether Snider could succeed in bunting the ball into fair territory, softly enough to get Reese safely to second base. We all have our weaknesses, even superstars, and Snider's were batting against left-handed pitchers and bunting, and now he was being instructed to bunt against a very good left-handed pitcher.

As Byrne went into his stretch to hold down Reese's lead off first, Snider prepared to bunt. In baseball language, they call it squaring away, which means directly facing the pitcher with the bat held out over the plate. Snider, however, was not so much squaring away as facing third base, the direction in which he intended to bunt the ball. As usually happens at the beginning of such a play, there is a ballet in the infield, as the third baseman (Gil McDougald) and first baseman (Bill Skowron) charge the plate, while the second baseman (Billy Martin) moves to cover first and the shortstop (Phil Rizzuto) runs over to cover second.

Snider bunted the ball perfectly, to the third-base side of the pitcher's mound and softly. Byrne, an excellent fielding pitcher, got to the ball quickly. When he picked it up, the old film of the play shows him pausing very briefly to look at Reese running toward second, deciding in an instant that a throw there might be too late, and throwing the ball directly at first base. Seeing that Snider was totally committed to bunting in the other direction, Skowron had stopped his charge and was still moving back to the bag when Byrne's throw reached him.

Skowron was perhaps one step in front of the bag when he caught the ball one-handed in his glove. With Snider almost upon him in the baseline, he made a sweeping motion to record the out by tagging the Dodger center fielder. Glove and ball touched Snider on his chest, and the motion more than any hard collision kept Skowron turning clockwise.

To the surprise of Snider, Skowron, and everyone watching the game, the ball then came flying out of his glove as he turned, and bounced back across the infield. After assuming Snider would be out, I remember being puzzled by Skowron's odd behavior as he looked around for the ball; that was the indication that Snider had in fact been safe. It was a ball Skowron definitely should have held on to, so the play was properly ruled an error by the first baseman.

Now there were Dodgers on first and second, no one was out, and that is called a threat. Roy Campanella was coming up—thirty-two home runs on the season and another two in the World Series—but there was no doubt at all now that another sacrifice bunt was coming. With two men on base, this is a somewhat more difficult play to stop, because the third baseman must stay close to his bag for a possible throw, putting more of a burden on the pitcher to make the fielding play.

As Byrne delivered his pitch, Campanella was truly squared around to bunt, and he did so cleanly, a bit closer to the third-base line than Snider's bunt had been. Byrne fielded the ball cleanly; again, he looked at both runners but quickly made his decision and his throw—to Billy Martin covering first base. The ball was caught this time and the first out of the inning recorded.

Now, however, there were runners on second and third, with just the one out, and more power due up in the person of Carl Furillo. With Bob Grim warming up in the Yankee bullpen, the situation virtually dictated that Furillo be walked intentionally to create a possible force out at any base or a double play on a ground ball. Byrne got the signal from Berra and threw Furillo four outside pitches, at which point Casey Stengel made the slow trudge to the mound.

Byrne told me he wanted to remain in the game to pitch to the next batter, Gil Hodges. He still felt strong, had excellent control, and could thus be counted on to keep his throws low.

The other point of view is called playing the percentages in baseball. In those days especially, long before today's bewildering assortment of breaking and sinking pitches, it was a truism that right-handed hitters batted more effectively against left-handed pitchers (and vice versa) because the curveball breaks toward their swing. Stengel was a notorious, and successful, percentage player as the Yankee manager, he asked for the ball and made a slight flick of his right wrist, the signal to bring Grim in from the bullpen. A disappointed Byrne slowly walked back to the Yankee dugout, a frustrating end to a season of inspiring personal triumph.

When Grim arrived at the mound, there was only one instruction from Stengel, an obvious one. Grim was to keep his pitches low to lessen the chances of a fly ball that could score a run. Vin Scully was reminding my father and me, and millions of other viewers, that Hodges had already driven in the first Dodger run. I don't recall believing or not believing that he would do it again, just realizing that the biggest moment in the game to that point had arrived.

Gil Hodges could hit, and hit with power, to all fields. Because he often went with outside pitches and hit them to right field he did not specialize in the home run quite the way sluggers like Snider and Mickey Mantle did. Hodges's real specialty was the run batted in. On the other hand, he was also famous for his record for hitting grand slams.

The pitch from Grim to Hodges was about waist high and toward the outside of the plate—almost certainly a strike. Hodges stepped into it and swung hard. For me it was another one of those moments when I instantly sat up. What was clear at first was that the ball had shot out beyond the infield very fast; what wasn't clear was how far it was going on an arc into right-center field. In the outfield, Bob Cerv had been positioned in straight-away center, and the first glimpse of him shows a man sprinting at top speed. He was running in the direction of the sign on the wall in deepest right-center field that said 457, as in feet.

Gradually, it dawned on me that Cerv was going to get to the long fly ball. He ran under it not very many strides in front of the dirt warning track in front of the wall. There was no doubt at all that from such a distance it was impossible for him to even try to throw Reese out at home. The camera showed Reese jogging home, but I was wondering what happened to Snider. As it turned out, he, too, had tagged up and run to third base after the catch, while Furillo stayed at first.

The next batter was Don Hoak. With Jackie Robinson's injury, there was no option for the Dodgers to pinch-hit for Hoak, so he stepped into the batter's box. A .240 hitter on the year, he was the man to end the inning, and Grim bore down hard pitching to him, perhaps too hard, because his pitch sailed away from the plate. Yogi Berra couldn't block it, and the ball bounced away from him.

It was not far enough away from him to give Snider a realistic chance of scoring, and Grim alertly rushed to cover home plate. However, it was more than far enough away to permit Carl Furillo to get to second base. Once again, the Yankees were without the chance of a force out in the event of a ground ball. From the dugout the order came to walk Hoak intentionally and load the bases again.

In shorthand reconstructions of the game, the emphasis has always been placed on what Alston tried to do with the bases loaded for the second time. What has been forgotten is that it was Grim's wild pitch that created the situation—which would have no offensive consequences but giant defensive ones that same inning.

According to the late Dodger manager—after the game and in two books he wrote—the intentional walk to Hoak caused him to change his thinking and maximize the chances of an extra-base hit or home run. That meant as a practical matter sending a pinch-hitter up for the next man, right-handed batter Don Zimmer—a .239 hitter on the year who had some power (fifteen home runs) and two hits that Series but could not be considered a consistent threat.

Alston had two choices, both left-handed hitters. The one who usually gets forgotten is Sandy Amoros, who had been batting well over .300 for much of the season, until back troubles limited his effectiveness, but who was now healthy. To that point in the Series, he had collected four hits in twelve times at bat, including Sunday's long home run.

According to Dodgers at the time and ever since, however, Alston never hesitated and George Shuba was seen in the dugout grabbing a bat. No one recalls even a discussion about the choice, much less an argument.

George Shuba's nickname was Shotgun because of his propensity for hitting hard line drives. He was thirty years old and had been on the Dodgers since 1948. A left fielder by trade, he was used sparingly as a regular; his most active year by far had been

1952, when he appeared in ninety-four games. He was very familiar with pinch-hitting in clutch situations, however, and had a
World Series home run (in 1953) to his credit; on the other hand,
he had not been in the Series at all to that moment. Shuba was
also very popular with his teammates; in fact, the previous year
several of the Dodgers, Jackie Robinson included, had urged
Buzzie Bavasi not to sign the highly regarded young Puerto Rican
outfielder, none other than Roberto Clemente, to a "bonus" contract because Shuba almost certainly would have been the player
let go to make room for him.

Now nearly eighty and still living in the Youngstown, Ohio,
area near where he grew up, Shuba remembered his appearance
well, in part because it turned out to be his last at-bat in the major leagues.

"Grim threw me a fast curveball," he told me. "I swung hard
and I hit it hard, but on the ground."

Bill Skowron fielded the ball cleanly well behind the first-base
bag, flipped it to Grim covering the base, and the long half inning
was over.

As a broadcaster would summarize it, the Dodgers had one run
on one hit, there was one Yankee error, and three men were left
on base; officially, the run was Byrne's responsibility but was not
recorded as "earned" because of the error by Skowron, without
which Reese would not have scored. Again, officially, because
walks and sacrifices don't count, just two of the seven Dodgers
who arrived in the batter's box during the sixth inning were
recorded for statistical purposes as having actual at-bats.

Because of the wild pitch and the resulting decision to pinch-
hit for Zimmer, Alston faced additional decisions as the Yankees
ran off the field and the Dodgers prepared to resume their positions. First, he needed a new second baseman; that one was
obvious—Gilliam, his usual position.

Now he needed a new left fielder to replace him. According to
Alston, he considered Shuba, but only briefly. After all, precisely
because of his defensive ability, Amoros had been used all season
long in left field in this very circumstance late in a game. The

arrival of Amoros the previous year had made the Dodgers a stronger, more versatile team. As with the decision to use Shuba as a pinch-hitter, Amoros was sent into left field by Alston without any discussion on the bench.

Through the years, Alston's actions have often been portrayed as somewhere between inspired and heroic. He did not see them that way, nor did any other Dodger at the time or since, from Podres on the mound to Bavasi in the front office. Instead, Alston was seen as having been wise all year to use Zimmer, Gilliam, and Amoros this way. Alston always considered himself "lucky" that things turned out as they did, but that would seem to apply more to using a pinch-hitter for Zimmer than sending Amoros to the outfield.

Vin Scully told me he is positive that he announced the defensive changes—Amoros to left field, Gilliam to second base—into his microphone as the Dodgers ran out onto the field. I cannot recall noticing; what I remember is feeling that the Dodgers had missed an opportunity to blow the game wide open. Instead of increasing my confidence that the Dodgers would win the game, this only caused my sense of foreboding to get stronger. In this context—a 2–0 lead with four innings to go—I had no experience with confidence, much less hope.

The productive middle of the Yankee lineup was due up.

For as long I could remember, my father had an almost visceral reaction when a Dodger pitcher walked an opposition batter—a look of distaste on his face or some noise like a groan. It was such a waste, a gift of opportunity to the other team, summarized in the old, dirgelike baseball lament. "Oh, those bases on balls."

To begin the Yankee half of the sixth inning, Johnny Podres walked Billy Martin on four pitches. It was the second and last base on balls Podres issued that day, the first since the two-out walk to Phil Rizzuto in the third inning. Podres told me he does not remember feeling any different on the mound after the

Dodgers scored their second run and that he never felt that his arm was tiring at that point in the game.

The shadows had arrived at the mound by then, and this was when Campanella began calling exclusively for fast pitches, on the assumption that his changeup had done its job and it was time to bear down the rest of the way. Should Podres's arm get tired, there was a bullpen full of potential replacements for the final innings, led by Clem Labine.

It is possible that in making this transition Podres might have thrown a bit too hard to Martin. Tommy Byrne had learned through bitter experience that control was a function of his attitude as much as abilities or, as Yogi Berra put it in another possibly apocryphal aphorism, "Ninety percent of this game is half-mental."

A fan could feel disappointment or concern at a walk in a tense situation, but a professional pitcher trying to throw a ball into a small strike zone from sixty feet away at ninety miles an hour understood that sometimes you missed and that you concentrated on the hitter you were facing, not the last one or the next one.

Gil McDougald, who already had sort of a single that day (the ground ball in the third inning that Rizzuto slid into), did not go up to bat to sacrifice Martin to second base. McDougald did, however, notice that Don Hoak was playing behind the base at third, protecting against line drives headed down the left-field line. He decided to try to bunt for a base hit.

Only when Podres came out of his stretch to throw the ball did McDougald change his grip on the bat, sliding his right hand up the handle in preparation for his bunt. He dumped the ball expertly onto the ground, where it proceeded to roll toward third. By the time Podres scampered over, there was no question it was going to remain in fair territory and no question that McDougald was going to be safe at first base.

Nonetheless, Podres made a rare fielding mistake and after an instant's hesitation flung the ball off balance toward Hodges at first anyway. It is in such situations that players often make wild throws. Podres was fortunate that his afterthought of a throw, which had nothing on it and sailed toward Hodges, was caught by the first baseman near the bag.

In barely two minutes, the Dodgers had gone from the team that had taken a 2–0 lead to one in the distasteful position of facing the gravest threat to them of the game. It was the same threat they themselves had presented to the Yankees in the top half of the inning—men on first and second with none out. For the Dodgers, the key play had been Skowron's error after Snider's bunt; for the Yankees, it had been the walk to Martin.

I remember watching Walter Alston slowly walk to the mound. Campanella was already there, Pee Wee Reese was on his way in from shortstop, and Podres was in the familiar pitcher's position for such meetings—head down, right foot kicking at the pitching rubber. Labine was throwing in the bullpen.

Podres says he does not remember what was literally said during those moments, only that the result was that he was still in the game, still throwing fast pitches, still trying to throw them away from spots from which they could be hit with power.

Later that day and until they died, Alston and Campanella had the same memory. The Dodger manager asked his catcher how Podres was doing before he reached the mound. The phrase he used, give or take a word, was, "Has he still got it?" Clearly, Campanella was trusted explicitly to make the judgment call. Campanella replied that Podres had lost none of his effectiveness. End of subject.

That left the matter of how to pitch to the most dangerous hitter imaginable to be coming up at a critical moment like this one—Yogi Berra. The Yankee catcher was not merely an excellent hitter. He was one of the best-hitting catchers of all time, because he not only hit for average and power but also could hit for average and power to all parts of a ballpark. His normal tendency was to pull balls sharply that he could reach easily; however, he was also famous for his eagerness to chase pitches that were outside the strike zone. He swung an unusually long bat.

At the mound, Alston and Campanella assumed Berra would be swinging away, not bunting. They each stressed the vital importance of keeping the pitches away from him and preferably low. They were intent on avoiding what the Yankees most likely would be seeking—a big inning. Alston slowly walked back to the dugout while Reese and Campanella returned to their positions.

At the plate, Berra was not content when he saw no bunt sign from the third-base coach, Frankie Crosetti. Berra walked toward the Yankee veteran. Crosetti was a regular on the championship teams of the 1930s and a fixture in the coaching box ever since who had been on the field for more World Series games than anyone, ever. They met halfway down the third-base line, where Crosetti told him the instruction was to hit away. Casey Stengel confirmed after the game that he never for a moment considered a sacrifice, that he wanted the big inning the Dodgers assumed he wanted.

Behind the plate, Campanella called for a fastball that even Berra would not swing at—above the shoulders and inside, to set up the outside pitches that would follow. Berra took the pitch for ball one.

For Podres's second pitch, Campanella called for a curveball low and outside and set himself and his target accordingly. As usual, Berra held his long bat high. In the field, the Dodgers played him to pull the ball; everyone was farther toward right field than normal. In the outfield, Sandy Amoros was not playing Berra all that deep—about midway between the infield and the outfield wall. He was positioned way off the foul line in left-center field, roughly behind where Reese was at shortstop, which was shaded toward second base. From right after the game until he died in 1992, Amoros always insisted that before returning to the dugout Alston had motioned him a few more steps toward straightaway center field, which Amoros interpreted as meaning that Alston still worried that Podres might be tiring and was mostly concerned about Berra pulling the ball.

It made what was about to happen all the more improbable.

According to my stopwatch, it took 11.97 seconds from the instant the ball left Johnny Podres's left hand until it arrived in Gil Hodges's glove to complete the play.

The pitch from Podres came in fast and slightly higher than Campanella's low target. Berra swung at it—sort of. His swing was late, bordering on the tentative, the way a good hitter swings when he intends to foul off a pitch.

At the instant of contact, the frozen film frame shows the Yankee catcher with his weight back, almost facing third base, with his bat fully extended. Berra followed completely through with his swing, but the act supplied no additional power behind the ball. At that moment of contact, it was more as if he had punched at it. In a game often ruled by millimeters, he had also swung slightly under the pitch from Podres.

In the outfield, Sandy Amoros did what only ability and instinct formed by experience can produce in a baseball player. He shifted at the crack of Berra's bat to face the left-field foul line and exploded like a sprinter coming out of starting blocks.

From the mound, Podres sensed an out and turned to pick up the white resin bag from the dirt behind him.

From the plate, Berra had no idea beyond a sense that he hadn't hit the ball hard. This was long before the free-agent era, when zillionaires could afford to stand at home plate to admire the flight of balls they had hit. He turned, discarding his bat, and started running to first base.

From behind the plate, Campanella discarded his mask as he stood up and began to mumble a prayer.

From a box next to the Dodgers' dugout on the third-base side of the field, Buzzie Bavasi was the instantaneous pessimist. The Dodger executive, aware that the left-field seats were a mere 301 feet away, next to the foul pole, thought Berra had hit a home run.

From the Yankee dugout on the first-base side, which afforded a clear view at field level, Tommy Byrne and the other players in the dugout thought: *Foul ball.* Berra had not truly sliced the ball, but it appeared to them on a gradual arc that would carry it well into the stands.

Down the foul line, the young Dodger assistant in the front office, Billy DeLury, was sitting by himself at the game and looking directly at Sandy Amoros, who seemed to be headed right at him. From the trajectory, he was certain the ball was not hit far enough to be a home run. What he could not be certain about was whether the ball would land foul, land fair, or be caught. If it landed fair, he was almost certain it would bounce into the stands for a ground rule double—scoring Martin and leaving Berra and McDougald on second and third, still with nobody out. The only way for a complete disaster to unfold would be if Amoros tried for a catch and dropped the ball.

From second base, Billy Martin was uncertain. He trotted halfway to third base and stopped. From first base, Gil McDougald immediately decided, as he would say later, that there was no way Amoros could get to the ball before it hit the ground and began sprinting toward second base at full speed.

No one had a better view than the people in the press box, well behind and well above home plate. From this ideal perch, Vin Scully not only had the right view; he also was concentrating with special intensity because he had to describe to the television audience what was unfolding. Scully has a standard phrase that he uses for possible or actual home runs; "cut on and belted." He told me he is certain he said nothing of the kind; instead he said he described a fly ball that was hit very high (in fact, very, very high) down the left-field line.

Back on the pitcher's mound, Podres said his second thoughts began as he picked up the resin bag and noticed no one in left field was nestling under the fly ball he had assumed would be an out; he called it a banana ball that seemed to be gradually moving beyond Amoros's reach. With deep misgivings, Podres turned and began jogging into foul territory behind third base to be in position to back up any throw from the outfield. Next to the Dodger dugout, Buzzie Bavasi now realized the ball did not appear to have been hit far enough to reach the seats for a home run; beyond that, he had no idea what would happen.

Down the line, DeLury stood up as he saw Sandy Amoros,

looking larger with each sprinting step. DeLury saw the ball, too, and realized it was an open question which would get to it first—the dirt just in fair territory or Amoros's glove.

I remember the first camera shot that widened beyond the home plate–centered view when Berra completed his swing. It showed the outfield, with Amoros coming into view at a point directly behind the normal shortstop's position. It was a moment of intense suspense in the race to the corner between the baseball and the outfielder. It was a hold-your-breath moment; the crowd was not yelling.

Amoros did not stop sprinting. In a quotation after the game in some of the few English words he knew, Amoros said, "I don't know I get it. I just run like hell and stick out my glove."

Pete Reiser's tragic heroics aside, it is not natural to run full speed directly at a wall. With about thirty yards to go, Amoros's stride changed—from all-out sprint to choppy. Whether he was decelerating to survive a collision or already certain he could reach the ball is uncertain; what is certain is that he was decelerating.

About three strides from the foul line and perhaps ten feet in front of the stands in fair territory, Amoros can be seen using his right heel as a brake, digging it into the ground. After another stride, he stuck the glove on his right hand straight out at about eye level, the inside of it facing him.

On television the ball was visible for the first time when it fell into the glove. Amoros's heel was planted in the dirt, but his left foot was at an anticipatory angle—pointed at third base. The play was at most half-completed. At that instant, Podres, head down, was just jogging across the third-base line to his backup position.

In the Dodger infield, Pee Wee Reese was the player with the responsibility to be on the move. On a ball hit into left field with runners on base, he had gone onto the grass in short-left field after the ball was hit. As it seemed to carry toward the foul line, he kept moving over as well until he was almost directly behind third base. His job would be to take a throw from the outfield and send it on its way with fresh gas toward home plate or to some other base, which demanded an accurate sense of where the base runners were.

With Martin stopped halfway from second, he was close enough to have an excellent chance to make it back to the bag if the ball was caught; though Martin was the lead runner, Reese decided on the spot to ignore him. McDougald, however, had run so far so fast that he had already rounded second base; he could not have been more exposed.

As the ball was falling into Amoros's outstretched glove, Reese began screaming to get his attention. At the same time, Reese held his own glove high above his head and waved it frantically.

Amoros heard him and saw the glove, he would say later. As he caught the ball, he pivoted, turning counterclockwise as his momentum from the long run took him into the left-field corner. In one motion he threw the ball straight at Reese's outstretched glove about sixty yards away.

From the press box, Vin Scully said he could see out of the corner of his eye that McDougald had stumbled as he realized the fix he was in and had begun moving to retag the bag and start the long sprint back to first base.

Reese was backing up as Amoros's beautiful perfect throw came toward his glove. When he caught it, he was one full step onto the infield dirt behind third base. With a graceful counterclockwise move of his own, Reese turned as the ball reached his glove and threw an equally beautiful line drive directly across the infield at Gil Hodges.

Hodges stretched to the limits of his long frame—left arm out stiff, right leg out stiff, left leg bent at the knee. He needn't have. The throw from Reese was in Hodges's glove while McDougald was still in the air before sliding.

Double play.

People who were in the stadium said that at first there was no great noise, as if the crowd was pausing to be sure it had actually seen what appeared to have just happened. This was followed by what was typically described as an excited buzz, a kind of "Did you see that?" reaction. The buzz got louder, there were many

Yankee fans applauding in tribute, but there was never any roar of the sort there is after a game-winning hit or home run, and the buzz continued even after Hank Bauer stepped into the batter's box with Billy Martin still on second base.

Spent, I turned from the couch, half-wondering if the sphinx at the dining table would at last speak. I found him staring at me, eyes ablaze, lips pursed so tightly they seemed to disappear. I think I half-smiled at him, but he continued to look at me, even as we both heard Scully's voice in the background saying that Bauer had hit a routine ground ball at Reese, who cleanly fielded an in-between hop at shortstop and threw him out to finally end the inning—eleven batters, two modest base hits, an error, a wild pitch, and a play that has survived for fifty years.

It is referred to as the Amoros Catch, but it really was a spectacular run, catch, and two picture-perfect relays—all directly connected to the bizarre events in the Dodger half of the inning.

Every Dodger that day and in the decades since has always made the same analytical point about the play. Junior Gilliam could not have made it had he still been in left field. Running directly at the short wall and needing to reach for the ball while moving forward, he would have had to reach across his body as a right-handed fielder to catch the ball backhanded. Even in the highly improbable event he could have done that, he would have had to stop, set himself, and then throw. Even in the highly improbable event he could have done that smoothly, precious instants would have been lost. The point is unanimous and apparently inarguable.

By contrast, very little attention has been paid to a final factor that may have had a significant influence on the play—the wind. It was a clear fall day, the wind was not strong and constant, but it blew hard in gusts. On a ball hit extremely high, there are informed eyewitness opinions that it played a role—both in keeping the ball in the air and in keeping it over fair territory.

That was Sandy Amoros's strong opinion after the game as he described the ball he never took his eyes off as he raced toward the left-field corner. To him it seemed to be trying to slowly curve into the stands but never managed to do so. That was also the considered view of Johnny Podres, once his second thoughts about the ball he first assumed was an easy out began. What he called a banana ball should have kept curving into foul territory, especially given the likely spin on a ball hit to the opposite field by a left-handed hitter.

Reflecting the view from the Yankee dugout, that was also Tommy Byrne's judgement. He told me that on windy days a breeze was often much stronger on the field and swirled intensely—especially in the left-field corner.

If the wind was in fact involved, it was a gift to the Dodgers that fate had rarely provided, helping keep a high fly ball aloft a little longer while Amoros ran toward it and helping keep it fair, which made possible the crucial double play. In the next day's *Daily News*, homage was paid to the wind as "a breeze that grew in the Bronx"—a nice play on Betty Smith's *A Tree Grows in Brooklyn*.

Nonetheless, for all the unforgettable drama, the score was still only 2–0 with three full innings to go. After the excitement began to wear off, the emotional residue is best described as relief, as people resumed the long vigil.

I have heard some people—Buzzie Bavasi, for example—say that from that moment on they had no doubt that the Dodgers were going to win the World Series. I have yet to meet a player who confessed to such supreme confidence. I know I didn't feel it; the burden of history was too heavy.

Still, those who followed the Dodgers all over the country could sigh with a relief that was rare enough in their experience.

13

Nine Outs

As the sixth inning came mercifully to a close, the Dodger players trotted off the field. The huge crowd—62,465, according to the notation on Lt. Gary Hymel's scorecard after the seventh-inning announcement on the public-address system—continued to buzz from the shock of Sandy Amoros's breathtaking play in the outfield. Reaching the dugout parallel to the third-base line, they briefly forgot that their left fielder had been suffering serious back pains since the middle of the season; repeatedly, large hands smacked the grinning Cuban player on his tender back. Despite his enormous language handicap, Amoros was always happy to be on the integrated Brooklyn Dodgers, and his teammates, aware of the long-standing hole in the field he was helping to fill, as well as pleased at his affable, hustling approach to the game, made him feel welcome. For much of the season he lived on a boat Campanella owned.

Most of these Dodgers had many years together. They were all children of the depression and of world war, astonished to be paid for playing a game, although their paychecks were meager by today's standards. Both as a team and as individuals, they were imbued with blue-collar, hardworking values. Many had been recruited and raised under Branch Rickey, whose baseball philosophy (beyond tightwad-ism) was that if you played hard as a team the individual accomplishments would follow. They had, over the years, been through hell together.

Twenty years later, playing on a Boston Red Sox team packed with large egos and wallets as it played for a championship, right fielder Dwight Evans famously observed of the commuting habits of his fellow loners, "Twenty-five players, twenty-five cabs." These Dodgers car-pooled from the ballpark.

The last player into the dugout, finishing his energy-conserving slow walk from the pitcher's mound, was Johnny Podres. He briefly joined the knot of players around Amoros, looked his teammate in the eye, and slugged him repeatedly on the back with both hands. Podres got a bat, walked to the plate, and promptly grounded out to second.

Then, as he had done whenever the rest of the Dodgers were up at bat, Podres disappeared. He walked down the steps that led from the dugout to a dimly lit passageway that connected the field to the clubhouse.

And there, a ballplayer in a different era, he lit a cigarette. From the dugout the Dodgers regularly heard a disembodied voice shout from the darkness that he was to be summoned when there were two outs. They left him alone.

As he told me about his between-innings routine, it was clear that Podres was relieved to be removed from the intense atmosphere on the bench. Players continuously paced, kibitzed, talked strategy; Podres was intent on simply hitting Campanella's target with the pitch he had called for. The atmosphere on the bench was electric; Jackie Robinson in particular seethed with slow-burning energy he was unable to use on the field. Avoiding this highly charged atmosphere was itself good strategy for the young pitcher who knew exactly what he was supposed to do in the late innings.

For an inning or so by now, the change-up had been shelved as the shadows gave the pitcher an advantage with fast pitches coming out of the bright light. Keeping it simple was the wise course, and if a quick cigarette served the purpose of today's yoga exercise and bag of sunflower seeds, then big deal.

Across the way, in the Yankees' dugout, Byrne described an atmosphere of determination salted with more than a little confidence. Winning really is habit-forming; most of these Yankees had made a habit out of beating the Dodgers. Fans in Brooklyn loved to compile lists of examples of storied "Yankee Luck," but the truth was that they played superbly and hard year after year, filled with a powerfully motivating sense of tradition.

The frustration after the sixth inning was less about the big inning Sandy Amoros had taken them out of than it was about the run the Dodgers had scored in the top half of the sixth. Bob Grim, in getting the assignment to replace Byrne, had been given the task of not giving Gil Hodges a pitch he could hit for distance and had failed.

Tommy Byrne had not tired, had pitched at least as well as Podres, and had made no mistakes with the four Brooklyn batters he faced to start the miserable inning. He was a veteran, he had reacquired his control, and he knew how to pitch away from power. Grudgingly but forthrightly, Casey Stengel told Byrne after the game he had been wrong to take him out.

It was also beginning to dawn on Stengel that he had also erred in his strategy toward Johnny Podres. The assumption behind Stengel's instructions to avoid first-pitch swings and wait for fastballs in the strike zone was that the more pitches the left-hander had to throw, the sooner he would tire. The risk, and it was becoming clear that the risk was the reality, was that the Yankees would lose some of their fabled aggressiveness and that in fact Podres would not tire appreciably. Stengel often appeared to the public as a disheveled, absentminded older man (he was sixty-five that summer)—hence the Old Professor moniker—in fact, he was a wise baseball man, a fervent believer in the percentages, and a person who had hustled all his life and pushed his players to hustle.

By the late innings, it seemed as if Stengel began trying to will his team back into contention, to overcome what he was becoming certain had been his own mistaken strategy for the game. Whenever a Yankee hitter got ahead in the count or got on base,

Stengel would appear with his left foot on the dugout's top step, on the left side closest to home plate, waving and shaking his fists at the action in front of him. Nine outs was a long way to go against the Yankees when a few swings could win the game.

With two runs instead of one to play with and their journey through the sixth inning a success, the Dodgers did not go to sleep or fall into the worst of all sports habits—protecting a lead. At the plate, however, their record slugging of the previous six games continued to be missing.

Grim found his poise and strength in the seventh inning. After Podres made out, however, Junior Gilliam went with an outside pitch and drove it into right field for a single. Grim, a right-hander, had nothing like Byrne's deceptive pickoff move, and Gilliam took off on an attempted steal of second base.

Yogi Berra nailed him—a snap throw from behind the plate got to Phil Rizzuto covering, in time. Pee Wee Reese then struck out and the Yankees got their next chance to score.

Johnny Podres would not oblige them. He continued to pitch with power, and the Yankees had trouble adjusting to the now-steady diet of fastballs and sharp-breaking curves, and the sudden absence of the changeups to which they had become accustomed. Neither Bill Skowron nor Bob Cerv got around well on Podres pitches, and each grounded to Reese at shortstop without incident.

Elston Howard did get around. His swing sent a fastball into left field that dropped in front of Amoros for a single. There was some stirring in the Yankee dugout as Mickey Mantle went to grab a bat and came up the steps to hit for Grim. Mantle walked very slowly, favoring a leg that was clearly hurt badly. To that point in the series, Mantle had one monumental home run in Ebbets Field and little else and had been unable to run effectively in the outfield. However, Stengel had noticed that Mantle had an easier time planting and shifting his weight when he was batting right-handed, while the most famous switch-hitter of his time could get nothing behind a left-handed swing.

In the box score, it shows up as an at-bat by a pinch-hitter with two outs and a man on first. In fact, it was as electric a moment as when Berra came to the plate the inning before. Mantle couldn't run, but he could hit right-handed and he could tie the game.

Sometimes, with so much on the line, hitters—even the very best of them—swing too hard, just as a pitcher can throw too hard. Mantle made a couple of basic errors in the seventh inning, both traceable to his intensity. First of all, he swung, as they say, for the fences—too hard and with an upward motion instead of level. He also made contact a half inch below the middle of his bat.

The result was a pop-up for which the adjective *towering* does not do justice. It went far into the afternoon sky but only a few yards out of the infield. Don Hoak alertly moved out of the way as Reese ran into position underneath the ball, behind third base. He could have recited the alphabet waiting for the thing to fall out of the sky; eventually, it did and the final out of the inning was recorded. But for an overswing that undercut the ball, that pop-up could easily have been something much different and more consequential.

For the Dodger halves of the eighth and ninth innings, Bob Turley got another chance to do his job, and this time he came through—just one hit and a walk were yielded over the last two innings. For the third time in the game, the Dodgers went quietly and in order in the eighth (Snider, Campanella, and Furillo).

And then, in the Yankee half of the inning, it happened all over again. The sixth inning is part of history because of what happened after Berra came up with two men on first and second and no one out. In the eighth it was no less nerve-racking a threat because two men were on first and third and there was one out. In fact, it was even more scary, with the first Yankee run just ninety feet away from home. Only Berra had been that close—with two outs back in the fourth inning.

Once again for New York, it was the top of the order—in the person of Phil Rizzuto, in his last World Series at-bat—that produced the trouble. In Game Seven, six of the eight Yankee hits came from the first four men in the batting order; to the extent the team failed to come through offensively in the game, it was a case of the people put in the lineup to drive in runs who didn't drive in any runs. Rizzuto's last hit was a line drive into left-center field that put him on first base with a single.

Billy Martin was next. Behind by two runs, the Yankees would not be wasting an out on a sacrifice, but to move Rizzuto along the smart move would be for Martin to try to hit a ball to the right side of the infield.

He did better than that. Martin slapped at a pitch that might have been slightly outside and sent toward right field a soft line drive that almost immediately began to sink (a dying quail, as it's known in baseball). Carl Furillo began to charge immediately, but for a split second it appeared the ball might hit the ground. It stayed up, however, just long enough for Furillo to grab it at full speed, slightly below his belt.

This was not a game that offered relief. The next batter, Gil Mc-Dougald, proceeded to get his third hit of the afternoon, a single. McDougald hit an extremely hard ground ball at Don Hoak, the third baseman. He was in position to field it (if he had it would have been an easy double play), but on its way at him the ball took a bad hop, changing direction just enough. Hoak did not react fast enough as he was backing up on McDougald's smash, and the ball glanced off his shoulder and rolled into left field.

Seeing all this, Rizzuto reacted instantly, sprinting around second and sliding into third before Sandy Amoros was able to get to the ball.

As Yogi Berra walked toward the plate, Walter Alston made his last walk to the pitcher's mound of the day. This time there was no question from the manager about Podres's condition: the sixth inning had given Alston confidence in his pitcher; he was still throwing hard and with control.

Instead, Alston wanted to reiterate his certainty that Berra would once again be looking for something to hit out of the ballpark and that Podres's job was to make sure he pitched away from Berra's power. Alston also kept the Dodger infield at its normal playing depth, rejecting any idea of moving them in closer to throw a possible ground ball home in time to get Rizzuto. Once again, a two-run lead, while small, offered a little breathing room and a chance of executing a double play on a normally hit ground ball.

The admonition to pitch to Berra carefully may have resulted in Podres pitching to him a bit too carefully. Three of Podres's first four pitches were balls. This at-bat I remember vividly, because it was every bit as tense and consequential as the one two innings earlier; this was the part of the game where every pitch was obviously crucial.

The fifth pitch to Berra was a curveball, on the inside of the plate. The Yankee catcher got around on it but appeared to make contact somewhere on the lower half of his bat near his hands. The fly ball was almost softly hit and appeared so at once. I did not tense up on the couch.

Carl Furillo ran in from right field to get under the ball. He was in short-right field. With his famous arm, there was no chance at all that Rizzuto would try to score on the play. Now there were two outs, as Hank Bauer stepped into the batter's box.

Hank Bauer was a very good baseball player for fourteen seasons and a good manager after that (he had the Baltimore Orioles when they swept the Los Angeles Dodgers in 1966). He had decent power and a reputation for hitting well in the clutch (he had a four–home run World Series in 1958). He had fought in the war and some people would have been forgiven after reading years of sports page writing for thinking his full name was Ex-Marine Hank Bauer. He had pulled a hamstring muscle near the end of the season that remained tender, but he was still very dangerous.

It was a classic confrontation, the exclamation point for the famous game's late innings. Podres remembers all of it with justifiable pride. He told me he threw fastballs throughout—a ball inside, a called strike, a foul tip straight back to the screen, and a second ball outside.

The fifth pitch—as Vin Scully would have said, the deuces were wild: two on, two out, two-and-two on the batter—was, in baseball patois, a high hard one. It was over the plate, up about at

Bauer's New York letters. He had a beautiful swing at the ball—hard, smooth, and straight—but just a bit late and a bit below it.

Roy Campanella caught the pitch cleanly, one-handed, in his upraised catcher's mitt.

"That was the moment when I understood what was at stake, that this was for real," Podres told me. "As I was walking back to the dugout I realized I could not let this game get away, not after all this."

The meaning of the strikeout was clear enough: the Yankees would be batting in the ninth inning with a Dodger World Series championship on the line after all those years. In the continued silence of our apartment, what I remember is not feeling excited or even specifically aware of the stakes but instead taking my cues from my father and trying to concentrate even more on every pitch. For a kid of almost ten, following a baseball game all the way through took special effort; what I remember is feeling spent, almost exhausted.

Turley narrowly averted trouble in the top of the ninth inning. After Gil Hodges fouled out to Bill Skowron, Turley gave Don Hoak a belt-high fastball toward the outside part of the plate that the third baseman stayed with and drilled into right-center field for a single. A patient Sandy Amoros then drew a walk to put two Dodgers on base.

This was 1955, long before one-inning relief pitchers had arrived to take over games in the final inning, regardless of how the starter was faring. Johnny Podres had pitched a marvelous game to that point, he was still strong, and that meant he would be on the mound in the bottom of the inning. That also meant he would take his turn at bat in the middle of a Dodger scoring threat. He succeeded in hitting the ball in the air, but it was a routine fly ball to Bob Cerv in center field for the second out.

Junior Gilliam, a switch-hitter, batted left-handed against Turley. At his best, Gilliam was a line-drive hitter, and he jumped on an inside pitch to hit a ball that shot out of the infield, jerking me up off the cushion. It looked a lot like the double Skowron had hit in the first inning and the home run he had hit the day before as it went toward right field. Unfortunately, it went straight at Hank Bauer, who caught it very deep on the track in front of the right-field stands.

The Brooklyn Dodgers had never played a ninth inning ahead and thus in position to win the World Series. There was no frame of reference, especially for a young fan who now could not avoid realizing what was on the line and hoping against hope that this time they would finally win. There was only Johnny Podres and the next batter. Had I been with contemporaries, I would have been shrieking and jumping; with my father and his still-inexplicable silence, I was experiencing the game, living it. There was an intensity and intimacy about our afternoon that blocked everything else out.

When Podres emerged from the dark tunnel off the dugout after one last cigarette, many Dodgers remember a torrent of last-inning "advice" pouring out at the determined pitcher—inside, outside, up, down, curveball, fastball. It was what he had largely avoided by disappearing between innings, and now it was pouring out of his wired teammates.

Roy Campanella almost immediately blew up at them as he finished strapping on his catcher's gear—baseball's storied "tools of ignorance." Above all else, a catcher who is also a leader protects his pitcher. Give or take a syllable, Campanella screamed: "Leave the kid alone. He did fine by himself for eight innings, so shut the hell up and stop telling him how to pitch. That's my job."

He walked behind the plate, took Podres's warm-up pitches, started the game's final, ritual throw-around—to Gilliam, to Reese, to Hoak, to Hodges, back to Hoak, and then a soft toss to the pitcher—squatted down, and started calling for fastballs.

Bill Skowron had hit Johnny Podres hard in both games. Skowron was not all that tall, but he had the powerful build of a onetime Big Ten athlete at Purdue. Behind the plate, Campanella's signs did not vary—fastball—only the target moved.

Skowron hit one right on the nose at the ground about ten feet in front of home. It was on Podres in an instant; the frozen frame of the film actually shows the ball almost to him while he was still standing, arms crossed after his follow-through. At the last moment, Podres reached up with his glove hand and snared the ball.

"I did not find that ball," he told me. "The ball found me."

It went so deep and hard into the webbing of his glove that it took out a stitch or two on its way. As he turned and took a few steps toward Gil Hodges at first base, Podres said he quickly realized that the ball was stuck in the glove. He began jogging toward Hodges, all the time tugging at the ball with his left hand.

Podres told me that if necessary he would have tossed the glove to Hodges with the ball still embedded in it. As it was, about two-thirds of the way there, his hand finally grasped the buried ball, which he flipped underhanded to the first baseman for the first out. Skowron missed a single by an inch or two.

Bob Cerv was next. He was just as big as Skowron but faster, so he played the outfield—and well. He was twenty-nine that year. He fit well into Casey Stengel's platoon system and by then was getting into fifty-plus games a year. He did not hit for the power he showed later in his career with Kansas City, but he was developing into a high-average hitter.

In the World Series, however, Johnny Podres had owned him. Cerv struck out three times in Game Three and had already grounded out three times in the seventh game. The fastball Podres threw Cerv was in toward his fists, and while he got around on the pitch, the result was a lazy fly ball to left field for the second out. For a Dodger fan or Yankee hater it was a beautiful sight to see Sandy Amoros trot under it and catch it effortlessly.

That left Elston Howard, who in his rookie season breaking the Yankee's unforgivably long resistance to desegregation had shown all of the signs that eventually produced a dangerous, versatile hitter. He was twenty-six that year, still mostly an outfielder (catching and first base would come later), and already had a home run in the Series in addition to his seventh-inning, seventh-game single.

After all the Dodgers and their fans had been through that Series, that decade, and that century, it was the most fitting of climaxes—agonizing.

Throwing nothing but fastballs, Podres and Howard had a see-saw duel through the first four—two balls and two strikes, one swinging. The deuces were wild again.

Howard then fouled a pitch straight back. He sliced another foul to the right. And another. And another. And another.

After the fifth foul ball, Campanella briefly took off his mask to wipe the perspiration off his face.

Back behind the plate, he signaled for another fastball. On the mound, Podres told me, he began to get a sense that Howard was starting to "time" his pitches better and that he was going to hit one hard eventually if this kept up. Podres decided he wanted to throw one last changeup.

At this point, memories diverge. Campanella, in his two books, said he signaled for another fastball, outside, for the tenth pitch and then noticed that Podres was shaking his head no, where-upon he signaled for a hard curveball, only to be shaken off again. Podres remembers only the first sign.

In any event, so complete was Podres's dependence on Campanella's wisdom and strength that this was the only occasion in the entire game when he shook off a sign. In a book he did in the third person with sportswriter Milton Shapiro more than forty years ago, the catcher's dilemma was explained thus: "It was obvious to him that Podres wanted to throw the change-up again. The pitch had been his best weapon all through the game, but for that very reason Roy felt Howard would be looking for it. And it was important to try to fool the batter on the pitch. Suddenly, Roy realized that Podres was supremely confident in his change of pace. He knew that he had to signal for it. More important than anything was the fact that a catcher had to imbue the pitcher with confidence in his talent, not destroy it."

From the silence in our apartment, my father finally spoke for the first time during the game—one word.

"Changeup."

At the moment of contact between bat and changeup, Howard was a study in confusion. The frozen frame shows his bat way out in front of his body—a hitting no-no. His weight is so far forward that he is almost down on his bent left knee. He was, in short, completely fooled. Howard did not so much swing as lunge at the ball.

The result was a ground ball that slowly rolled toward shortstop, so slowly that Pee Wee Reese charged it. I can see him fielding the ball cleanly, and then I remember a moment more of bewilderment than panic.

Reese had a very brief problem getting the ball out of his glove and then stopped to aim his throw across the infield to Gil Hodges—a fielding no-no, often ironically a precursor of wild tosses.

Reese's throw was to Hodges's right and quite low. It was, however, well within range of the big man's famous stretch. He caught the ball perhaps six inches off the ground—a step, maybe two, ahead of Howard's arrival at the bag.

It was over.

There was a pause, in the apartment and in Yankee Stadium—similar to the pause after Sandy Amoros's catch and the relays that completed the double play—before all hell broke loose. The television camera stayed with the Dodgers in the infield, but I remember hearing the roar.

I had this feeling, very deep inside, that is like the welling up that happens just before you burst into tears. I then remember hearing, and memorizing on the spot, the words from Vin Scully that are part of broadcasting lore as well as Dodger history: "Ladies and gentlemen, the Brooklyn Dodgers are the champions of the world."

Today, at the entrance to the Dodgers' offices at Chavez Ravine in Los Angeles, those words are at the top of a wall that is covered with a giant picture of the joyous chaos on the field that was unfolding while he spoke them. Scully did not want to interfere with the dramatic scene with broadcaster babble, but he also told me he could not have spoken another word without his voice breaking.

260 | *Praying for Gil Hodges*

That was when it really hit me, much, much more than when Hodges stretched to the low throw from Pee Wee Reese. I turned to look toward the dining table.

My father had stood up, tears streaming down his face, his arms outstretched.

I took the cue as always and lost it myself. I sprang off the davenport and flew into his arms.

I never saw another second of the television.

14

Glowing

My father held me for the longest time—a minute, maybe longer. He wasn't sobbing, neither was I, but I could feel moisture on the top of my head. He held me very tight, and as best I could, I squeezed back. Normally, very little went unsaid between us, but this was a moment whose broadest context didn't require any words. We were a comfortably demonstrative little family; we just held on.

Eventually, he spoke. He told me to put some shoes on and grab a jacket because we were going to go downtown to find my mother.

"Let's go to Brooklyn," he said.

He picked up the phone. The fact that he got through was a miracle; five minutes later and it probably would have been impossible. Shortly after the game ended, the phone system in New York went bonkers. In particular, it became next to impossible to get a call through into Brooklyn and Long Island from Manhattan, especially the East Side. The jammed area especially included the exchanges for our home phone (Murray Hill 5) and our apartment building phone (Lexington 2). Hundreds of thousands of calls were being placed, to no avail. The phone company said that despite all its improvements of the last decade, this jam-up was at least as bad as and probably worse than what had happened on V-J Day ten years before.

I ran into the next room to find shoes and on my way down the short hallway grabbed a jacket out of the closet. Sometime during my absence, my father must have turned off Scarlet.

The celebratory scene in the locker room has never interested me all that much as an event. The fact that there was joyous bedlam could not surprise even a casual observer. The fact that this person whooped and hollered and another person hollered and whooped always struck me, to paraphrase George Bernard Shaw, as descriptions of the obvious enlivened only by a manufactured sense of discovery.

That night, and ever since, I have looked for telling details that hinted at human reactions as opposed to ritual hysteria. For example:

- The locker-room drink of choice was Schaeffer beer, not champagne, and the suds also flowed at the official party tossed by the Dodger management at the old Bossert Hotel in Brooklyn.
- For the second time after a gigantic game, Clem Labine sat down and cried.
- Johnny Podres couldn't find his dad in the crush. His uncle had to fetch him from his car in the small parking lot, where he sat for a half hour after the game sobbing.
- When Podres's dad finally arrived, the first of several Dodgers who went over to him was Russ Meyer, who said, "Mr. Podres, you must be the proudest man in America. That kid of yours has more guts than the law allows."
- Billy Loes stood alone in the chaos, his face lathered with shaving cream—buck naked.
- The Yankees who walked over to the dressing room to congratulate their opponents were Phil Rizzuto, Yogi Berra, and Casey Stengel (who made a beeline for Sandy Amoros).

None of these images, however, holds a candle to what happened over in Belle Harbor in John Sexton's basement room on Beach 136th St. He had been kneeling there in prayer with his best friend, Bobby Douglas, each with a hand on the small, metal crucifix between them. At the moment when Pec Wee Reese's last throw arrived in Gil Hodges's glove, they each leapt skyward. Douglas let go of the crucifix as he jumped up. Still gripping it, Sexton drove the tip into his mouth, chipping one of his front teeth.

As a badge of honor, John Sexton left that tooth unrepaired for more than forty years. A dentist finally prevailed on him to fix it around the time he became president of New York University.

We were out the door, down the elevator, and out on 42nd Street in no time. We walked up the wide street to get the subway at Grand Central for the ride downtown. I don't think we talked much. My father had his arm around me, and what I remember is periodically smiling and then, when our eyes met, just laughing out loud. It was shortly before the rush hour and there were always fewer people going downtown at that hour anyway, so we had no trouble getting a seat on the train.

On the subway, I asked him why he didn't say anything during the game. Socratic as ever, he asked me about my crossed and uncrossed ankles. Age aside, I could be a wise guy sometimes, so after I got his drift I asked him how come he didn't smoke when the Yankees were up. Now we were both laughing, partly because we were so indescribably happy, partly because neither of us had to come right out and say he had used superstition.

We got off at Wall Street, a mere half block from my mother's office building. When we got to the top of the stairs coming out of the station, I could see piles of paper pouring out of a few of the buildings. There was no order to it. A huge blizzard would come out of one window; a half minute later another pile would come out of a window across the street or down the block. The blizzard of ticker tape on Broadway during a parade for somebody famous would be steady, almost orderly. This was deliciously chaotic and improvised.

My mother must have seen us coming, because the first time I saw her she was running toward us in her heels, her long hair flowing behind her. She had a smile on her face like she'd just won the Irish Sweepstakes. When she reached us, she picked me up (she could still do that) and smeared lipstick all over my forehead; the three of us hugged one another, with her in the middle, laughing. I had never seen this expression of unrestrained joy on her face before; I thought she was pretty anyway, but her smile made her look gorgeous. I can't remember anybody saying anything.

There was a younger woman with her, a friend and Dodger fan from her office. Her name was Mary Alice and she lived somewhere in the East Flatbush section of Brooklyn. My father could never remember her name, so he called her Mary Alice Something out of her presence, which was frequently enough that I only remember her as that. She was single and had short red hair and wore black suits and dresses and black glasses, but on this afternoon she was a little mussed up and laughing; I didn't see her that often, but she, too, smeared lipstick on my forehead and picked me up. Some years later, when my mother and I were reconstructing that joyous afternoon and I remarked that she and Mary Alice Something had seemed so flushed and buoyant, my mother began giggling as I realized that the two of them had knocked down a couple of belts in a bar before we arrived.

My father gallantly suggested another subway ride, and off we went; he and my mother had their arms around each other as they walked; Mary Alice Something decided to hold my hand, and I let her.

We got off across the river at Atlantic Avenue. I am eternally grateful that no one suggested we head for the Hotel Bossert, where we would have stood behind police barricades looking for arriving Dodgers like we were at some movie premiere. Naturally, there was a huge crowd over there, but I have always thought the most interesting reaction was that tens of thousands of people—like us—simply poured out of their dwellings and hung around on the streets.

The first thing I noticed was the traffic; Brooklyn could get jammed, but almost never like midtown Manhattan except around the bridges at rush hour. This was like midtown at its worst; hardly anything on the avenue was moving. Unlike Manhattan at five o'clock, there was no sign that anyone cared, the police included. Being on foot was a huge advantage.

The second thing I noticed was the church bells. I knew the sound well, but this was different—two or three church bells just ringing randomly, a phenomenon that was being repeated all over Brooklyn. The absence of melody or rhythm told me that it had all just happened.

The third thing I remember noticing was faces. Everybody looked like us, beaming and laughing, unrestrained. Every so often a car would inch by filled with obviously drunk young people screaming, but the overwhelmingly dominant impression was of mass joy, not bedlam.

We walked a few blocks down the avenue to where the crowds on the street thinned a bit. My father gestured at the stairs of some walk-up and led me, my mother, and Mary Alice Something halfway up the stairs, seated us as if we were at a café, and then went back down the stairs and down the block into a candy store. He emerged a minute or so later carrying a paper bag that turned out to contain four White Rock cream sodas and four large salty, doughy pretzels.

I sat on the top step of the walk-up with Mary Alice Something while my mother and father were a few steps down. We drank, ate, and watched the impromptu parade of happy people. No one seemed to be simply walking home from work or going about some business. There was instead this continuous stream of Brooklyn's marvelous diversity, laughing and talking excitedly.

In particular I remember two fairly old ladies, in black dresses with black laced shoes, greeting each other and gushing on about the Dodgers while they casually held on to each other's forearms. They were almost dancing. The other sight I focused on was the continual encounters between little groups of people and other little groups of people walking toward each other; they would greet, begin talking about the Dodgers, and then you could monitor their rising decibel levels. Eventually Mary Alice Somebody and I started poking each other to watch this or look at that.

At length, she poked me in the ribs and pointed down. My mother and father were in midkiss—a heavy, wet one. Mary Alice had her hand over her mouth in an expression of mock horror, still pointing down to where I could see my father's left hand inching down the back of my mother's skirt. Mary Alice and I both burst out laughing.

We were on the stoop for maybe ninety minutes. It was getting dark, and I didn't object to the suggestion that we start home. We walked back to the subway, saying good-bye to my mother's friend at a bus stop, which meant more lipstick on my forehead.

Back in Manhattan, we got as far as Third Avenue from Grand Central when my mother made the sudden suggestion that we duck into my favorite restaurant, the Automat. I don't remember what we had, but it was always my enjoyable chore to put the coins in the famous window slots for desserts. The family favorite was rice pudding.

Since my father and I had been together all day, we let my mother do the talking. We laughed as she told us how grumpy the law partners became after each inning as the Yankees fell behind. She said she and her girlfriend Dodger fans were rooting and screaming in the refreshment room around the radio, in dramatic contrast to the funereal atmosphere in the conference room. Normally, she was a relatively reserved person and a stickler for detail and order; I think a lot of the time she was also very tired. That night she was aglow and loud, and it wasn't just the postgame whiskey. She had another horse laugh when my father and I confessed our superstitious rituals to her.

I also couldn't help notice how intimate my father was with her. Usually they made me the center of attention when we were together; on this evening, it was he who interrupted me to describe in detail Sandy Amoros's catch, which she had missed seeing when she changed rooms. I enjoyed watching them together.

When we got home, it was well after nine o'clock, borderline late for a school night, but there was no pretending that the return to routine would start before tomorrow. At some point after the game or on the way home we had heard that Johnny Podres would be the guest on the fledgling *Tonight Show* (then hosted by Steve Allen), and I didn't even have to ask permission to stay up for it. It was simply assumed I would.

After we had freshened up and my mother had gotten out of her work suit, it must have been ten or so, because my father suddenly suggested with the Indiana cornball phony seriousness that he always telegraphed by calling me Son that I go to the corner and get every newspaper that had an account of the game in it. He knew that would be an additional thrill at that hour, so I collected a dollar bill from my mother, got my jacket again, and headed out the door, careful to leave it open a crack for my return.

Fortunately, Tommy was working late at the newsstand, so I didn't have to pretend that I belonged on the corner of 42nd and Second at ten o'clock in the evening. He saw me and my wide smile coming and waved. I was not the only customer; several people were lined up to grab papers for the same reason I was there in this snapshot of pre-instant replay America. Tommy shared my glee and set about arranging a stack of papers that had full accounts of the game in them.

As I walked back down the block, I had a sizable stack (from the favored *Post* to an early or special edition of the *Times*) in both my arms. Back in the building, my burden was graciously relieved by the lone elevator man on duty at that hour, a recent arrival from Ireland named Charley Kerrigan.

When there was no one else riding the elevator, Charley always let me operate it. Back then, push-button elevators were mostly in new buildings. This one ran with a large lever—which you pushed left to go up, right to go down, and moved to the middle to stop. I was pretty good at it and hit our floor cleanly on the first try, without having to adjust up or down.

I heard the noise right after I thanked Charley and stepped off into the hallway. It was a clarinet that got louder as I walked toward our door. We had no fancy high-fidelity set, just a portable player for our modest collection that was all 78s. I recognized the tune—the 1930s standard "So Rare."

I nudged open the door and stepped lightly inside. My father and mother were dancing near the dining table, locked in a close clinch, barely moving as they swayed. I could hear my mother humming softly.

I stood in the little hallway with my bundle of papers.

And glowed.

15

Afterward

I sat on the Gil Hodges Memorial Bridge for maybe a half hour, munching my doughnuts and drinking my milk. No more than a half-dozen cars broke the rural Indiana peace on a sunny, breezy October morning not unlike the one I awoke to on October 4, 1955.

Eventually, I noticed that there was a plaque on the bridge as well as its identifying sign and I walked over to read it. It contained most of the basic facts of Hodges's baseball career and concluded thus: "Above all, he was dedicated to God, family, country, and the game of baseball."

There is a large open space between the end of the tribute and the bottom of the simple monument. I eventually learned the gap was left to make room for Gil Hodges's plaque at the Baseball Hall of Fame in New York, a more-than-deserved honor that had still eluded the best first baseman of his era as the fiftieth anniversary year of the Dodgers' World Series victory began. It remains one of the Hall's enduring outrages of oversight. For the record, among the eighteen first basemen who had been elected as of 2005, Hodges is hardly outclassed.

He had a higher lifetime batting average (.273) than Harmon Killebrew and Willie McCovey. He had more hits (1,921) than Frank Chance, Hank Greenberg, and George Kelly. Among modern era players he had more home runs (370) than Greenberg and Johnny Mize and was just nine short of Orlando Cepeda and Tony

Perez. Hodges's comparative weakness was runs batted in (1,274), but that was more than Chance had, and all this comes before recognition is given to his unmatched magnificence in the field, his character, and his role in leading the Amazing Mets to victory in 1969. Where Gil Hodges is concerned, Wait'll Next Year applies to the Hall of Fame.

Near the bridge, there had been a sign indicating the way back to Princeton. On a lark, I followed its instructions and took Highway 64 into the town. It still has roughly the population of 8,000 people or so as it did when Hodges was raised there before he went to high school in the much smaller community of Petersburg to the northeast.

But Princeton has changed. Its economy was rescued from its traditional overdependence on coal by Toyota's decision to build a major factory nearby that continues to expand. Gil Hodges is still everywhere, however—at the thriving public library and at the gorgeous baseball field and park that were named after him. The place has perspective, however, taking care to notice its other well-known baseball name, Dave Niehaus, the longtime voice of the Seattle Mariners, as well as its two links to fast-food culture—Orville Reddenbacher and Dave Thomas of Wendy's.

It was impossible while walking on the outfield grass of Gil Hodges Field not to think of his family's determination that he get the tools in school and in sports not to have to be in the coal mines that shortened his father's life. Hodges came from a lovely place deeply rooted in American culture, but in an act just as deeply rooted in American culture he moved on.

So did my mother and father and so did the Dodgers.

We didn't leave New York until 1959, not quite two years after our team did, but 1955 was a turning point for us.

It had been a wretched year for my father—two hospitalizations around a continuous string of setbacks effectively ended his professional career at the age of forty-six. That year, I finally got a chance to meet the oddball character (also from Indiana) who had roamed the West with him thirty years before. Still with family money, still a quixotic dreamer and schemer, and with his third wife and a bewildering assortment of delightful children from his various entanglements he had plans for a business venture. He wanted to set up shop in Southern California.

What I didn't know at the time was that he offered to bring us all out there—to a beach town on the northern fringe of San Diego called La Jolla—to work in the venture, a company making printed circuit boards for a fledgling industry called electronics.

My parents demurred at first. The man's plans were at that point vague, but my parents' real reason was me—a refusal to even consider moving while I was still in grammar school and working in the opera. The seed, however, was planted, and even more urgent circumstances three years later, combined with the end of my boy soprano career, induced them to say yes.

I went berserk, my first true fury directed at my parents. I was fourteen; I had a girlfriend, a fantastic school, friends there and in my neighborhood, and no conceivable frame of reference for a place on the Pacific Ocean that had no subway system. My rage lasted about a month.

I simply loved high school, I loved the ocean, I still had my piano, and while the business venture collapsed and my parents still faced some brutal years, I had my first stirring of an understanding that after all they had been through and still faced, they had the right to choose a better opportunity and an infinitely more pleasant setting.

They had a lovely little house on the ocean and after some hideous years, my father's health finally became tolerable after doctors figured out how to control the flow of digestive acids into his ulcerated organs. As it turned out, a brain tumor got him at the age of seventy-one. Another brain tumor got my hitherto healthy mother less than two years later. On the day she took her final turn for the worse she told me she had seen her beloved husband in a dream. He was beckoning to her.

The Dodgers' story is of course more complex, but California also first loomed on their horizon in 1955, if only behind the Byzantine scenes of New York politics.

After all these years, the hatred that move spawned still burns, especially brightly in Brooklyn, against the Dodgers as a business and against Walter O'Malley in particular. It is said that one evening over dinner the two writers Jack Newfield and Pete Hamill decided to make independent lists of the most evil people in history. Their top three were identical—Hitler, Stalin, and O'Malley.

This situation strikes me as long overdue for some peacemaking. The Dodgers, as much as any organization in baseball, have a strong devotion to all of their long history, symbolized by the huge picture of the post-Game Seven celebration, adorned with Vin Scully's famous quote, that frames the entrance to their Los Angeles offices.

Their new owner in 2004 was a real estate developer from Boston named Frank McCourt. He purchased them from Rupert Murdoch's News Corporation, which had bought out Walter O'Malley's son. McCourt made plans to observe the anniversary appropriately. But it struck me as sad that plans for a separate celebration in Brooklyn were also proceeding and that no effort to have the twains meet was even attempted. After all, the most recent members of that fabled Brooklyn diaspora that has existed for three hundred years make an effort to stay in touch with those who stayed behind. It would seem that enough time has passed for the wounds to be allowed to heal.

History can help. Brooklyn is special but not unique; it was as susceptible to the winds of post–World War II urban change as any other city or major part of a city was. Most of the reasons that propelled the Braves out of Boston to Milwaukee, the Browns out of St. Louis to Baltimore, the Athletics out of Philadelphia to Kansas City and then to Oakland, and the Giants out of New York to San Francisco were at work in Brooklyn in the 1950s.

All these years later it is clear that a superhuman effort was undertaken to remain in Brooklyn, or at least the New York area, and that its failure was by no means solely Walter O'Malley's fault. The actual decision to depart was cruel and selfish, but those are not adjectives unheard in the cowboy capitalist world of baseball. The entire saga is tragic but, in context, comprehensible as something other than a mere immorality play.

The team's natural fan base was immense and still expanding almost to the first shots of World War II; from the World Series teams of 1916 and 1920 through the Daffy Dodgers era to the revival under Larry MacPhail, it had always been clear that the team was beloved in its roomy geographical home. As a franchise the Dodgers had seen decent as well as horrid times, but the team's inherent potential was always apparent. From Branch Rickey's arrival through Walter O'Malley's coup that potential was realized; the team made serious money and by 1955 had salted away millions for a project—a new home—that had been seen as essential ever since World War II.

From almost the moment the war ended, it had become increasingly clear that something was wrong though the problems were slow to develop. In the first full season after the war ended, the Dodgers drew 1.8 million fans to Ebbets Field, leading the National League in attendance despite the ballpark's relatively small size, as they would do in 1947, 1949, 1951, and 1952. In 1947, Jackie Robinson's rookie year, their record draw at home was more than matched by another 1.8 million fans on the road, who turned out in large part to get a glimpse of history.

The Dodgers never matched either total again, however. From 1948 until they abandoned the town, the Dodgers drew more on the road than they did at home each year. In the year of their only championship, the attendance at Ebbets Field barely exceeded 1 million fans and was the occasion of much angry comment by the players as the season unfolded, including a famous tirade in print by Duke Snider. What was wrong was that people were moving from the city to the suburbs and from the Northeast to what would eventually be called the Sunbelt. To lure fans to an urban ballpark in the late 1950s would require more than just proximity to bus and subway lines; it would require parking space for cars from Long Island and New Jersey, which Ebbets Field famously lacked.

For some very obvious, indescribably painful reasons, the Dodgers cannot ignore their history of abandonment; it is at least somewhat to their credit that they don't hide it. The point was driven home to me in the fall of 2003, when I was in the state to watch the people get rid of their governor and select the movie actor Arnold Schwarzenegger to replace him. I took one morning off the campaign to swing by the ballpark to watch Walter O'Malley's son unveil an Internet site devoted to the team's full history and many of the late rascal and visionary's once-private papers.

Peter O'Malley has his father's face but a more distinguished air. His family's placement of the historical record where anyone can see it was not entirely selfless. It is good politics to soften the image of the ruthless decision to leave Brooklyn against a background of the city's refusal to help O'Malley put together a large-enough land parcel near downtown Brooklyn for a larger ballpark and the parking spaces required to attract at least the populace of the suburban pieces of Brooklyn's diaspora. Back in Brooklyn, the most hardened of the left-behind argued that it was also part of a campaign to help Peter O'Malley's eventual election to the Hall of Fame.

The documents are revealing and helpful. They beg the ultimate question—how business greed could have produced such a brutal abuse of the public trust as to pull up stakes and drive one of them through Brooklyn's heart, no matter the politicians' provocation—but do show clearly how Los Angeles did not become a genuine option until it was clear that the city of New York would not take even minimal steps to help the Dodgers build a new home.

The very first document was written by Walter O'Malley in 1946 when he was still a bank lawyer on the board of what was then a Branch Rickey–run operation.

"Your fertile imagination should have some ideas about enlarging or replacing our present stadium," he cajoled in a note to Emil Praeger, the architect/engineer eventually of the ballpark at the Dodgers' spring training complex in Vero Beach, Florida, and of Dodger Stadium itself in Los Angeles.

Less than a decade after MacPhail's improvements, Ebbets Field was already notoriously rickety, with equally notorious amenities like faulty plumbing. I never saw my mother at the ballpark without a small clump of toilet paper in her handbag, though in my childhood I can never recall being aware of anything wrong with the place. The real problem was not so much size (Ebbets

Field could have been expanded by several thousand seats) as it was parking (there was space for only seven hundred cars).

By 1948, O'Malley had begun scouting possible sites and exploring designs including the ultimate innovation of a domed stadium, on which he consulted in depth with the likes of R. Buckminster Fuller and Eero Saarinen. From the beginning, it was clear that the principal obstacle was New York's legendary planner and builder, Robert Moses.

The archetype of the best and worst of the era of "urban renewal" and "slum clearance," Moses's vision created affordable housing for poor, working families and retired people by the scores of thousands of units. His highways also destroyed neighborhoods and both made the suburbs reachable for commuters and hastened the economic decline of the city in which those commuters no longer lived. His beliefs in democracy and accountability frequently yielded to autocracy and ego. In my little progressive household I learned from my parents to detest four people in public life before I was fully aware why—Joe McCarthy, Richard Nixon, Carmine DeSapio (the last real boss of the decaying Tammany Hall political machine), and Robert Moses.

Over a period of roughly ten years, the O'Malley–Moses correspondence reveals a clash between the Dodger boss's dream and the Moses political philosophy. On the surface, each was a dreamer, schemer, and builder. O'Malley had, from the moment of his appearance on the Dodger scene in the 1940s, always been part of the business and political support structure that helped get Moses's megaprojects completed. O'Malley believed that the Dodgers, in Brooklyn but housed in a new complex suitable for modern times, fit perfectly with Moses's vision of a late-twentieth-century city. Gradually, however, it became clear that Moses himself did not share that belief.

As chairman or commissioner of the various supergovernment agencies and authorities in New York that transformed the city as they were transforming other urban centers in the country, Moses's power derived from authority delegated to such public officials by the federal government. In the legislation that enshrined the nation's basic housing and urban policies after the war, it was the authority to clear land (and the people who inconveniently might live on it) designated as a "slum," as long as the clearance and the construction that replaced it served a legitimate "public purpose."

O'Malley did not want direct financial help. The Dodgers, under both Rickey and O'Malley, made money and retained the team's earnings in accounts that swelled into the millions of dollars. The Dodger boss did not want to rent a publicly financed, new stadium; he wanted to own the land, the ballpark, and an adjacent parking lot outright. However, he needed Moses to use his condemnation authority to help him assemble property.

Moses could be ruthless with his power, but their correspondence makes it clear he did not agree that the public purpose requirement of federal law could be stretched to accommodate a privately owned baseball team. At a minimum he wanted a stadium built on land put together with government help and muscle to have more than one purpose, as Shea Stadium would have a decade later. Moses was deeply involved in plans for a vibrant Brooklyn Civic Center in the heart of the borough, but the intriguing possibility of a ballpark site right next to it at the corner of Atlantic and Flatbush Avenues (occupied by a huge eye- and nose sore called the Fort Greene Meat Market), hard by the Brooklyn station for the Long Island Railroad, and convenient to major highways, could not induce him to offer help in assembling an affordable land package for O'Malley's dream.

The O'Malley–Moses correspondence, increasingly pointed and then angry, had been going for at least two years. Moses repeatedly suggested other sites but never budged from his contention that the "public purpose" requirement of federal law could not apply to condemning property simply for a new Dodger stadium. O'Malley never slammed his mind shut, but increasingly focused like a laser on Atlantic and Flatbush. The exquisite irony is that in early 2004, prominent developer Bruce Ratner purchased the New Jersey Nets basketball team to move them to a new auditorium on that very site in Brooklyn, which will use public power to assemble land for a mixed-use complex.

The machinations of urban big shots were not prominently on my mind, but I actually remember one episode in the O'Malley–Moses battle that was very public during that championship season—the announcement that during the following year the Dodgers would play seven games in the old minor-league park across the Hudson River in Jersey City that would otherwise have been played at Ebbets Field. The announcement came in mid-August, as the team coasted toward its earliest-ever clinching of a pennant, and it followed a particularly acerbic exchange of letters between the two headstrong men.

The full text disclosed that the New Jersey experiment would continue in 1957 and that the team "will have to have a new stadium shortly thereafter." The public comments about moving the team were restricted at this time to Queens, New Jersey, and Long Island, but more than the immediate neighborhood was involved even then.

The very next sentence opened the door by implication: "We will consider other locations only if we are finally unsuccessful in our ambition to build in Brooklyn. In that event we would want to [not have to] keep the franchise close to our fans."

The Dodgers' real estate problems had caught the attention during 1955 of some very sharp young politicians who were actively scheming to graft big-time sports and culture onto the exploding population and economy of Southern California. Even as the team was moving toward the one triumphant moment in its long history, the seed that would sprout two years later was being planted.

Undeterred by a referendum defeat that June of a $4-million bond issue by Los Angeles County voters to pay for a new stadium fit for a major-league team, the city council in August voted with a public relations flourish to invite O'Malley west for an inspection tour and a chat. Early in September, O'Malley received a letter from Rosalind Wyman, a council member then all of twenty-four years old, who would become one of the modern city's leading figures and one of the Dodgers' most prominent suitors.

Wyman told O'Malley that she would be in New York for the World Series with a fellow council member (Edward Roybal, later a heavyweight congressman), staying at the Waldorf Astoria Hotel, and that the two of them were authorized to start talking to any team that would listen (she sent a similar letter to owner Horace Stoneham of the New York Giants).

O'Malley replied a week later that when he saw accounts of the city council vote in the newspapers he had assumed it was "a publicity stunt," but while he essentially blew Wyman off, he left his door temptingly open a crack. He said he doubted there would be time to talk during the Series and said he would have no part in any public maneuvering that might complicate life for Los Angeles' two minor-league teams (the Angels and the Hollywood Stars). However, he added that "at a later date perhaps there might be an occasion when a meeting would be appropriate."

Another exchange in that period shows that the Dodgers were already willing to consider this kind of contact appropriate. In Los Angeles, there was no bigger tub-thumper for a major-league franchise than Vincent X. Flaherty, a sports columnist for the Hearst paper the *Herald-Examiner*. In the old Hearst tradition, Flaherty was not above adding behind-the-scenes lobbying to his writing duties. That same month, he informed O'Malley by letter that he would be staying at the Plaza Hotel during the Series and was also looking for a meeting.

O'Malley responded via the Dodgers' assistant general manager, A. F. "Red" Patterson, who was more than a little encouraging.

"Hope we can have a session during the World Series," Patterson replied. "As you know, Walter will be only too glad to discuss the Los Angeles situation with you—off the record—but as you know we've got something started in Brooklyn which we plan to see right down to a conclusion."

On October 4, 1955, that something was the seventh game of the World Series as well as the ongoing struggle to arrange a new home without moving. The millions of Dodger fans who endured the tortures of hell that day were totally focused on the former; the stadium clock that had already begun ticking was completely inaudible to all but a few insiders.

Tick it did, however, until everyone involved ran out of time and viable options. It remains the only move by a sports team that has left such scars, produced such passionate, durable outrage.

What happened later when the Dodgers left, however, has never come close to the durability of what happened in 1955, still the source of wonder and joy.

The memory of that World Series is in fact the only one given formal recognition at the Hall of Fame. It was sort of an accident—an effort by a rich guy to give something to baseball's shrine that reflected his own memories and feelings. The people who run the place, though, had no difficulty considering the gift more than appropriate and worthy.

I came upon it by accident taking a break from my research work in the Hall of Fame's remarkable library for a short stroll outside. Sort of between the building's wings, there is a small courtyard with a couple of benches in it, which I noticed from some distance away. As I walked into it, I saw that there were two statues on the small lawn—one of a left-handed pitcher, the other of a catcher, with a bronzed home plate in front of him. They appeared to be separated from each other by the officially required distance of sixty feet, six inches.

From a distance of no more than ten yards it suddenly dawned on me that the pitcher was Johnny Podres and the catcher was Roy Campanella. Podres was in his follow-through, left leg in the air; Campanella had his mitt extended, with his mask on top of his head so a visitor could see his face.

On home plate, there was an explanatory inscription. The sculptor was Stanley Bliefeld, a highly regarded artist who lives in Connecticut and Italy; the donor was the New York restaurant entrepreneur Sheldon Fireman—Brooklyn boys both. It was presented in memory of 1955, but it was accepted in honor of all seventh games when everything is on the line.

For some silly reason, I stood where a right-handed hitter would stand, trying to mimic Elston Howard's lunge at Podres's last changeup. Eventually, as at that little bridge in Indiana, I simply let the memories and feelings flow again.

Johnny Podres was right. It all really is frozen forever.

Name Index